The Multinational Corporation as a Force in Latin American Politics

Adalberto J. Pinelo

The Praeger Special Studies program—utilizing the most modern and efficient book production techniques and a selective worldwide distribution network—makes available to the academic, government, and business communities significant, timely research in U.S. and international economic, social, and political development.

The Multinational Corporation as a Force in Latin American Politics

A Case Study of the International Petroleum Company in Peru

HD
9574
P54
I 55
1973

614745

Lamar University Library

Praeger Publishers   New York   Washington   London

PRAEGER PUBLISHERS
111 Fourth Avenue, New York, N.Y. 10003, U.S.A.
5, Cromwell Place, London S.W.7, England

Published in the United States of America in 1973
by Praeger Publishers, Inc.

All rights reserved

© 1973 by Praeger Publishers, Inc.

Library of Congress Catalog Card Number: 72-91103

Printed in the United States of America

PREFACE

In the fall of 1968, the Peruvian government seized the assets of International Petroleum Company (I.P.C.), a subsidiary of Standard Oil Company (New Jersey) which holds 99.5 percent of its stock. I.P.C. has about 150 additional shareholders. The move by the Peruvian military junta seemed out of keeping with the traditional role of the Latin American military establishments as defenders of the status quo and as friends of the United States. Military interventions in Latin America have traditionally been carried out to prevent change, or to cancel out an unacceptable national election. But the junta which took power in Peru in early October seemed bent on reform and on a confrontation with American companies operating in Peru.

In undertaking this study, I originally planned to analyze the military seizure of Standard Oil's assets in Peru, hoping that such an analysis would shed some light on the attitudes of the "new military." During the course of the study, it became increasingly clear that the seizure of International Petroleum Company property was incidental to the actual coup of 1968. At the same time, however, the controversy surrounding the company in Peru proved significant in a deeper sense than anticipated. Ownership and operation of the La Brea y Pariñas oil fields became a divisive issue which split and weakened the Peruvian coastal oligarchy, and undermined the United States Government's supportive role behind this ruling elite. In weakening the elite's cohesiveness as well as its good relationship with the United States, the I.P.C. controversy helped to set the stage for the eventual military take over. In 1968, the Peruvian military argued, with a measure of justification, that the civilian leadership had proved itself incompetent in dealing with national problems. La Brea y Pariñas was a long-term problem tackled by several generations of Peruvian leaders. While the I.P.C. controversy did not play a significant role as the immediate cause of the 1968 coup, the International Petroleum Company played a very important role in Peruvian politics for several decades.

The author wishes to acknowledge the contribution of Professor Howard Wiarda, of the University of Massachusetts, whose comments, suggestions and encouragement made the preparation of this study both enlightening and enjoyable. The Department of Political Science of the University of Massachusetts provided a deeply appreciated measure of financial assistance.

The management of I.P.C. cooperated to the fullest extent on this project by facilitating my research at the company's offices in Coral Gables, Florida. I wish to thank in particular John Oldfield, and the other I.P.C. executives who all made generous contributions of time and insight. Former President of Peru Fernando Belaúnde Terry extended both his hospitality and a marvelous first-hand account of the events of his administration. Fernando Espinosa, former General Manager of I.P.C. in Peru, recounted his experiences in Peru frankly in a valuable interview.

In addition, I acknowledge the cooperation of General Marco Fernández Baca, Director of Petróleos del Peru, Bruce Sever, Peru desk officer at the U.S. Department of Commerce, Myles Frechette, U.S. desk officer at the U.S. Department of State and Alberto Ruiz Eldredge, Ambassador of Peru to Brazil. Finally, the staffs of the National Archives and the Library of Congress provided me with much of the raw material of this study, and their assistance was invaluable.

CONTENTS

	Page
PREFACE	v
INTRODUCTION	ix
Notes	xiv

Chapter

1   THE ORIGINS OF LA BREA Y PARIÑAS   3

      Notes   25

2   INTERNATIONAL ARBITRATION AND
     THE LAUDO OF 1922   31

      Notes   40

3   FROM POWER BROKER TO BELEAGUERED UTILITY   42

      The Revenge of the Inca   42
      Notes   60

4   A MULTINATIONAL CORPORATION PLAYS
     LATIN AMERICAN POLITICIAN   64

      Notes   84

5   ANATOMY OF THE ANTAGONISTS   89

      El Comercio   89
      The Social Progressist Movement   93
      The Military   95
      Alianza Popular Revolucionaria Americana   97
      Pedro Beltrán and La Prensa   99
      The Oligarchy   100
      The Presidential Campaign of 1962   102
      Notes   106

6	INTERNATIONAL PETROLEUM COMPANY AND BELAÚNDE FACE EACH OTHER	110
	The First Round	110
	Notes	126
7	THE END OF INTERNATIONAL PETROLEUM COMPANY AND DEMOCRATIC REFORM IN PERU	130
	Notes	145
8	CONCLUSIONS	149
	Notes	157
BIBLIOGRAPHY		159
ABOUT THE AUTHOR		172

INTRODUCTION

THE MULTINATIONAL CORPORATION

A multinational corporation is one that does most of its business across national boundaries. The scholar can set definite criteria as to the proportion of multinational business and the volume of that business. Typical multinational corporations such as Standard Oil (New Jersey), Pfizer, Singer, or International Telephone and Telegraph have at least half of their assets abroad, and either do more than half of their marketing in, or get more than half of their revenue from, countries other than the United States.[1]

The U.S. oil industry accounts for a larger share of American investment abroad than any other type of enterprise. In 1969, this investment totalled over $20 billion, and represented more than a quarter of all American foreign direct investment.[2] The oil industry is significant not only because of its large scale, but because it is a pioneer in an ever increasing trend for other American industries to expand across national borders. Beginning during the first decade of the twentieth century, American oil companies began buying producing and refining facilities in the Third World, including Latin America. It was not until the 1930s that other American industrial groups began to move toward establishing manufacturing operations in Latin America.

Given current conditions in Latin America, with economic nationalism on the upswing in Chile, Peru, and Bolivia, American-owned subsidiaries throughout Latin America are bracing themselves for what could be a very difficult period, characterized by official hostility from host country governments. With the Alliance for Progress over, and the after-effects of the Cuban Revolution nearly forgotten, Latin Americans have begun taking a closer look at economic problems, and more than ever, at the mushrooming role played by multinational corporations in their economies. Yet, to argue that Latin America is on the threshold of a wave of nationalizations and open confrontations with American economic interests might be as unfounded as the predictions of continental upheaval made after the Cuban Revolution.

The problem of assessing the impact of the multinational corporation on Latin American social, economic and political life is a very complex one. Increasingly, Latin Americans have taken the view that these corporations have played a detrimental role in their national affairs. A variety of arguments—social, political, and economic—have been advanced to support this point of view.

On the sociological level, the American subsidiaries have changed the ownership patterns in Latin America. As these enterprises move in and purchase or dominate industries, they co-opt whatever local entrepreneurial talent is available, thus transforming the national bourgeoisie into a "transnational technocracy," void of any legitimacy as a national ruling class, according to scholar Osvaldo Sunkel. The middle class is also affected; part is incorporated into the new economic structure and part is left out—effectively barred from upward mobility and terrified by the prospect of proletarianization. The working class is simply divided—those few who find employment with the American subsidiary companies become a privileged elite within the working class. The balance of the labor force is left to endure the problems of unemployment and marginal economic existence. This division of the working class makes it difficult to organize labor, and the corporate absorption of local talent interrupts the development of a native entrepreneurial class. Consequently, national development along the lines historically followed by Great Britain and the United States is impossible.[3]

The economic argument has been well articulated by the Chilean Ambassador to the United States, Orlando Letelier. When asked whether the government of Salvador Allende was frightening foreign capital away from Chile, the ambassador replied:

> In general terms, we have been exporting capital, not importing it . . . between 1950 and 1967, 17 years, $450 million flowed into Chile as direct investments. Now deduct depreciation for such investments during that period, which the companies took back out of the country, and the net figure would be only $257 million. In the same period, the outflow of profits and dividends just on investments was $1.056 billion, about four times the net investment.[4]

The Chilean argument is probably valid for the rest of Latin America. From 1960 to 1968, there was a flow of $1 billion of fresh capital from the U.S. to American owned subsidiaries in the underdeveloped world. During that same period, incoming capital from the less developed areas to the United States in the form of income alone amounted to about $2.5 billion. This is a rather conservative estimate, according to economist Raymond Vernon, and if other factors such as royalty payments were included, the difference between what the United States sends to the Third World and what it receives from there would be even greater.[5] However, there are counter arguments.

The U.S. Department of the Treasury suggests that the effect of American foreign investment is more than the cited figures indicate.

The Treasury Department holds that when an American subsidiary establishes producing facilities in a Latin American nation, for example, a process known as "import substitution" takes place. That is, products which were previously imported into that country are henceforth produced locally. Given this import substitution, the obvious advantage which the U.S. has in net capital flow is minimized if not reversed.[6] This argument assumes that import substitution would not have taken place without the presence of the American subsidiary company. Furthermore, in the case of extractive industries geared for exports, there is only minimal import substitution. For example, Chile does not need to import copper. But then, Chile would be unlikely to import copper in any quantity in any event.

Related to the economic impact of multinational corporations on the Latin American balance of payments is the taxation problem. Since corporate subsidiaries often conduct their transactions with other subsidiaries of the same parent company, that parent company can arbitrarily choose to show profit in a certain transaction and not another. For example, if an oil company in Ecuador produces oil at $1 per barrel, it could conceivably sell that oil to another subsidiary of the same company at $1.01. The profit margin reported to the host country would be minimal. The subsidiary receiving the oil could then market it in the U.S. or elsewhere at $2 per barrel, with a profit margin of nearly 100 percent. The host-country could not tax the profit because the transaction took place outside its national boundaries, between corporate entities over which it had no jurisdiction.

Latin Americans have grown increasingly suspicious of multinational oil companies. As they develop a more sophisticated understanding of economic complexities, they are reassessing their relations with foreign companies. This reassessment has brought about more critical attitudes. Latin Americans are no longer viewing the foreign investment in their countries as an unqualified blessing, bringing with it Western capital and technology. The role of the U.S. in particular as an economic missionary bent on industrializing the Third World has come into question.

The political impact of the multinational corporation is even more complex than the sociological and economic effects of such corporations, and the corresponding theories are even more controversial. The basic question raised is whether multinational corporations intervene in the politics of their host countries, and if they do, how far do they go? Do such giants as Standard Oil (New Jersey) or the Royal Dutch Shell Company distort the precarious balance of power that might exist within a relatively underdeveloped nation?

Opinions range very widely. In his book World Crisis in Oil, Harvey O'Connor referred to Peru as Standard Oil's province. The thrust of his argument was that Standard Oil has dominated Peruvian politics in all matters affecting its own interests.[7] A similar thesis has been advanced by a number of Peruvian political leaders.[8] Yet, the spokesmen for the oil industry flatly deny any meddling in the politics of host countries by the oil companies. Writing in International Affairs, Geoffrey Chandler, Trade Relations Coordinator for Shell International Petroleum Company, attempted to put to rest what he sees as the myth that oil companies influence the politics of their host countries. He stated that:

> if an affiliate of an international group were to meddle in internal politics in order to serve its own ends, this would amount at the least to folly and at the most to suicide which would provoke no sympathy.[9]

Chandler suggested that the oil company is part of the society within which it operates. The company will argue its case to the fullest, "but the strength of its argument will rest on the economic factors it can adduce to encourage or discourage particular measures affecting itself." He finally dismissed the widely held suspicion that bribery was an oil company technique on the grounds of inexpediency, for "lasting marriages are not based on venal affection."[10]

This utilitarian morality, to the extent that it exists, surely must be a relatively recent development. Earlier in the century, Chandler's own employer Royal Dutch Shell apparently financed the illegal coup d'état of Augusto Leguía to a considerable degree. The financial assistance granted Leguía was no corporate philanthropy meant to aid Peru along the path to authoritarian bliss; rather, it was a trade. Royal Dutch Shell financed the coup, and in return Leguía was to give that company favorable concessions in Peru. The record does show that this move on the part of the multinational corporation was pure "folly," for Leguía got a better deal with Shell's competitor Standard Oil, and being somewhat less than trustworthy, he favored the American company during his administration at the expense of Shell.[11] This incident merely proved that Shell was outmaneuvered in Peru, and not that the technique used was inherently inexpedient. And in any case, to argue that political meddling and bribery is unwise does not prove that it does not take place. Chandler's argument has limitations.

While generalizations about the size and recent growth of multinational corporations abound both in studies and in the press, the problem of actually defining their role in various countries and their impact upon the political development of those countries is very difficult. The impact of a given multinational corporation on one country might be considerably different from the effect of that same corporation on the country's next door neighbor. Standard Oil's subsidiary, I.P.C., was nationalized in Peru. However, its Colombian subsidiary was able to iron out its difficulties with the Colombian government. It probably employed similar tactics in both countries, and it was in fact represented by the same executive in both cases. However, there were very different results.

Within two weeks of the nationalization of Standard Oil (New Jersey) properties in Peru, a military junta seized the assets of Gulf Oil Corporation in Bolivia. Even the most superficial analysis would show that Gulf's historic role in Bolivia and its position in that country did not bear any resemblance to the position of I.P.C. in Peru. Multinational corporations and their host countries interact on a wide variety of levels. It is possible to make any number of theoretical assertions which can then be supported by any number of examples; but given the variety of multinational corporate experiences, any number of mutually incompatible hypotheses may be supported.

It is precisely because of this variety that it is necessary to proceed cautiously. One research technique which yields particularly fruitful results is the examination of an industry or even of a specific corporation and the analysis of its impact on one or two countries. Beginning with Department of Commerce statistics on the largeness of multinational corporations and simply drawing the conclusion that huge size means involvement in host country politics is of little use in illuminating the operations of multinational corporations. The scholar must discern the types of involvement and the impact upon different categories of countries.

The fact that corporation "A" is very large and powerful and that it operates in country "X" which is small and underdeveloped in itself tells us nothing about the relationship between corporation "A" and country "X". It is possible for corporation "A" to dominate the political system of the host country, but perhaps the corporation's assets in the country do not merit the time, effort and money which such domination would entail. Furthermore, country "X" might be weak in nearly every respect except in its ability to deal with foreign capitalists. In other words, the relationship between any country and the foreign subsidiaries which operate in its national territory is determined by many variables, and not by any global theory which postulates that foreign subsidiaries co-opt national elites into a rootless and illegitimate "transnational technocracy." National elites may be co-opted, but not necessarily so. The nature of the subsidiaries functioning in the country and the national elite itself are the factors which determine the outcome of international corporate investment.

Moreover, it is not enough to study a particular industry's operation in a country during a brief period of time. Some corporations have operated a Latin American subsidiary for many decades, and their more current policies should be placed in historical perspective. It is quite possible that instead of finding global theories to explain multinational corporations in the world today, we might find an historical theory which explains the existence of such enterprises and their impact in terms of predictable phases or stages.

The objective of this study is to illuminate the impact which a United States company as large and as powerful as Standard Oil (New Jersey) had on the politics of a relatively feeble and underdeveloped country such as Peru. How did a company which during the 1960s had annual revenues three times larger than Peru's gross national product operate as a citizen of that country? How did a company whose 1969 payroll was about 25 percent larger than the entire budget of the government of Peru operate as a subject of that government? The answer to these questions varied through the years of I.P.C.'s stay. The relationship of the company to the government of Peru was shaped by many economic and political factors which were essentially dynamic. What factors molded the nature of this economically uneven relationship? What generalizations can be made about the effect of large corporations on small or medium countries with limited industrial development?

Even though they were unevenly matched from a financial point of view, in 1968 the government of Peru dared to do what generations of Peruvian political leaders had wished to do for decades: the military junta seized Standard Oil's assets in Peru. The road from the 1910s to the 1960s was a long one, and one from which the student of politics can gain valuable insights into a widespread phenomenon—the coexistence of multinational corporate giants in the midst of national pigmies—pigmies, however, whose internal dynamics are changing and who are no longer willing to accept their traditional subservience to such giants.

NOTES

1. Jonathan F. Galloway, "Multinational Enterprises as World Interest Groups," Paper presented to the 66th Annual Meeting of the American Political Science Association, Los Angeles, California, September 8-12, 1971, pp. 4-5.
2. Raymond Vernon, Sovereignty at Bay—The Multinational Spread of U.S. Enterprises (New York: Basic Books, 1971), p. 27.
3. Osvaldo Sunkel, "Big Business and 'Dependencia,' a Latin American View," Foreign Affairs, L, No. 3 (April, 1972), pp. 517-531; Sunkel takes as his point of departure a similar argument by Celso Furtado, "La concentración del poder económico en los EE. UU. y sus proujecciones en América Latina," Estudios Internacionales, I, No. 3-4 (1968).

4. Orlando Letelier, as interviewed by Geoffrey Smith, "As They See It, Expropriation: Why Do They Do It?" Forbes, CVIII, No. 1, (July 15, 1971), p. 34.

5. Vernon, Sovereignty at Bay, p. 172.

6. Ibid., pp. 173-78.

7. Harvey O'Connor, World Crisis in Oil (New York: Monthly Review Press, 1962), pp. 225-32.

8. Alfonso Benavides Correa, El Petroleo Peruano. . . o La Autopsia de un Clan," (Lima: Papel Grafica Editora, 1961); José Macedo Mendoza, Nacionalicemos el Petroleo! (Lima: Ediciones Hora del Hombre, 1960).

9. Geoffrey Chandler, "The Myth of Oil Power, International Groups and National Sovereignty," International Affairs, XLVI, No. 4 (October 1970), p. 717.

10. Ibid., pp. 718-19.

11. See the "Strictly Confidential (To be kept in locked files)" enclosure attached to a report by Carlton Jackson, U.S. Trade Commissioner in Lima to the Bureau of Foreign and Domestic Commerce, August 5, 1920, U.S. Department of State Document No. 823.6363/32.

The Multinational Corporation as a Force in Latin American Politics

CHAPTER

1

THE ORIGINS OF LA BREA Y PARINAS

The center of the conflict between International Petroleum Company and the Government of Peru was a very large hacienda in Northwestern Peru—La Brea y Pariñas. Ownership of the subsoil of that hacienda was in dispute well before Standard Oil (New Jersey) entered the Peruvian oil business, and these problems of ownership remained to plague the company and the country until the late 1960s. By 1968, the controversy had grown from the dispute over the hacienda alone to all other properties and installations connected with the refining, marketing, and distribution of petroleum products from that field.

In order fully to appreciate the nature of the conflict between Standard Oil's subsidiary, I.P.C. and the Government of Peru it is necessary to trace the history of the dispute to its origins, and to follow its development to the present. Without historical perspective, the actions of most of the Peruvians involved would seem highly irrational, and understanding the causes of the apparent viciousness with which the political leaders of Peru persecuted a beneficial, well-run and efficient company serving the petroleum needs of their country would be difficult, if not impossible. While historical perspective will not in itself vouch for the rationality of Peruvian policies during the 1960s, it does illuminate the sources of their irritation with the oil company.

The management of I.P.C. fought desperately to preserve what they considered the legitimate role of their company in Peru. That very struggle led them to a deep involvement in the political process of the country, covering the whole gamut of political action, from veiled international intrigue from 1915-25 to outright financial underwriting of cabinets and governments in the 1930s, from gentle private persuasion of political leaders to heavily funded public relations campaigns aimed at convincing the population at large of the justice of the company's position.

The hacienda of La Brea y Pariñas was plagued by anomalies from the time that Peru secured its independence. Hence, the legal problems over the title to the soil and subsoil existed for as long as the country has existed as an independent republic. It was to this early confusion that I.P.C. and the Peruvian government trace their arguments.

The extensive lands which are now called La Brea y Pariñas were first explored by a Spaniard about 1629. Captain Martín Alonzo Granadino, a resident of Paita, acquired usage rights over the land in 1642. However, the property belonged to the King until after sixty years of possession, when in accordance with Spanish law, it finally became private property. Granadino's heir, Don Juan Benito de las Heras, formally acquired the title to the property in 1689. Eventually, the land became the property of the Roman Catholic Convent of Belen through inheritance. It remained in the hands of the clerics during most of the 18th century and until 1815, when usage rights were sold to Don José de la Lama for a period of 150 years. By 1830, the convent was forced to close down, and de la Lama bought the property. He no longer simply had usage rights to the property; he was the complete owner of the hacienda, then known as Máncora.

In accordance with Spanish customs and law, the subsoil of the hacienda remained the property of the King. The land gave off surface emanations of a black substance alternatively called brea or copé. The Incas reportedly used the substance to light up their pre-Columbian ceremonies. After the establishment of the colony, the Spanish crown directly exploited this mineral. Brea, which was nothing more than petroleum, was heated to evaporate the lighter elements. The resulting thick black substance, mineral pitch, was used by the Spanish government to waterproof ships. In 1735 the Crown decided to lease this very primitive mining operation to Montero de Ugarte. After two successive leases, the Spanish government rented the property to Juan Cristóbal de la Cruz in 1802.

With the achievement of independence in 1824, the mine became the property of the Peruvian state, and in order to raise revenue to pay the public debt, the Peruvian Congress enacted a law directing the government to sell all kinds of state property. This law, dated March 5, 1825, provided "that all kinds of goods, haciendas, mines, houses and whatever real estate or property which belonged to the State, and of which the State might freely dispose of, be used towards the liquidation of the public debt."[1] The law was signed into effect by Simón Bolívar on March 9, 1825.

Soon thereafter, on September 22, 1826, the "pitch mine," which up to that point had been the property of the State, was sold to Antonio

de la Quintana, in consideration of a debt owed him. The mine was
valued at 2,695 pesos by the government's assessor, but Quintana
was willing to settle his 4,964 peso debt for the mine. After the
necessary legal paperwork was cleared, the sale was effectuated,
and the Lima government issued a decree which stated in part that
the representatives of the State "take away and separate from the
State which they represent, from the operation, property and dominion
of the pitch mine of reference, which is given, ceded, renounced to
and passed on to the buyer . . ."[2] Hardly four months had passed when
Quintana sold the mine for an unspecified sum to Don José de la Lama,
the owner of the hacienda within which the mine was located. From
that point, De la Lama owned both the surface—the Máncora hacienda,
and the Amotape mine—the subsoil.

De la Lama died in 1850, and his property was divided between
his widow and his daughter. The executors of the estate decided
to name the daughter's portion La Brea; it apparently contained the
bulk of the known pitch deposits. The widow's share was called
Pariñas. In 1857, De la Lama's widow died, and her daughter inherited her part of the estate. Henceforth, the property was known not by
its old name—Máncora, but by a name which was carried down to the
present—La Brea y Pariñas.

Originally, the estate was larger than it was to be in the 19th
and 20th centuries. The hacienda stretched from the Chira River
in the South to the Tumbes River in the north, and from the Pacific
Coast in the west to the foothills of the Andes in the east—an area
comparable to that of the state of Delaware. Through inheritance
and partition, the area was reduced considerably until it was about
one-fourth the original estate. During the 19th century, the hacienda
covered approximately 643 square miles—an area about half the
state of New Hampshire.[3] Lying on the northern coast of Peru, the
property covers terrain which can best be described as desert. Water
is available only from the outside, or from the sea via a desalinization
plant. During its early years La Brea y Pariñas was isolated not
only from the world, but even from the country within which it was
located, because of its remote location and the lack of lines of communication with Lima.

Peru had no laws or ordinances regulating mining from the time
independence was proclaimed on July 28, 1821 until 1824. On June
22, 1824, the Peruvian Congress enacted a law declaring that all
colonial ordinances were valid for the Republic. The effect of this
law was to place mining under the concession system: the State owned
the subsoil and gave exploitation rights to private parties in exchange
for a percentage of the minerals extracted, and/or profits obtained
from the property—a royalty. The law of 1825 which directed the
Peruvian president to sell state property including mines was

inconsistent with this long established Spanish policy. The present Peruvian military government maintains that the original award to Quintana was illegal insofar as it was inconsistent with the Spanish ordinances valid for Republican Peru.[4] However, that conclusion seems unwarranted considering that the Spanish ordinances had validity only through the 1824 law. What the Peruvian Congress did in 1824 could be freely contravened or undone by that same congress a year later. In other words, the sale to Quintana cannot be considered "illegal" on the grounds that it violated an 1824 law when, in fact, it was carried out in accordance with another later law which would take precedence over the earlier one.

In 1859, Edwin Drake drilled the first oil well in Titusville, Pennsylvania. Four years later, on November 2, 1863, A. E. Prentice, an engineer working for the Compania de Gas de Lima, drilled the first oil well in Peru, in an area just north of La Brea y Pariñas. During the 1860s, as a result of the expanding Industrial Revolution, interest in petroleum skyrocketed. Reflecting this new interest, the Peruvian Congress enacted a mining law on April 28, 1873. Its purpose was to promote petroleum and coal production in the country. The law established that petroleum and coal seekers could "announce" their discoveries and establish pertenencias or claims which would be limited to an area of 200 by 200 meters, or 400,000 square meters. The pertenencias were given as concessions—their holders had to work them continuously in order to preserve their right to extract mineral. The law also provided a four-month period within which mine operators would have to present their papers to the Mining Court in Lima for revalidation. Otherwise, old claims would be considered null and void.

The owner of La Brea y Pariñas at the time of the initiation of this new ordinance, Genaro Helguero, did not submit his title for validation. He simply assumed that since the law dealt with mining concessions, and he owned his mine, it did not apply to his property. In 1875 Helguero hired an American to do some exploratory drilling on his property. The venture proved a success—petroleum was found in commercially exploitable quantities.

On January 12, 1877 the Peruvian government enacted another mining law simply establishing a surface tax on mining. Instead of requiring continuous exploitation of the mine, the new law required a semi-annual payment of fifteen soles* per pertenencia. Again,

---

*In the late 19th and early 20th centuries, the sol was worth about $0.50 in U.S. currency. Since then the value has decreased considerably. By fall of 1968 the official rate of exchange was 38.70 soles to the dollar, and the unofficial rate was 47 to the dollar.

THE ORIGINS OF LA BREA Y PARIÑAS

Helguero assumed that the law did not apply to his property. He took no action, and the government made no move to enforce the law—a fact that could be interpreted as either confirming Helguero's stand, or showing that La Brea y Pariñas was so far removed from national life by physical factors that the question of enforcement never arose.

Helguero apparently intended to exploit his oil holdings outside the confines of Peruvian mining regulations. From his point of view, La Brea y Pariñas had a special status—the mine had been sold to him, not given as a concession. The status of the property might never have become problematical except for the fact that in the next decade British oil promoters became interested in the property and Helguero decided to sell. The idea of an untaxed and untaxable oil field privately owned and therefore outside the reach of the Lima government must have appeared very tantalizing indeed. The situation seemed too good to be true to the British investors. They demanded clarification of the status of the mine before proceeding with the purchase.

In response to these pressures, on January 14, 1886, Helguero petitioned the Court of Claims of Paita to have his title to the surface property and the mineral subsoil of La Brea y Pariñas confirmed. In the petition Helguero argued that the subsoil of his property "remained outside the law which authorized prospecting and claims, inasmuch as the nation could not dispose in favor of third persons of what it had previously disposed of by legitimate sale."[5] On February 12, the Judge of the Court of Claims ordered that the unopposed petition be granted. Apparently, the British investors were not completely satisfied, and they demanded some assurance from the government in Lima. On October 12, 1887, Helguero filed a new petition with the Peruvian government asking that it recognize that he, and not the state, was the "absolute owner" of the minerals underlying his property, that his dominion was complete and total, and that no one could prospect or make claims inside the boundaries of his property, insofar as Quintana had acquired the land by sale and hence it was not subject to the procedures created by the ordinances.[6]

As fate and the whims of the Peruvian bureaucracy would have it, Helguero's petition was handled by both the Mining Department and the Acting Attorney of the Supreme Court—with opposite results. The Mining Department went along with Helguero's petition, and further stated that the Laws of 1873 and 1878 could not have retroactive effects detrimental to interests which dated back to 1826. However, the Attorney of the Supreme Court stated that Helguero was the rightful owner of the property, but subject to the mining ordinances. On October 29, 1887, the government issued a decree— a Supreme Resolution,[7] acknowledging the fact that the pitch mine had been adjudicated to Quintana, and that through successive transferences Genaro Helguero acquired the rights of the original buyer.

However, echoing the Attorney of the Supreme Court and his judgment, the resolution also stipulated that, "while the State has the right to sell its mining properties, it cannot exercise that right except in accordance with the restrictions of the laws covering the matter."[8] The decree went on to order that the property be inscribed in the official registry under the name of Helguero, and that the property be listed as three pertenencias until a proper measurement could be made. This decree had the net effect of hopelessly confusing the situation. On the one hand, it admitted that the mine had been sold to Helguero, and on the other it stated that this could not have been done since existing regulations did not allow such a sale. The decree ordered that the mine be registered as belonging to Helguero and at the same time be taxed as though it did not. The reasoning behind the decree was as muddled as its text—the assumption was that the Spanish ordinances covering mining had some sort of constitutional force which preempted parts of the 1825 law signed into effect by Simón Bolívar. More likely, the bureaucrat who actually issued the decree assumed nothing and merely attempted to reconcile the diametrically opposite conclusions of the Attorney of the Supreme Court and the Department of Mining. The result was a nonsensical decree.

Of particular concern to Helguero was the fact that the decree ordered that the property be surveyed in order to determine the number of pertenencias encompassed within its limits. After all, the ordinance had a ten pertenencia (400,000 square meters) limit and the property extended over 1,600 square kilometers. The problem was resolved by an executive decree, a Supreme Resolution dated November 16, 1887—only two weeks after the first decree. This decree, which made no mention whatever of any property and was presumably aimed at mining in general, established that in conditions where mineral deposits extend "irregularly" through the subsoil, a pertenencia need not be regular (200 by 200 meters) but may be measured irregularly. The "irregular" pertenencia may be larger than the prescribed 40,000 square meters.

On November 15, 1887, Helguero filed another petition asking for further clarification of his property's status. In the petition he clearly stated that he needed such a clarification to obtain capital for the development of the mine. In response, the government issued another Supreme Resolution dated December 22, 1887. This new decree reaffirmed the previous one, and in addition granted that "Genaro Helguero is the sole owner of the 'La Brea' mine. . . ."[9] It recognized that only Helguero could exploit its mineral wealth—however, the Law of 1877 governed the mine. Helguero must have been quite concerned about the measurement of his land into pertenencias and the resulting potential tax. As a concession to this concern, the 1887 decree established that the property would be measured in accordance with Article 10, Section 8 of the Mining Ordinance and the rule set in the Supreme Resolution of November 16, 1887, providing for "irregular pertenencias." It specifically instructed the Judge of Primary Jurisdiction of Paita to "designate the number and extension [Emphasis supplied] of the pertenencias encompassed by the property of 'La Brea'. . . ."[10] In other words, the government was willing to compromise with Helguero—the property would be taxed as if it were a common concession, except that since it was privately owned, the tax would be far less than otherwise, given the extent of the property.

In late December 1887, or early January 1888, the Judge of Primary Jurisdiction, accompanied by Helguero and an assessor, inspected the property. On January 10 the judge issued a report which stated in part:

> Taking into account the irregularity of the above mentioned deposits and the difficulties which must be encountered in their discovery, for in the exploitation of oil it often happens that great works are carried out at great expense with no results whatever, his honor, the Judge ordered the assessor to divide the whole extension of the lands within the above mentioned demarcation lines into ten pertenencias.[11]

On January 26, 1888, the Lima government issued a Supreme Resolution specifically acknowledging the validity of the judge's report.[12] Given this sequence of events and the actual texts of the two supreme resolutions and the judge's report, it may be surmised that this final arrangement reflected a compromise settlement between Helguero and the Peruvian government in Lima.

Since the Mining Ordinances imposed a limit of ten pertenencias for any one individual or corporation, Helguero would have lost well over 99.9 percent of the subsoil under his property if the exact maximum extension had been applied. The oil wells were widely dispersed throughout the hacienda. If the property had been taxed according to regular pertenencias, the tax of well over a million soles per year would have been burdensome even for a man of means such as Helguero. The government taxed Helguero only 300 soles a year. However, the government actually gained in the agreement, for since the mine had been sold to Helguero, it was not technically entitled to collect any mining tax geared for concessions from the privately-owned mines. Helguero gained from the agreement because he was then free to sell his mine to the British entrepreneurs on the assumption that its status of private ownership, as well as a favorable tax rate, had been satisfactorily settled. The status of the mine was in fact even more muddled—it was privately owned but "irregularly" taxed as a concession.

On February 3, 1888, Helguero sold his property to British oil promoter Herbert Wilkin Colguhoun Tweedle for £18,000 Sterling. Tweedle sold one-half interest to William Keswick, and the two of them organized the London and Pacific Petroleum Company with a capital of £250,000 and subsequently leased La Brea y Pariñas to the company for a period of 99 years beginning July 1, 1889. From that point on, with the influx of British capital, the petroleum operation grew by leaps and bounds.

The year after the London and Pacific Company took over La Brea y Pariñas the field produced about 8,000 barrels; ten years later, at the turn of the century, production had shot up to 200,000 barrels, an average annual growth of 215 percent. The rate of growth from 1900 to 1915 slowed somewhat, to 53 percent—but by 1915, the fields were producing 1,800,000 barrels per year.[13]

By 1910 it was obvious to all that La Brea y Pariñas was a success. The Peruvian government realized that the "nickels and dimes" settlement of the 1880s had become a multimillion dollar operation in which Peru had virtually no part. Almost simultaneously, Rockefeller's Standard Oil (New Jersey) arrived at the same conclusion—the oil giant had no part in what promised to be a most profitable operation.

It was during the first decade of the 20th century that Rockefeller's oil trust was broken. By the dissolution decree of 1911, the company lost its California oil supply and installations. Standard Oil depended on these western installations to supply its Far Eastern market, especially in China, which offered a vast potential profit. It was the need for a new western coastal source of petroleum which enticed Standard Oil (New Jersey) to Peru.[14] In 1913, Walter C. Teagle, a high company executive, persuaded Standard's president John D. Archbold to initiate negotiations for the purchase of the London and Pacific Petroleum Company. Because of the considerable bitterness which Standard's encounters with the United States Government had generated, the company management decided to utilize Standard's Canadian subsidiary, Imperial Oil, to carry out the purchase. The management felt that the British government was far more willing to back up British enterprises abroad than the American government, and therefore they played it safe and arranged to maintain their purchase under the British flag. In 1914, Jersey Standard organized the International Petroleum Company in Toronto, Canada. I.P.C., as it became known, was destined to serve as a holding company for Standard's operations in Peru and later in Colombia and Ecuador. The purchase of London and Pacific Petroleum Company was kept secret—that is, there was no direct acquisition. The stock was bought and by 1914 Standard Oil (New Jersey) had a dominant interest—it owned over 50 percent of the stock.

As previously mentioned, the prosperity of La Brea y Pariñas struck the Peruvians as well as Standard Oil. In 1911, Ricardo Deustua, a Peruvian engineer employed by the government and a relation of the prominent Peruvian philosopher Alejandro O. Deustua, traveled to northeastern Peru and "discovered" that La Brea y Pariñas was far larger than ten regular pertenencias. After returning to Lima, Deustua spoke before the Peruvian Geographic Society and "unmasked" the London and Pacific Petroleum Company for alleged fraud against the Peruvian treasury.[15] While there is no clear reason why Deustua journeyed to La Brea y Pariñas, there are two logical possibilities. As an employee of the Lima government, he might have been ordered there with specific instructions to inspect the land. Another alternative is that he might have been urged to conduct his inspection by Peruvian entrepreneurs who had become anxious to acquire a share of the booming petroleum interest, since he so suddenly reported his findings to the Geographic Society.[16]

As a result of Deustua's inquiry, the Ministry of Development issued another Supreme Resolution, dated March 31, 1911, declaring that the 1888 Supreme Resolution dividing La Brea y Pariñas into ten pertenencias was an administrative error because it failed to follow the prescribed pattern for dividing mining concessions into regular pertenencias. It also ordered that the property be remeasured. Ricardo Deustua was appointed to carry out the order. William Keswick, who by then had become the sole owner of the property, and his leasee, the London and Pacific Petroleum Company, objected to the decree and enlisted the support of the British legation in Lima to try to stop or at least delay the application of the decree. Due to pressure from the British, and even more likely, because of the internal turmoil that the Civilista Administration of Augusto Leguía was then encountering, the Supreme Resolution was never carried out. Augusto Leguía, the Civilista President of Peru from 1908-12 and future dictator from 1919-30, was well known for his rapport with foreign investors and it is unlikely that his administration would have acted unfavorably against as prominent a British enterprise as the London and Pacific Petroleum Company.

There were national elections in Peru in 1912, and the Civilistas were voted out of office. Their opposition, led by Guillermo Billinghurst, took over. The question of La Brea y Pariñas remained unresolved, but not forgotten as the American owners of London and Pacific might have wished. President Billinghurst was the grandson of a British soldier who had fought in the Peruvian War of Independence—a man who had a substantial business interest in the guano industry of southern Peru. While he made promises of social reform,

Billinghurst found that it was very difficult to move against the entrenched Peruvian Congress. It was this Congress which finally inspired a coup d'etat against Billinghurst and installed a new government under the leadership of Colonel Oscar R. Benavides in 1914.

And it was this military government which was destined to drag La Brea y Pariñas out of its splendid isolation and into the arena of Peruvian and, eventually, international politics. Several factors contributed to the new developments. World War I substantially diminished Peruvian foreign trade, and as a result, the government's income dropped. Benavides was forced to suspend payments on the foreign debt. His government looked around for new sources of revenue, and the prosperous La Brea y Pariñas operation, with an annual tax rate of about $150, figured prominently as a potential source of much-needed revenue. Another factor which made the move against the London and Pacific Petroleum Company plausible was the harassment which both the Americans and the British had been carrying out against the labor practices of Peruvian landlords. For instance, in 1912 the British and American governments carried out a joint investigation of slavery in Peru. This represented but the latest chapter in what had been a continuous campaign since the turn of the century conducted by Peru-based British and American officials. They were trying to focus world public opinion on the conditions of "virtual slavery" under which Peruvian farm workers labored. Along with other newspapers, the London Times deplored the "horrible evils" plaguing the poor Indians on the haciendas of Peru.[17] This ill-advised campaign, which might have diverted attention away from labor conditions in the sweat shops of Britain and the United States, created a great deal of animosity among the Peruvian gamonales— the landowners, who were very much in control of the Congress in Lima.[18]

The intellectual climate was not very favorable to Anglo-Saxon capitalism. Many wealthy Civilistas repudiated modernization. Their chief spokesman, Alejandro Deustua condemned the use of scientific knowledge in the pursuit of utilitarian objectives as the lowest form of human endeavor. Through his popular philosophy courses at the University of San Marcos, Deustua convinced many prominent Peruvians that man's highest endeavor was to seek the "ideal image of God." Naturally, such a goal was possible only for the selected few, and consequently society should be organized in such a way that its material benefits would go to that tiny, but intellectually capable minority who would pursue the highest of goals. At a policy level, Deustua favored a reduction of primary and secondary school enrollments— widespread education would only encourage the materialistic appetites of the masses.[19] While Deustua's ideas were not universally accepted in Peru, the gamonales reduced his philosophy to a rationalization of the Peruvian hierarchical society. These landlords disliked capitalism because it represented a sort of materialistic endeavor sprinkled with egalitarianism which they detested. They preferred a paternalistic authoritarian society based on Thomistic Catholic doctrine.

It was in the context of this political and ideological climate that the government of Colonel Benavides issued its decree of April 25, 1914, rejecting all the arguments presented by the London and Pacific Petroleum Company and ordering that the property be resurveyed. Engineers Héctor Boza and Alberto Jochamowitz went to northeastern Peru to survey the property. They apparently encountered considerable difficulty—the company refused to give them drinking water.[20] After their work was completed, they returned to Lima and announced their findings—La Brea y Pariñas covered not ten but 41,614 regular pertenencias. By the 1914 decree and subsequent ones issued the following year, the Peruvian government insisted that the company raise its tax payments from 300 soles to 1,240,000 soles per year. This would have represented an increase from $150 to $6 million.[21] The new tax rate would have amounted to approximately one-third of the gross revenues and somewhere between 50 percent and 60 percent of the net gains according to calculations of Peruvians friendly to the company.[22] The company objected, and the Peruvian government's answer came in the form of a decree ordering that the property be officially registered as consisting of 41,614 pertenencias, and that the tax be paid accordingly. On March 15, 1915, the government even went so far as to deny a company petition to have the La Brea y Pariñas problem submitted to the Peruvian Court.

On April 12, 1915, Standard Oil (New Jersey) sent an urgent and confidential telegram to the Department of State in Washington complaining that the Peruvian government was "imposing and enforcing destructive and actual confiscatory tax" on London and Pacific's operation. The telegram also advised the State Department that Jersey Standard had a "dominant financial interest" in that company, and asked that Washington intercede with the Peruvian government to delay enforcement of the decree until the company had an opportunity to argue its case.[23] Washington complied with the request immediately. On April 14, 1915, the Department of State sent a coded message to the American ambassador in Lima instructing him to do as Standard Oil suggested.[24] This fateful telegram signaled the beginning of what was to become a long and for the most part acrimonious tripartite relationship between Standard Oil (New Jersey), the United States government and the Peruvian government.

At this point in the history of this controversy, however, the partisans were not limited to the three mentioned above. The government of Great Britain, through its legation in Lima, also intervened on behalf of London and Pacific Petroleum Company, which was registered as a British business even though it was controlled by Standard Oil (New Jersey), and on behalf of William Keswick, the British subject who owned La Brea y Pariñas, even though the property was leased to London and Pacific. In a note to the Peruvian Foreign Office, the British Ambassador wondered "how one can demand, with justice, the claimed sum as specified in the decree. . . ." He went on to state: "It can be expected thereby, that in view of the above mentioned reasons and of the great and important interests which are involved, the Government of Peru will see to it that the Decree of March 15 be annulled."[25] Years later, Peruvian public leaders would bitterly remember the imperious tone of the British note as an example of the humiliations Peru suffered during this stage of its history.[26]

On April 17, 1915, American Ambassador to Peru Benton McMillin cabled Washington advising the Department of State that the Peruvian government had acquiesced to the Anglo-American demand. In a dispatch dated April 28, the ambassador advised the American government that according to the Peruvian government, Peru was not attempting to levy a new tax, but was merely trying to collect a general tax which the London and Pacific Petroleum Company had not been paying. The Peruvian Minister of Foreign Affairs persuaded the American ambassador that London and Pacific had been paying taxes for only the few acres which they were exploiting, and that the law required them to pay for the complete acreage.[27] This was an inaccurate interpretation from the company's point of view, for the 1888 settlement made it quite clear that the whole property was divided into ten irregular pertenencias, not that the company would pay taxes on only part of its territory. The ambassador also reported conversations with representatives of the company, who gave him their side of the story. What is most significant about this exchange is that up to that point the State Department seemed to have no information whatever as to the involvement of Standard Oil (New Jersey) in the Peruvian oil extraction business. With serious problems in the offing, the Department began to learn from the Peruvian government and from the company's management via the American ambassador about a problem which had been smoldering for several years. When taking over his duties as ambassador in 1913, McMillin was specifically instructed "to keep a look out for such resources in Peru as might prove profitable investments for Americans. . . ."[28] It appears that Standard Oil meant to keep its Peruvian operation secret, even from the American government, until its hand was forced by the need for diplomatic pressure from Washington. The State Department apparently did not take offense, for it intervened on behalf of the company, and then continued to

THE ORIGINS OF LA BREA Y PARIÑAS

exercise a careful watch over the situation once the enforcement of the 1915 decree was indefinitely postponed.

1915 was an election year in Peru, and the Civilista Party's presidential candidate was victorious. In August, José Pardo began his second term as president. His administration seemed more willing to negotiate with Standard Oil than had the administration of Benavides. No sooner was the new government in power than negotiations were initiated with R. V. Le Sueur, I. P. C's chief counsel. However, these conversations continued for several months without achieving a conclusive settlement.

On November 7, 1915, Walter Teagle, Standard Oil's overseas entrepreneur, reputed architect of the London and Pacific purchase,[29] and I. P. C. president, arrived in Callao in what must have been one of the earliest corporate yachts. Teagle and his entourage spent some time visiting La Brea y Pariñas on their way down the coast. They declared that the Peruvian oil fields would never become "great oil producers . . . that the deposits are already showing signs of exhaustion. . . ." These statements were promptly cabled to the New York press, with a corresponding flurry of concern in Peru. Teagle conferred with Le Sueur, the company's chief negotiator in Lima. Soon thereafter, a satisfactory agreement from the company's point of view was concluded.[30]

This agreement was presented in a bill submitted to the Civilista-controlled Senate on December 7, 1915. As amended by the Senate, the bill provided that La Brea y Pariñas covered a territory of 41,614 regular pertenencias. However, provisions were made for dividing the property into two parts taxed at different rates. The pertenencias currently exploited would be taxed at the regular rate of 30 soles per year; the remaining area would be taxed at the special rate of one sol during the ten years after 1915, two soles between 1926 and 1935, three soles from 1936 to 1945, and fifteen soles from 1946 to 1965. The bill fixed the tax rates for fifty years beginning in 1915; however, the proportion of exploited to unexploited land would vary. It was expected that London and Pacific would be using about 1,000 pertenencias in the beginning, while the remaining area would be considered inactive.[31] Under this formula, the company's tax payments would increase to 3,000 soles—a considerable sum, but far short of the previously demanded annual tax rate of 1,240,000 soles.

The government's bill was debated by the Senate Legislative Commission, and after much discussion lasting through 1916, a favorable report was issued by the Commission's majority against bitter opposition of the minority. From 1915 to 1918, La Brea y Pariñas ceased to be a dispute between the Peruvian government and a private enterprise with occassional interference from the British and American governments—it became a hotly contested internal political issue in Peru.

The Pardo administration had good reason to insist that the compromise solution reached with London and Pacific be accepted. The Peruvian economy had overcome the financial difficulties faced by the Benavides administration, thanks to the booming exports of items such as petroleum. The government's revenue, highly dependent on export taxes, went from 28 million soles in 1915 to 40 million soles in 1918. In addition, Pardo wanted to enlist the aid of the United States in the settlement of the touchy Tacna-Arica dispute with Chile.[32] Unfortunately, Pardo was unable to persuade the opposition and some very prominent members of his own party of the wisdom of his compromise solution. Many Civilista legislators preferred to remain loyal to Alejandro Deustua's philosophy—anti-capitalist.

Leading the group of twelve dissenting Senators, and writing the minority report, was Antonio Miró Quesada, a member of the government Civilista Party and editor of the influential Lima daily, El Comercio. Miró Quesada contended that the government's bill would "place the owners of La Brea y Pariñas in a privileged condition. . . ." He argued that the state would grant the London and Pacific Petroleum Company a reduced tax burden and furthermore tie its hands for fifty years. Peru would abdicate its sovereign privilege of taxation for half a century. Basing his argument on the fact that throughout the transactions of the 1880s, the property had been referred to only as "La Brea," Miró Quesada and his fellow dissenting senators insisted that the Pariñas side of the property could not even be discussed. No viable claim on its subsoil could be made by any private party. He maintained that the mine bought by Quintana consisted of a few wells in the Prieto Mountains with insignificant territory, and that the current owners could not claim ownership over the subsoil of thousands of square kilometers on the basis of that original purchase. In any case, he argued that what was purchased was brea (pitch) and not petroleum. The dissenting senators inferred that an administrative error was made in allowing such large pertenencias, and that bad faith or corruption entered into the granting of the 1889 decree. Some of their arguments were pragmatic; they pointed out that with the new technology, La Brea y Pariñas would soon become more fully exploitable and as such a very important world oil field. Finally, Miró Quesada and his friends appealed to the wounded Peruvian national pride: "Peru has lost the guano and the saltpeter, but now generous Nature offers it petroleum. Our duty is to conserve it."[33]

During the month of November 1917, the partisans of the compromise produced a sharp rebuttal. Senator Manuel Vicente Villarán led the attack on the dissenters. He declared that there had been no error and that the government knew of the extent of La Brea y Pariñas in the 1880s. He emphatically rejected the allegations of corruption, noting that the government in power then was supported by the Civilista Party. The Pardo administration feared that the opposition was attempting to place responsibility for the problem at the Civilista doorstep. The senators favoring the compromise presented a well-researched legal case stressing the validity of the private title to the subsoil of La Brea y Pariñas. Given the validity of the private title, it would be logical for the government to reach a compromise solution so that the state could receive more income while preserving the sanctity of private property. The supporters also had pragmatic arguments—they stated that it would be expedient for Peru to attract foreign investment. Senator Villarán exhorted Peru not to look with suspicion upon foreign enterprises and "to note that they represent a step ahead in what is most important to us, the industrial development of the country."[34] Villarán and his supporters in the Senate favored the kind of utilitarian capitalism which had been so resoundingly rejected by the Civilista Party's leading thinker—Alejandro Deustua.[35]

The bitterness of the battle, with its partisan and philosophical configuration well-delineated, soon grew. During 1917, the Pardo administration published the speeches of Senators Villarán, Arturo Osores, and other pro-government legislators in booklet form. In an acrimonious preface, the administration charged the opposition with "pitiful sterility for the good," and with "using subterfuge to distort reality so as to mold passion to their own interests."[36]

A week after the speeches of Villarán and Osores were delivered, the Senate passed the La Brea y Pariñas bill, and it was sent on to the Chamber of Deputies, where it soon became evident that it faced an uphill battle for acceptance. The opposition in the Chamber of Deputies refined some of the same arguments which had been offered in the Senate. The possibility of defeat was very real, and the management of I.P.C. decided to bring pressure to bear.

On January 12, 1918, the West Coast Leader, an English language newspaper which generally reflected the interests of the Anglo-American entrepreneurs in Peru, published an article declaring that "a fortnight ago the Canadian Government requisitioned the steamer tanker Azof," one of the two carrying oil from Talara to Lima-Callao. At the time, the Lima-Callao area needed some 6,000 metric tons of petroleum per month. The remaining tanker, the Circassian Prince, could carry 5,000 metric tons per month. The metropolitan area faced a petroleum deficit of 1,000 metric tons. The article made it clear that while the Canadian government had allowed the two tankers to remain in service "if thereby a favourable settlement of the controversy could be effected with the Peruvian government," the pressures of war and "the failure of the Peruvian government to take definite action . . . has removed the essential cause for the Canadian Government's forbearance in the question of the tankers, and as a result one of them has been withdrawn and the second will probably soon follow."[37]

The warning could not have been more explicit—either the Peruvian government reached a compromise acceptable to the company, or else it would face first a shortage and possibly a complete lack of petroleum with resulting hardship to the economy of the country.

The battle continued unabated during 1918, and it intensified as time passed. I.P.C., which had already stopped all new exploration and development, leaked information to the effect that it might stop all work at its oil fields. On September 24, Le Sueur publically confirmed the rumors that the company was considering a work stoppage and gave as the reason the lack of progress in the settlement of the La Brea y Pariñas tax controversy. The Lima press widely interpreted the company's move as an attempt to pressure the Chamber of Deputies into passing the bill approved earlier by the Senate. Miró Quesada's El Comercio demanded that the government take over the oil fields and form a Peruvian corporation to run the operation. Even La Prensa, Lima's other major daily newspaper, joined in counseling that if I.P.C. carried out its threat, the government should expropriate the fields.[38]

The Peruvian government, which was under heavy pressure from the U.S. and the oil company, then faced the acute displeasure of the oil workers at Talara, who appealed for an early settlement of the controversy. The government's response was to agree confidentially to submit the dispute to arbitration, perhaps to the Hague Tribunal. This agreement appeared to have been reached at the urging of the American ambassador in Lima, although the evidence is not entirely clear.[39] October brought no relief in Congress. The opposition vigorously argued against any compromise on the grounds that the original sale to Quintana was null, and that the concession was given subject to the general mining laws. The sale of a pitch mine could not be turned into the sale of a petroleum field, and since the surface property was separate from the subsoil there was no reason to assume that the subsoil sold to Quintana corresponded to the entire hacienda, Máncora. When word of the government's proposal to submit the question to international arbitration was made public, the opposition countered with demands that I.P.C. should pay back taxes amounting to some $16 million. The inflexibility of their argument was well illustrated by the statement of one of the outspoken opposition leaders, Oscar C. Barros.

> Now, even assuming that it would be possible to submit our sovereign rights to arbitration in a conflict with a

THE ORIGINS OF LA BREA Y PARIÑAS 19

> private party which should disappear as a pigmy, as a
> germ before the magnificence and greatness of a State,
> it turns out that we have always arrived at solutions
> which were prejudicial to Peru.[40]

With hindsight, it is simple to recognize that Oscar Barros's premonitions about an international arbitrary award were quite correct; however, his assessment of I.P.C. and its parent company, Standard Oil (New Jersey), was very unrealistic. The "pigmy" prevailed for many years.

It was Standard Oil and not the Canadian government which withdrew the steamship Azof from its Peruvian route. By October the second ship was also put out of service, thus effectively cutting Peru off from its petroleum supply.[41] The American, British, and Canadian embassies in Lima kept quiet about the ship requisition scheme and played Standard Oil's game—effectively pulling the rug out from under Peru.[42] Joining in this concerted effort was the only other significant oil producer in Peru, the Lobitos Oil-Fields Co., Ltd.

Realizing that without oil Peru's railroads and electric power plants would come to a grinding halt, the Peruvian government ordered the Lobitos Oil-Fields Co. to transport 20 percent of the oil it usually exported to Canada to Callao. The British company refused with the backing of the British ambassador. The company argued that the ships used by the Lobitos company were under the control of the Canadian government.[43]

By October 28, 1918, the situation became untenable for the Peruvian government. In a final effort, the Pardo administration, through its ambassador in Washington, requested "that the government of the United States kindly use its good offices to the effect that the British Government recommend the aforementioned Oil Companies to observe the laws of Peru."[44] The Pardo government was brought to its knees—Peru begged Washington to intercede with London so that a private company would obey its laws. The American government, however, was an accomplice to the oil company maneuver, and the State Department merely shuffled papers without taking any action. The Department forwarded the Peruvian request to the War Trade Board, which had already obtained the German ships Peru had held. Peru had nothing further to bargain with, and the War Trade Board responded that it "would be reluctant to take any action in this matter, except upon the express request of the Department of State."[45] No such request was forthcoming, and Pardo was left to fend for himself against the recalcitrant and proconfiscatory forces in the Peruvian Congress and press.

During the early weeks of November 1918, the Peruvian Congress debated the question of La Brea y Pariñas, apparently unconvinced that the battle was lost. The Lima press, with Antonio Miró Quesada and El Comercio in the lead, recommended that the legislators consult Mexican laws dealing with oil. At last, Washington showed some concern. The Department of State feared that "General Carranza will seize this opportunity to . . . induce the Peruvian Government to adopt a policy similar to that of the Mexican Government." The American ambassador in Lima was ordered to watch the situation closely, and "to report to the Department any evidence of Mexican influence."[46]

This concern proved unfounded, for on December 24, 1918, the Peruvian Congress passed Law 3016, which proclaimed in its single article:

> The Executive Power is authorized to come to an agreement with the Government of His Britannic Majesty for submission of the controversy pending between the State and the mining enterprise "Brea y Pariñas" to the final decision of an international arbitration.[47]

Representing the legislative branch, Antonio Miró Quesada, President of the Senate, editor of El Comercio, and arch foe of I.P.C., signed the bill and forwarded it to President Pardo.

The Civilistas were once described by an American ambassador to Peru as:

> the reactionary, ultraconservative faction of Peru, corresponding to the group of large landowners so powerful in Mexico in the days of President Dias. They are anti-foreign, anti-industrial and wish Peru to be solely an agricultural country without development outside their own haciendas,—with the country administered entirely for their own benefit.[48]

The question of La Brea y Parinas proved a watershed in the history of Pardo's Civilista Party—the oil issue divided the party hopelessly. Pardo and his supporters wanted to reach an expedient compromise with American capitalism and one of its foremost representatives in Peru, I.P.C. Opposing him were men of considerable prominence, led by Antonio Miró Quesada, who so bitterly contested the government's action that the Civilistas could neither heal their wounds nor face the challenges of the election year 1919.

Widespread strikes in Lima-Callao, an untimely reduction of the military budget, and an overanxious opposition candidate for the presidency provided the ingredients for a coup d'état in July 1919. Before the year was over, most important Civilista leaders, including Pardo and Miró Quesada, were exiled—the golden age of oligarchy in Peru had come to an end. Henceforth:

> The wealthy families would continue to be a force in politics . . . but from now onwards the oligarchy would not have it all its own way. A new force had begun to play its part in Peruvian politics—the urban working and middle-classes. Their growing influence could no longer safely be ignored either by the men of wealth or the soldiers . . . Peru by 1919 had already taken a first important step into the modern age.[49]

According to Francois Bourricaud, the Coup of 1919 ended the Civilista dream of "an aristocratic republic," under the tutelage of the great Lima families, and initiated for the first time in the 20th century, a "duality between the governing [or rather dominating] and the political class. . ."[50]

With the antiforeign and anti-industrial oligarchy shocked and in disarray, the Peruvian scene looked more promising than ever to American capital in general and to Standard Oil's Latin American subsidiary, I.P.C. in particular. In August 1919, the Department of State sent a circular to all American embassies and consular offices impressing upon the personnel "the vital importance of securing adequate supplies of mineral oil both for present and future needs of the United States. . . ." They were instructed to obtain and forward information regarding the discovery of oil, the granting of concessions, and the "change of ownership of oil property or important changes in ownership or control of corporate companies concerned with oil production or distribution."[51] The American diplomatic personnel in Peru took the message to heart, for during the 1920s American diplomatic channels were saturated with information concerning the moves of American and European petroleum interests in that country.

The key to the new American optimism rested not only on the broken back of the oligarchy, but on the personal background of the new strong man—Augusto Leguía. The new president of Peru learned fluent English early in his life—an important asset in his very successful business career. Prior to his entrance into politics, Leguía served as the general manager of the Peruvian, Bolivian, and Ecuadorian operations of the New York Life Insurance Company. After a trip to London, he became manager of the British Sugar Company in addition to his duties as president of the National Bank of Peru.[52] He served as Minister of the Treasury in the first Pardo administration from 1904 to 1908. At that point he became the presidential candidate of the Civilista Party and won the election. His term in office was marred by Congressional stalling on his legislative program and even a theatrical uprising in which he was actually captured by his adversaries and marched through the streets of Lima. An unperceptive American attaché who witnessed the event reported that Leguía had gone mad and joined in a demonstration against himself.[53]

As time passed, Leguía grew more bitter and suspicious of democratic institutions. He plotted to rig the congressional elections and when his machinations were discovered, he found himself in opposition to his own party's congressional delegation. Leguía remained in office—a prisoner of the circumstances of his own creation. However, he learned a valuable lesson. "Never again would the future dictator of Peru allow himself to be pushed around by the oligarchy, or indeed by politicians of any political creed."[54]

Following the expiration of his term in 1912, Leguía went abroad. He spent most of that time between the end of his first term and the 1919 coup d'etat in London, apparently selling British businessmen on the idea that he would be the future leader of Peru. In exchange for an unspecified sum which he planned to use in the financing of his coup, Leguía promised the Royal Dutch/Shell Company that once he was in power he would grant that company exclusive exploration rights in Peru. The international oil giant fell for Leguía's proposition.[55] On his way from London to Lima, Leguía stopped in New York and in Washington during the spring of 1919. He held conversations with important American businessmen, and while the nature of these conversations and even the identity of the businessmen remains unclear to this date, chances are that Leguía tried to strike deals similar to the one he reached with Royal Dutch/Shell. It is known that Leguía talked with the president of the National City Bank of New York about his desire to "consolidate the various government agencies and monopolies operating in Peru . . ." and about refinancing the Peruvian public debt.[56]

In the words of James Careye:

> There is no evidence to conclude that the prospective president of Peru and the head of the National City Bank entertained other than honorable intentions. When it is noted, however, that the conversations took place before the elections were held in Peru, it is evident that some presumptuous planning was done with a man who had not yet returned from a five-year absence.[57]

Leguía proved to be a more skillful politician than his British and American promoters might have suspected. He refused to honor or

THE ORIGINS OF LA BREA Y PARIÑAS

even acknowledge his commitments to Royal Dutch/Shell. Instead, he began to bargain with British and American businessmen to see who would offer the most for the favors of his government.

When word of his dealings with some British promoters leaked out, the Department of State instructed its Lima embassy to make it known to Leguía that Washington would not look favorably upon any Peruvian oil concessions to any oil concerns reflecting any future exclusion of American oil companies.[58] Leguía promptly responded "that Americans would be given equal or preferential opportunities for investment and development in Peru."[59] However, in spite of Leguía's pledges, Washington remained skeptical. The American Embassy in Lima carefully monitored everything going on in the country. Even a Swedish scientific expedition was suspect as a cover operation for the exploratory activities of Royal Dutch/Shell, the worldwide archenemy of Standard Oil (New Jersey). The American chargé d'affaires talked with Leguía regularly, yet he commented in a dispatch to Washington dated March 5, 1920, that he would be "obliged to discount his statements as I do not believe he is giving out full information."[60]

By the middle of March, William Walker Smith reported that "the President again brought up the question of financial assistance to the country." Noting that Peru was hard pressed for capital and that Leguía's success depended on aid from abroad, Smith went on to conclude: "Whoever can come to the financial assistance of Peru at this time will gain a great commercial advantage."[61] With a clearer understanding of Leguía's strategy, the United States government and I.P.C. moved; the first to promote the entry of American mining enterprises in Peru, and the second to consolidate its very profitable operations by settling the still pending La Brea y Pariñas issue. In late March, 1920, a memorandum from Alvey Adee, Second Assistant Secretary of State, went to the Department of Commerce, advising that:

> there is great activity for the development of oil at the present time in Peru, and I earnestly recommend that the Department so place the matter before American interests that they may enter this field with the least possible delay.[62]

In accordance with this recommendation, the Department of Commerce issued a confidential three page report entitled "Peruvian Oil Development" to major American oil companies. A covering letter from Philip B. Kennedy, Director of the Bureau of Foreign and Domestic Commerce, informed the companies that "since so much interest is now being displayed by European companies in Peru, it behooves

American oil interests to look carefully into the possibilities of the Peruvian fields. . . ."[63] The U.S. government, knowing that the Royal Dutch Shell Company was attempting to gain a foothold in Peru, warned the American giant Standard Oil to engage in counter-maneuvers.[64]

The message was not wasted, for in April 1920, Walter Teagle called on the government to give his company "all possible and proper assistance."[65] The company needed to settle the La Brea y Pariñas question. Such a settlement, however, might have to be reached in the context of a larger package deal. During the spring or summer of 1920, I.P.C. offered the Peruvian government $10 million in exchange for an oil monopoly in that country—the compensation would cover the La Brea y Pariñas problem as well. Leguía neither accepted nor rejected the offer—he merely kept everyone in suspense, pending counter offers from Royal Dutch/Shell, British Oil Fields, Sinclair Oil, or from promoter Lewis Emery, Jr.[66]

Leguía wanted a $25 million loan, and he wanted Standard Oil (New Jersey) to finance "the civic and general sanitary improvements" which he had planned for Peru. Since the company was paying taxes of about $1 million annually, Leguía proposed to pledge that annual tax to service the loan. He also proposed . . ."to settle in the company's favor certain long-continued disputes with the government over the titles of certain oil lands in the Talara district."[67] The executives of Standard Oil well understood their predicament— the Peruvian Congress authorized the president to settle the La Brea y Pariñas controversy by international arbitration, but as of 1919 it was up to Leguía to initiate this action. He was not willing to do so unless Standard Oil was willing to underwrite his public works program. The company rejected Leguia's proposal, and its relations with the Peruvian strongman rapidly began to corrode. Leguía continued his coy strategy during the first half of 1921, keeping the American ambassador partially informed of loan offers by the representatives of the Shell Company and the serious consideration they were being given. At the same time he earnestly declared his almost passionate partisanship for American capital.

> You know, he was quoted as saying by the American Ambassador, that if I could have my way, Peru would be practically American within ten or fifteen years. But, Mr. Ambassador, what can I do when the business interests of the United States refuse to take advantage of the opportunities given to come into Peru and lay the foundation for such conditions.[68]

Leguía's strategy was clear. He sought to pressure Standard Oil (New Jersey) into underwriting his government while hinting that he

THE ORIGINS OF LA BREA Y PARIÑAS

had other bidders whom he would have taken up long ago had it not been for his love for American business.

The company resented Leguía's attitude. From the middle of 1920 to the fall of 1921, International Petroleum's manager in Lima, William Montavon—a former representative of the U.S. Department of Commerce in that city, openly attacked the administration of Augusto Leguía. Ambassador Gonzales reported to Washington that Montavon was "favorable to any revolutionary movement that might cause an overthrow of the present government."[69] The ambassador admonished Montavon against further public comment, but Montavon, upon departing for a trip to the United States, promptly declared that an insurrection by one Captain Cervantes then in progress in Iquitos signaled "the beginning of the end of Leguía." This was particularly distressing to the ambassador, since American military intelligence received reports that oil interests were financing the insurrection.[70] Another would-be anti-Leguía revolutionary, Augusto Durán, also approached American oil companies seeking a $100,000 loan in exchange for future concessions of oil lands in Peru.[71] While there is no evidence of whether or not the loan was made, it was apparent that Standard Oil (New Jersey) wanted to depose Leguía, or at least frighten him into a compromise.

Standard Oil's "get tough" policy was deeply disturbing to the American diplomatic personnel in Lima. William Gonzales, the U.S. Ambassador, noted that the manager of I.P.C. was "one of the most prominent Americans in Peru," and poignantly concluded that "any tendency of American businessmen in foreign countries to become 'King-makers,' should be discouraged if for no better reason than in behalf of the sound general business interests of the United States."[72] Unfortunately, Standard Oil's influence in Washington was great, and Gonzales's assignment was cut short. Even so, the logic of his statement would live to haunt the company's Peruvian operation to the end of its days.

With Gonzales replaced and Standard Oil threatening to finance a new revolution, Leguía opted for settlement with the company. On August 27, 1921, Leguía's Minister of Foreign Affairs and a representative from Britain signed an Agreement for Arbitration in Lima. This agreement signaled the beginning of the diplomatic phase of the La Brea y Pariñas controversy.

NOTES

1. The entire text of the law was reproduced in a pamphlet issued by the London and Pacific Petroleum Company in 1916 and later reissued by International Petroleum Company in 1960. Historia

de La Brea y Pariñas: Articulos y Documentos Publicados en 1916 por la London & Pacific Petroleum Company, Ltd. (Lima: International Petroleum Company, 1960).

2. Ibid.

3. Historical Resumé of "La Brea y Pariñas" (International Petroleum Company, August, 1967).

4. Revolutionary Government of Peru, National Office of Information, Petroleum in Peru—The History of a Unique Case for the World to Judge (Lima: Petróleos del Peru, 1969), p. 27.

5. "Chronological History of 'La Brea y Pariñas' Oilfields of the International Petroleum Company, 1826-1963," Peruvian Times, July 28, 1967, p. 13.

6. Historia de La Brea y Pariñas.

7. In the press and often in conversation, Peruvians refer to their government as El Supremo Gobierno. Decrees are called Supreme Resolutions officially and colloquially.

8. The entire decree is reproduced in ibid.

9. Ibid.

10. Ibid.

11. The entire text of the judge's report is reproduced in ibid.

12. The decree stated in part: "The measurement performed and the assessment of ten pertenencias which had been determined by the Paita Judge are hereby approved, with the extension which corresponds to each pertenencia according to the enclosed topographic sketch . . ." ibid.

13. International Petroleum Company, "100 Años de Industria Petrolera en al Peru," FANAL, XVIII, No. 68 (1963), p. 28.

14. Harvey O'Connor, World Crisis in Oil (New York: Monthly Review Press, 1962), pp. 225-226.

15. José Macedo Mendoza, Nacionalicemos el Petroleo! (Lima: Hora del Hombre, 1960), p. 22.

16. That the Geographic Society was in effect a kind of chamber of commerce for entrepreneurs became obvious later when the Society attempted to get exclusive privileges to explore for certain minerals, including petroleum. See the telegram from William Smith, Chargé d' affaires ad interim in Lima to Secretary of State, U.S. Department of State Decimal Files, Record Group 59, No. 823.6363/20, March 5, 1920.

17. James C. Carey, Peru and the United States, 1900-1962 (Notre Dame, Indiana: University of Notre Dame Press, 1964), pp. 25-27.

18. Fredrick B. Pike, The Modern History of Peru (New York: Praeger, 1967), pp. 183-184.

19. Ibid., pp. 184-186.

20. Macedo Mendoza, Nationalicimos el Petroleo, p. 23.

21. O'Connor, World Crisis in Oil, p. 226.

22. "Discurso del Doctor Manuel Vicente Villarán, Senador por Junín, Sesión del 15 de Noviembre de 1917," Arturo Osores, et al., La Brea y Parinas: Discursos ante el Senado, (Legislatura Ordinaria de 1917) y Dictamenes Juridicos (Lima: International Petroleum Company, "Noticias de Petroleo," 1963), p. 40.

23. A report on this telegram appears in a dispatch. William Libby to Secretary of State, April 12, 1915, U.S. Department of State Decimal Files, No. 823.6363/5.

24. Secretary of State to the American Legation in Lima, April 14, 1915, U.S. Department of State Decimal Files, No. 823.6363/5.

25. The text of the diplomatic note is reproduced in: Revolutionary Government of Peru, Petroleum in Peru, p. 35.

26. Augusto Zimmermann Zavala, La Historia Secreta del Petróleo (Lima: Editorial Gráfica Labor, 1968), p. 46.

27. Benton McMillin to Secretary of State, April 26, 1915. U.S. Department of State Decimal Files, No. 823.6363/7.

28. The fact is reported by McMillin himself in a memo dated dated February 2, 1916.

29. O'Connor, World Crisis in Oil, pp. 225-226.

30. The entire affair is covered in a memo from William Hadley, U.S. Consul-General in Lima-Callao to the Secretary of State, November 14, 1915, U.S. Department of State Decimal Files, No. 823.6363/9.

31. Osores, et al. La Brea y Pariñas! Discursos ante el Senado, p. 45.

32. Pike, The Modern History of Peru, pp. 209-210.

33. Luis Humberto Delgado, Historia de Antonio Miró Quesada, 1875-1935, Vol. I (Lima: American Express Limited, 1938), pp. 161-171.

34. Osores, et al., La Brea y Pariñas, p. 48.

35. Francois Bourricaud, Power and Society in Contemporary Peru, trans. Paul Stevenson (New York: Praeger, 1970), pp. 61-62.

36. Government of Peru, La Cuestión "Brea y Pariñas," Discursos Parlamentarios (Lima: Emprenta del Estado, 1917), p. 3.

37. A copy of the article entitled "Petroleum Famine" is included in a memo from the American Consulate in Lima-Callao to the Secretary of State, January 23, 1918, U.S. Department of State Decimal Files, No. 823.6363/10.

38. See telegram from Benton McMillin to the Secretary of State, September 27, 1918, U.S. Department of State Decimal Files, No. 823.6363/11.

39. Ibid; See also No. 823.6363/12.

40. Oscar C. Barros, <u>Discursos Parlamentarios: Asunto Brea y Pariñas</u> (2nd. ed.; Lima: Imprenta Minerva, 1960), p. 77.

41. Earlier in 1918, U.S. Secretary of State Frank Polk inquired whether the Canadian government was requisitioning the two ships serving Peru. The Canadian reply left no doubt: "Neither the <u>Azof</u> nor the <u>Prince</u> have been requisitioned by the Canadian Government." Richard Crawford to Frank Polk, January 20, 1918, U.S. Department of State Decimal Files, No. 823.6363/9½.

42. The United States, Britain, and Canada may have decided to support Standard Oil due to hard feelings in the State Department over Peru's refusal to allow the Allies to use certain German ships which were interned in Peruvian harbors. At one point, the Secretary of State reminded the Peruvian government that such hesitation "has produced an unfortunate impression upon the American people." Carey, <u>Peru and the United States, 1900-1962</u>, pp. 29-31.

43. The relationship between the Lobitos Oil-Fields, Ltd. and I.P.C. has been complex and somewhat obscure. The Lobitos company began operations in northern Peru in 1902. During the first two decades of the century, both I.P.C. and Lobitos were represented by the same managing firm in Lima. Furthermore, a State Department memo dated December 30, 1918 stated that "both the Lobitos Oil-Fields Company and the London and Pacific Petroleum Company are now owned by the International Petroleum Company." A check with documents subpoenaed during U.S. Congressional investigations during the 1940s showed that Lobitos was not listed as a subsidiary of Standard Oil (New Jersey). Company officials of I.P.C. expressed bewilderment when presented with the document and emphatically denied that Lobitos had ever been owned by I.P.C. The State Department memo identifies the source of the information as Walter Penfield, counsel for the London and Pacific Petroleum Company. The scholar is left with two alternative interpretations: either the two companies were owned by I.P.C. and that fact became one of the best kept secrets in American corporate history, or else, the memo was in error. If the former conclusion is correct, then I.P.C. operated a virtual petroleum monopoly in Peru that has not to this date been verified. However, the fact that the information was only mentioned in two memoranda in 1918 and 1919 and not dealt with in diplomatic correspondence through 1939 would seem to indicate that the information was a mistake. The evidence is inconclusive. U.S. Department of State Decimal Files, No. 823.6363.12, December 30, 1918; No. 823.6363/11, February 10, 1919.

44. M. de Freyre, Peruvian Ambassador to the United States, to the Secretary of State, October 28, 1918, U.S. Department of State Decimal Files, No. 823.6363/12.

45. See the memorandum from the War Trade Board to the Department of State, November 2, 1918, U.S. Department of State Decimal Files, No. 823.6363/13.
46. See notes from the Department of State to Benton McMillin, November 7, 1918 and November 16, 1918, U.S. Department of State Decimal Files, No. 823.6363/14.
47. The La Brea y Pariñas Controversy, Vol. I (International Petroleum Company, February, 1969), Exhibit 1.
48. American Ambassador to Peru Miles Poindexter to the Department of State, April 23, 1925, U.S. Department of State Decimal Files, No. 823.6363/491.
49. Sir Robert Marett, Peru (New York: Praeger, 1969), p. 135.
50. Bourricaud, Contemporary Peru, p. 52.
51. See the circular from Alvey Adee, August 16, 1919, U.S. Department of State Decimal Files, No. 823.6363/23.
52. Pike, Modern Peru, p. 195.
53. Ibid., p. 196.
54. Marett, Peru, pp. 32-34.
55. Memorandum to the U.S. Department of Commerce from Carlton Jackson, Trade Commissioner in Lima, August 5, 1920, U.S. Department of State Decimal Files, No. 823.6363/32.
56. Testimony by Claude W. Calvin, representative of the National City Bank in Peru, before the Committee on Banking and Currency. Quoted by Carey, Peru and the United States, 1900-1962, p. 34.
57. Ibid.
58. Telegram from the Department of State to the American Legation in Lima, February 10, 1920, U.S. Department of State Decimal Files, No. 823.6363/17a.
59. William Walker Smith, Chargé D'affaires ad interim to the Secretary of State, February 19, 1920, U.S. Department of State Decimal Files, No. 823.6363/21.
60. William Walker Smith to the Secretary of State, March 5, 1920, U.S. Department of State Decimal Files, No. 823.6363/20.
61. William Walker Smith to the Secretary of State, March 15, 1920, U.S. Department of State Decimal Files, No. 823.6363/22.
62. Memorandum from Alvey Adee to the Department of Commerce, March 25, 1920, U.S. Department of State Decimal Files, No. 823.6363/21.
63. Report and letter from Philip Kennedy, May 7, 1920, U.S. Department of State Decimal Files, No. 823.6363/24.
64. Official concern with American oil interests was at one point interpreted as favoring the entry of any American company into Peru. However, when Standard Oil of Indiana attempted to negotiate with Leguía to secure an oil monopoly, the State Department instructed its ambassador in Lima not to introduce the company's

representative because it would be "tantamount . . . to favoring said businessman's proposals . . ." in the eyes of the Peruvian president. The question was long debated. The Department justified its position on the grounds that an oil monopoly for Indiana Standard would damage the "established" interests of Jersey Standard, and furthermore would errode the open door policy the Department sought to establish in Peru. The fact is that Standard Oil (New Jersey) also attempted to establish oil monopolies without incurring the disfavor of the State Department. Standard Oil of Indiana's proposed oil monopoly did not necessarily threaten I.P.C.'s holdings. See the diplomatic correspondence from May to August, 1930.

65. As reported in an interoffice memorandum, April 8, 1920, U.S. Department of State Decimal Files, No. 823.6363/23.

66. James Roth, Vice-Consul at Lima-Callao to Secretary of State, August 3, 1920, U.S. Department of State Decimal Files, No. 823.6363/29.

67. Carleton Jackson, American Trade Commissioner in Lima to Department of State, August 5, 1920, U.S. Department of State Decimal Files, No. 823.6363/32.

68. Augusto Leguía, as quoted by American Ambassador to Peru William E. Gonzales in a dispatch to the Secretary of State, July 26, 1921, U.S. Department of State Decimal Files, No. 823.6363/48.

69. William E. Gonzales to the Secretary of State, September 26, 1921, U.S. Department of State Decimal Files, No. 823.6363/48.

70. Ibid.

71. Henry S. Waterman, American Consul in San José, Costa Rica to the Secretary of State, U.S. Department of State Decimal Files, No. 823.6363/407.

72. William E. Gonzales to the Secretary of State, September 26, 1921, U.S. Department of State Decimal Files, No. 823.6363/405.

CHAPTER 2

INTERNATIONAL ARBITRATION AND THE LAUDO OF 1922

Any settlement of the La Brea y Pariñas controversy necessarily had to involve several parties: the formal owners of the property—the British heirs of the Keswick estate, the London and Pacific Petroleum Company—the British firm which held a 99 year lease on the petroleum fields, International Petroleum Company—Canadian owner of the London and Pacific Petroleum Company, Imperial Oil Company—Canadian owner of International Petroleum Company, and finally, Standard Oil (New Jersey)—American owner of Imperial Oil Company, and thus, International Petroleum Company and London and Pacific Petroleum Company. Stripped of corporate complexities, Standard Oil (New Jersey) controlled and operated the La Brea y Pariñas property through its Canadian and British subsidiaries. The heirs of the Keswick estate had a stake in the form of the royalties due them from the production of the Peruvian fields. It was the fact of British "ownership," however, which made an agreement between the Peruvian and British governments diplomatically plausible.

The Agreement for Arbitration contained a statement of the respective positions of the Peruvian and the British governments:

> The Government of the Republic of Peru contends that the Supreme Resolutions or Decrees of the 31st March, 1911, 15th March and 22nd May, 1915, relating to the Mineral Property of "La Brea y Pariñas" are valid and legal and should be enforced, and that the said Mineral Property is subject to the general body of mining laws which may be in force in Peru now or in the future.
> The Government of His Britannic Majesty, on the other hand, contends that the said Mineral Property

has a legal status distinct from that of mineral property
acquired and held in the usual manner under the Mining
Ordinances or the Mining Code of Peru; that the said
Mineral Property is not subject to the general body of
mining laws or to legislation inconsistant with such
distinct status, and that the Supreme Resolutions or
Decrees above mentioned are invalid and cannot
legally be enforced.[1]

This document also stipulated that the Tribunal would be composed in the following manner: Peru and Great Britain would each appoint an arbitrator, and the third jurist would be the President of the Federal Court of the Republic of Switzerland. The subsequent articles of the Agreement for Arbitration set forth the task of the Tribunal. However, in Article X, Paragraph II, was the key provision of the agreement.

In case the Tribunal should, before rendering its award,
suggest terms which the two Governments may accept
as satisfactory, or <u>in case the two Governments should
themselves agree upon terms of settlement, the Tribunal
shall, in either case, incorporate such settlement in an
Award, which shall be treated as the Award of the Tribunal.</u> [Emphasis supplied][2]

In other words, the Agreement provided that should the Peruvian government and the British government reach a compromise outside the auspices of the Tribunal, the compromise itself would not suffice—it would have to be incorporated into the award of the international tribunal. What was the reason for this peculiar requirement?

The Leguía administration was willing to settle for a compromise even more favorable to the company than the agreement worked out in 1915 and eventually rejected by the Peruvian Chamber of Deputies. Since the President had no legal power to reach a settlement without getting it approved by Congress, and since any compromise he forced down the throat of Peru would only last as long as his stay in power, the solution was simple. He would legitimize any compromise he reached by transforming it into the award of an international tribunal.

The compromise took the form of a bilateral treaty between the governments of Peru and Great Britain. It was signed in Lima, rather than in Paris where the Tribunal was meeting. On March 2, 1922, the British representative Arthur Grand Duff, and the Peruvian Minister of Foreign Affairs Alberto Salomón, signed the compromise agreement, and on April 24, the Tribunal in Paris issued the Lima agreement as its award, over the signatures of the presiding officer

Fritz Ostertag, President of the Federal Courts of Switzerland, the British aribtrator, Robert Laird Borden, and his Peruvian counterpart, José Varela Orbegoso.

In its first article, "the High Contracting Parties" agreed that the property comprised 41,614 claims of 40,000 square meters each as the Peruvian government had claimed all along. In the most important article, it stipulated that for a period of fifty years, beginning January 1, 1922, the company would be liable for annual taxes 30 soles per pertenencia under exploitation and one sol per unexploited pertenencia.[3] This settlement was far more advantageous to the company than the earlier compromise which had been defeated by the Civilista-controlled Congress. In the earlier proposal, there was a graduated tax on the unexploited pertenencias which started at one sol during the first ten years and escalated to fifteen soles during the last twenty years of the fifty year period covered by the agreement.

The Award of 1922 also provided that at the end of the fifty year period for which there was fixed taxation, the property would "be subject to the tax base on surface, tax on production, royalties, and all other contributions and taxes which may be established by the laws then in force. . . ."[4] Article V stipulated that:

> For the aforesaid consideration the owners of "La Brea y Pariñas" will pay the Government of Peru the sum of one million dollars ($1,000,000) American gold, which will include the payment of all contributions accrued up to December 31st, 1921, and every other claim which may exist in relation to the property "La Brea y Pariñas."[5]

For $1 million, La Brea y Pariñas was granted a clean slate so far as all possible claims to back taxes were concerned. But why should the British owners pay Peru $1 million U.S. currency?

Perhaps the British played only a formal and symbolic role in all the negotiations. When an irate member of Parliament in London inquired who was going to pay for the arbitration, the British Undersecretary of State for Foreign Affairs replied that "the International Petroleum Company have undertaken in writing, through their solicitors to indemnify His Majesty's Government against any remuneration of the arbitrator and agent respectively."[6] In fact, the London and Pacific Petroleum Company—of British registry, had been under liquidation since 1916. It was under the direct control of I.P.C. and its board of directors was dissolved in 1916. The real beneficiaries of the Award of 1922 or Laudo as it became known in Spanish was the Standard Oil Company (New Jersey) through its subsidiary I.P.C.

The profits of I.P.C. in Peru are confidential, and buried in a consolidated statement of the company's profits throughout Latin America. However, an economic study by J. Fred Rippy originally published in 1959 was most revealing. After noting that most British investments in Peru were disastrous, the author noted the exceptions—Lobitos Oil-Fields Ltd., and . . .

> More remarkable still was the financial record of International Petroleum Company, Limited . . . For three decades beginning in 1921, International Petroleum paid an average annual dividend of 40 percent on a nominal capital of approximately $36 million! No year passed without a reward to its shareholders; the return was no less than 100 percent annually for four consecutive years (1935-1938)! But English investors probably did not own more than a fourth of its securities, perhaps not more than an equivalent of 2 million.[7]

While some Peruvians were aware that the London and Pacific Company had a tremendously profitable operation,[8] and while they must have suspected that I.P.C. was not any less lucrative, they did not have proof. Secrecy on the part of the company and partial knowledge and suspicion on the part of the Peruvian government henceforth created an atmosphere of mutual distrust. Peruvians imagined the company profits as astronomical.

With renewed confidence, Standard Oil moved to simplify the complex legal status quo of La Brea y Pariñas. In 1924 it acquired title to that property and thus terminated the lease arrangement which had prevailed up to that point. By acquiring La Brea y Pariñas after the Laudo of 1922, Standard Oil's I.P.C. hoped to have a clean slate. The company maintained that the arbitral award took place between Peru and the British and that since the company did not acquire the property until 1924, it had nothing to do with the agreement.[9]

International Petroleum Company gained only time with the 1922 settlement. In 1924, Royal Dutch/Shell took action signaling "the commencement of a new campaign between the European and the American oil concerns for the domination of the oil market."[10] The new offensive was to center on Standard's Peruvian production and its distribution in Canada. It did not take long for Peru's President Augusto Leguía to realize that the rivalry would mean new opportunities for his regime.

In the fall of 1926, President Leguía's son Juan departed for Europe with the task of selling the Royal Dutch Shell Company a monopoly on the distribution of gasoline in Peru. Ample opportunity was given for American interests to learn of his intention, and I.P.C.'s general manager in Lima even managed to acquired a copy of the proposed contract. In the newest of Leguía's schemes I.P.C. would be allowed to continue its operations. It would, however, have to sell enough petroleum products to supply Shell's monopoly at specified rates, and under penalty of confiscation, I.P.C. would be banned from marketing any gasoline in Peru. The company would remain free to export whatever oil surplus Peru's fields produced.[11]

Leguía's plan became a casualty of the dictator's failing health. When, in 1927, it became known that he would need surgery, foreign capital became fearful that Leguía would die or be overthrown. This fear was replaced by the economic catastrophe in 1929—the Great Crash—as the major cause of lagging dollar inflow into Peru. "When the inflow of capital stopped . . . Leguía's downfall was not long coming."[12] Leguía's demise in power ended a sort of carnival for foreign capital which he and his son had been running. Juan Leguía would travel to New York and arrange loans of up to $50 million; the banks would charge exorbitant commissions and then sell the bonds to the American public. Juan Leguía usually got a percentage of the proceeds and everyone benefited except the Peruvian nation and the Americans who bought the default bond securities. Six months after the end of Leguía's Oncenio, Peru began to default its sizeable foreign debt. The Sanchez Cerro administration indignantly pointed out that as of January 1932 servicing the foreign debt would have amounted to 34.3 percent of the national revenues.[13]

International Petroleum Company fared well during the cataclysmic events of the early 1930s. The Peruvian populace, which had a vague understanding of Leguía's proforeign business policy, struck back by attacking American businesses. The Cerro de Pasco Corporation suffered heavy damage from riots. In contrast, however, I.P.C.'s installations in Peru's distant northeast corner remained undisturbed. I.P.C. moved cautiously to protect its $45 million investment. The new nationalism prevalent in Lima, with its xenophobic connotations, was very dangerous, but at the same time, Peru's precarious financial position presented many opportunities.

The government of Sanchez Cerro wished to institute a tough policy towards foreign companies and I.P.C. in particular. In the minds of most Peruvians, foreign companies had a long and guilty partnership with Augusto Leguía—it was thus politically attractive to hit these companies hard. On the other hand, Leguía left the country bankrupt and badly in need of funds—only the American capitalists had the cash to save the situation. As a result of this dilemma, the government followed a two-faced policy. For public consumption, the Sanchez Cerro Administration made dramatic moves to invalidate the 1922 Award. But in secret his government continued

Leguía's policy in an attempt to persuade, cajole, and even blackmail
I.P.C. into giving Peru financial support. Sanchez Cerro had two
weapons: diplomatic assaults on the Award, and a law passed by the
Leguía government in February 1930 which authorized the creation
of a petroleum marketing monopoly. Ironically, that law was passed
in anticipation of such an arrangement between Peru and I.P.C. In
spite of its pious antimonopolist platitudes, the U.S. Department of
State gave its blessing to that proposed monopoly, and it even went
so far as to torpedo an attempt by another American company, Standard Oil of Indiana, to outbid Jersey Standard's I.P.C.[14]

Reflecting its public policy, in April 1931 the Peruvian government announced that it considered the 1922 Laudo nonbinding since
it had never been ratified by the Peruvian Congress, and that it
intended to collect 22,000 soles in back taxes beginning with 1924,
the year in which I.P.C. formally purchased La Brea y Pariñas.[15]
This action by the government triggered a new offensive against I.P.C.
by its traditional Peruvian enemies who once more had the virulent
backing of Antonio Miró Quesada and his newspaper El Comercio.
As is often the case in Peruvian politics, appearances did not tell the
whole story. For months prior to the new official pseudo-offensive
against the company, the Peruvian government reached what can only
be described as a cozy modus vivendi with I.P.C. Shortly after the
Sanchez Cerro government took power, funds dried up and the government found that it could not pay its army, navy, or police. As a career
military officer, Sanchez Cerro knew that a government which cannot
pay the armed forces does not endure. His solution was simple—get
the money from a party you can trust and pay off those you cannot.
In late November or early December 1930, the "revolutionary" government sent its Minister of Finance to confer with a most important
American in Peru—the general manager of International Petroleum.
The minister pleaded for the company to advance secretly the Peruvian
government 1.5 million soles. After urgent consultations with the
company's high command, the loan was granted and the government
saved.[16]

Unaware of the company's financing of the Peruvian government,
many of Peru's political leaders hastened to the attack against I.P.C.
A Constituent Assembly was called to draft a new constitution, and it
took up the question of La Brea y Pariñas. The same topic was
simultaneously being considered by the Peruvian Congress. Fearing
that the situation would get out of hand, the Sanchez Cerro government
anticipated the Assembly and the Congress by a few days and cabled
its representative in Geneva to request the Permanent Court of International Justice to revise the 1922 Award. Subsequently, the Peruvian
Congress passed a law authorizing the executive to do what it had
already done. The Congress explicitly outlined the reasons why the

Award should be revised. First, the Award did not settle the classification of property to which the subsoil of La Brea y Pariñas belonged. Second, it did not have provisions for Congressional approval of the arrangement. Third, the Award legislated on matters of taxation, and hence impinged upon the powers of the Peruvian Congress, and finally, it exceeded the limits set out by the Law of 1918 authorizing the arbitration.[17]

Of course, the Permanent Court of International Justice had no jurisdiction over the decision of another International Tribunal, or for that matter over any dispute unless both parties to the dispute were willing to submit to its judgment. Great Britain was not about to reopen the question, and thus this move by the Peruvian government was purely political. If anything it undermined its previous position. If Peru did not consider the Award binding in 1931, how could it now ask that it be revised in 1932? Diplomatic moves notwithstanding, Peruvian politicians in the Constituent Assembly now competed with each other to see who would champion the anti-I.P.C. crusade. On March 21, the Assembly approved appointments to a special committee on the revision of petroleum laws. Eight days later Congressman Calmell del Solar introduced a bill which provided for the construction of 4,000 schools to be financed through the profits of a petroleum monopoly.[18] Through all of this stormy political situation, I.P.C.'s management remained notably calm. While at times they wondered whether the situation would snowball out of control, for the most part they knew that the executive branch was in their pocket. In fact, while the pseudodiplomatic offensive was going full steam ahead, the Peruvian Minister of Foreign Affairs privately assured the company's manager, Walter Reed, that "so far as he . . . was concerned, the matter of altering the treaty between Peru and Great Britain was a closed issue."[19]

Not only did the company save the day for Peru's government in December 1931, from that point on I.P.C. regularly began to advance the Sanchez Cerro administration from £25,000 to £30,000 a month through an Italian bank in consideration of future export taxes. When this advance allowance did not suffice, the Minister of Development pleaded for larger advances from International Petroleum and went so far as to suggest that I.P.C.'s Lima manager Walter Reed deceive the company's home office by stating that the Peruvian government was forcing I.P.C. to make larger advance payments. Walter Reed refused, not for ethical but for political reasons. He explained to Ambassador Dearing that "in view of the precarious nature of the Government, the fact that it might be forced out of office, and that its successor may not take it kindly that a foreign corporation assisted to prolong its existence by conniving with it to deceive the public . . ."[20] the International Petroleum Company would not advance the Sanchez Cerro government additional funds.

International Petroleum's involvement in Peruvian politics reached even further than this incident indicated. Sometime during the first half of 1932, the Minister of Development and President of the Council of Ministers, Francisco Lanatta, approached I.P.C.'s manager and asked for an advance on the customs payments at a 15 percent discount to I.P.C. The money was needed to get the Peruvian Navy's shipbottoms scraped. Lanatta embezzled the money. In a confrontation involving several government ministers and the President of Peru, Walter Reed unmasked the corrupt Lanatta, was instrumental in getting him fired, and established "very friendly contact with the President."[21] It appears that during this stage of Peruvian history, many members of the Council of Ministers consulted individually with I.P.C.'s general manager about their efforts to meet the payroll, carry out their programs, and even secure personal wealth.

International Petroleum Company was also involved in Peru's foreign affairs. During the latter part of 1932, Peru's border dispute with Colombia flared up, and when war became a distinct possibility, the Peruvian government began to seek weapons purchase money so that it could fight the impending war. Washington imposed an arms embargo on both Peru and Colombia; therefore, the Japanese and French arms dealers were quite active. In January 1933, the Peruvian government asked I.P.C. for $800,000 worth of petroleum, the value of future export duties, so that Peru could use the oil to buy French weapons. The company balked, but the Peruvian government pressed its request. I.P.C. claimed that it had already advanced the government the equivalent of one year's worth of taxes and export duties, and the requested sum of $800,000 would pay in advance all taxes for three and a half years. While the company's financial allegations were technically correct, the foremost reasons for its refusal were political and diplomatic. First, the American Embassy made it known that "approval of the proposal would annul the effect of the Department's embargo on arms plan."[22] Also of great concern to the company was the fact that it had operations both in Peru and Colombia, and it did not want to imperil its position in either country by aiding the other.[23]

By the end of the Sanchez Cerro administration in 1933, the pattern of interaction between the Peruvian government and I.P.C. was established. Unlike during its relationship with Augusto Leguía, the company was not celebrated as the foremost foreign benefactor of Peru. Rather, I.P.C. was regarded as a kind of necessary nuisance. Privately, the government knew it could count on the company for advance taxes with discretion. In a financially troubled nation such as Peru this was an important consideration.

International Petroleum Company entered into similar arrangements with succeeding governments of Peru not because it was corrupt, but because in a world of unmitigated commercial competition it had to adapt to the Peruvian rules of the game or risk being dislodged by its archcompetitor, Royal Dutch/Shell. The operations in Peru were extremely profitable, but profit alone was not necessarily the primary motivating force behind corporate behavior. Rather, there existed a kind of corporate nationalism or "corporatism"—devotion to the growth and well-being of the corporation. This force drove the management of the company into what can best be described as an extralegal relationship—a relationship which was doomed from the start, and would eventually lead to confrontation between Peru and Standard Oil's I.P.C.

Peru was a sovereign state, but within its borders there existed another state—not necessarily an American colony, but part of a multinational concern with supranational loyalties. To Standard Oil (New Jersey), the United States was not necessarily the object of supreme loyalty. More often than not the company kept the Department of State in the dark about its activities. Corporate memory is long, and the dismemberment order of 1911 was a very painful blow to the international oil giant. The company informed the American embassy of its activities only when it was expedient for it to do so.

Peru's problems with I.P.C. stemmed not from the fact that it was an American company somehow geared to exploit Peru on behalf of the U.S. but rather from the fact that its parent company, Standard Oil (New Jersey), was a far larger organization and commanded more resources than the Peruvian state. The United States broke up Rockefeller's oil trust when the corporate giant seemed to be getting out of hand domestically. When Standard Oil, through I.P.C., moved into Peru, the company was already too large and too powerful for the Peruvian state to do the same. For example, it would be inconceivable for an American company to refuse cooperation with the U.S. government during World War II because it might have had interests in Germany or Japan. But it was possible, and actually happened that I.P.C. refused to cooperate with the Peruvian government when it anticipated a war with Colombia because the company had interests there as well.

In theory, for Peruvians the state was majestic and sovereign—the state was the supremo gobierno. In practice the Peruvian government was a weakling in comparison with one of its corporate citizens. The incompatibility of this theoretical conception with practical conditions made it difficult for both parties to function. Peruvian nationalists from the "right" and "left" never forgave I.P.C. for operating in their country as if it were a banana republic—buying off cabinet members and even total administrations, blackmailing duly constituted legislatures into submission to company demands. I.P.C., for its part, could not very well accept the constant threat of fleecing promoted by corrupt Peruvian politicians. After all, it was company expertise and capital which transformed La Brea y Pariñas from a barren desert into a boom town employing thousands of Peruvians and indirectly providing a decent living for many more. The company attempted to bargain in good faith, only to discover that its concessions merely incited Peruvian chauvinism to ever more preposterous demands. What was originally a difference over taxes grew into a giant of mistrust and hatred bridging two generations of Peruvian political leaders. As time passed, this bitterness grew and the principal contending parties froze their minds against compromise.

Who were these parties, and why did they act as they did? Besides the company and its constant ally, the American embassy, there were three distinct groups in Peruvian politics actively participating in the controversy: first, the Miró Quesada family and its journalist friends, the traditionalists—nationalistic people with a long-standing enmity for the company, who seized every opportunity to attack and embarrass the company; second, the Peruvian leftist radicals, who naturally singled out I.P.C. as the most prominent member of what they considered the exploitative club of American capitalists in Peru; finally, Peru's industrial and commercial elite in Lima, which could and apparently did profit from the activities of I.P.C.—the group which comprised the company's most important Peruvian allies.

NOTES

1. The La Brea y Pariñas Controversy, Vol. I (International Petroleum Company, February, 1969), Exhibit 2, p. 2.
2. Ibid., p. 7.
3. Ibid., pp. 9-10.
4. Ibid.
5. Ibid., p. 11.
6. As quoted in a dispatch from Robert T. Kennedy, American Consul General in London to the Department of State, February 15, 1922, U.S. Department of State Decimal Files, No. 823.6363/59.
7. James Fred Rippy, British Investment in Latin America, 1822-1949—A Case Study in the Operations of Private Enterprise in Retarded Regions (2nd. ed.; Hamden, Connecticut: Archon Books, 1966), pp. 131-132.
8. Ricardo A. Deustua showed data that London and Pacific Petroleum paid dividends of $37\frac{1}{2}$ percent and 20 percent of capital investment in 1914 and 1915. Ricardo A. Deustua, El Petroleo en el Peru (Lima: Imprenta Americana, 1921), p. 68.

9. "El Laudo de La Brea y Pariñas y la posición de la International Petroleum," Noticias de Petróleo, XIII, No. 117 (May, 1960).

10. Report from the Dutch press sent from the American Legation in The Hague to the Department of State, September 24, 1924, U.S. Department of State Decimal Files, No. 823.6363/67.

11. Memorandum from Leland Harrison, Assistant Secretary of State, to Charles Evans Hughes, Secretary of State, December 14, 1926, U.S. Department of State Decimal Files, No. 823.6363/91.

12. James C. Carey, Peru and the United States, 1900-1962 (Notre Dame, Indiana: University of Notre Dame Press, 1964), p. 62.

13. Ibid., p. 78.

14. See the diplomatic correspondence from May 2 to September 3, 1930. U.S. Department of State Decimal Files, Nos. 823.6363/111, 117, 120, 122, 125, 126, 127, 128.

15. Fred Morris Dearings, American Ambassador to Peru, to the Department of State, April 7, 1931, U.S. Department of State Decimal Files, No. 823.6363/133.

16. Fred Morris Dearing to the Department of State, December 19 and 26, 1930, U.S. Department of State Decimal Files, Nos. 823.6363/131 and 132.

17. H. P. Starrett, American Charge d'Affaires ad interim in Lima to the Department of State, April 25, 1932, U.S. Department of State Decimal Files, No. 823.6363/151.

18. Fred Morris Dearing to the Department of State, March 21 and 31, 1932, U.S. Department of State Decimal Files, No. 823.6363/146 and 148.

19. Ibid.

20. Fred Morris Dearing to the Department of State, November 14, 1932, U.S. Department of State Decimal Files, No. 721.23/511.

21. See Enclosure No. 1 in a dispatch from Fred Morris Dearing to the Department of State, April 6, 1932, U.S. Department of State Decimal Files, No. 823.51/821.

22. In a telegram to the Department of State, Ambassador Dearing suggested that Standard Oil of New Jersey be informed of the consequences of accepting Peru's proposals. Fred Morris Dearing to the Department of State, January 13, 1933, U.S. Department of State Decimal Files, No. 721.23/729.

23. I.P.C.'s management expressed preoccupation with this point to Ambassador Dearing, who in turn reported it to Washington. Ibid.

CHAPTER

3

**FROM POWER BROKER
TO BELEAGUERED
UTILITY**

THE REVENGE OF THE INCA

The influence of I.P.C. on Peruvian politics reached its peak during the 1930s. Due to improved technology such as deeper drilling and artificial stimulation of oil flow from the ground, the production of La Brea y Pariñas grew from a daily average of 26,800 barrels to an all-time high of 41,300 barrels daily in 1936.[1] From then on, the production began a slow descent to about 14,000 barrels a day in 1968, the year the property was finally nationalized.[2] Though internal oil prices were artificially low due to government price controls, large exports combined with a miniscule domestic consumption managed to produce huge profits for International Petroleum.

On the average Peru consumed less than 10,000 barrels daily, and thus the company exported three-fourths of the total oil produced during the 1930s. In 1937, for instance, I.P.C. exported a total of 13.5 million barrels of oil from Peru. Given the relatively low labor costs, proximity of the oil fields to port facilities and high quality of the crude oil, as well as the minimal taxes set by the Laudo of 1922, the company managed to turn profits which amounted to a 100 percent return on the investment for four consecutive years (1935-38).[3] The 1930s represented a golden era for I.P.C.—an era soon to disappear under the stress of an antagonistic landed oligarchy. The factors contributing to this erosion of the company's power were varied, but the most important was the willingness of the Peruvian government to make concessions to the lower classes at the expense of I.P.C.'s profit margin.

In 1939, shortly after the beginning of World War II, the Peruvian government imposed a price freeze on most consumer items. After the war, the government hesitated to lift the price controls for political reasons, but finally in 1949 it yielded to economic pressure and eliminated the price controls on most items with two exceptions, bread and petroleum products. The government simply figured that I.P.C., the country's major petroleum producer, did not wield voting power, and that in a country where the populace had grown accustomed to low fuel prices, these prices could not be raised without political repercussions.

While the fact of frozen domestic prices was not too important at first since Peru consumed a relatively small proportion of the oil it produced and the rest was sold abroad at world markets, internal consumption increased dramatically during the 1940s and continued to increase up to the present—in part as a result of artificially low prices. International Petroleum Company operated under two laws which had a pincer effect on its profits. Law 4452, passed in 1922 at the instigation of the Leguía government, provided that I.P.C. would have to satisfy Peru's internal markets before selling abroad. While this provision had little importance in 1922, by the middle 1950s Peru was consuming as much as La Brea y Pariñas could produce, and by the early 1960s the country had a petroleum "deficit"—it actually had to import some oil. The second government action affecting profits was the previously mentioned price freeze and subsequent government price control. As a result, petroleum derivatives in Peru remained at their 1939 level until 1948. During that year, the prices of diesel fuel and residual oil were raised, and in the following year the price of kerosene was increased. In 1953, the price of kerosene was again increased and for the first time since the 1930s the price of gasoline was raised. Since the prices were fixed in Peruvian soles, inflation had the net effect of actually reducing the price of gas over the years. Thus, while the price of gasoline remained at 42 Peruvian cents per gallon from 1934 to 1953, in U.S. currency the price went from ten cents a gallon in 1934 to about three cents a gallon in 1953.[4]

As a result of the artificially low prices imposed by the government, the consumption of kerosene—a petroleum derivative—rose steadily over the years. In the 1960s, it was calculated that 90 percent of the homes in the Lima-Callao area used kerosene as a cooking fuel. People also used kerosene throughout Peru for illumination, refrigeration, heating, as a cleaning fluid, and finally, as a substitute for more expensive fuels or as a cheaper additive. About 18 percent of the 8,500 barrels of kerosene used daily in Peru served as a substitute for more expensive fuels.[5] The price of kerosene during the 1953-59 period was 0.95 soles per gallon, or the equivalent of seven cents in U.S. currency.[6] Even after the prices were raised in 1959, "the Peruvian kerosene at S. 1.10 per gallon [was] extraordinarily cheap... The prices in the world market [were] two or three times higher..."[7]

Prices were deliberately kept low because the government knew that the lower classes, particularly those living in Lima-Callao, Cuzco, and other urban centers, relied on these low prices, and any substantial alteration could create civil unrest. The oil companies were required by Laws 4452 and 11780 to provide kerosene for Peruvian consumption. Had it not been for this legal requirement, the oil companies would have used the petroleum to produce gasoline and diesel fuels, and not kerosene. Because the Laudo of 1922 set forth the operating procedures of La Brea y Pariñas, these laws had no technical application to the I.P.C. property. However, for political reasons and to its financial disadvantage, the company produced 66 percent of all kerosene in Peru, and the Talara refinery processed over 98 percent of it.[8]

During most of the 1950s the prices for gasoline, diesel fuel, and residual oil were not much higher than kerosene. With the exception of premium gasoline which sold for S. 5.20 per gallon, all other fuels sold at prices ranging from S. 1.05 to S. 1.17 per gallon. Not only were prices kept low by decree, but the companies were forced to have the same prices throughout Peru, regardless of varying costs for transportation.

These laws and regulations had the effect of turning the I.P.C. and the British-owned Petrolera Lobitos, the major private concerns in the Peruvian petroleum business, into virtual utilities. Like an American electric or telephone company, I.P.C. had constantly to haggle over the price of its products and over what would be a reasonable return for its parent company; but unlike the American utilities which can count on stockholder support in their communities, I.P.C. had virtually no constituency of its own other than the workers in Talara and their dependents, who proved to be more of an impediment than a help to the company.

Beginning in the late 1940s, I.P.C. actively campaigned to get legislative changes introduced. With alarm, the company pointed out that the petroleum legislation governing concessions in Peru was unattractive to foreign capital, and therefore no new companies had explored for Peruvian oil since the administration of Augusto Leguía. Actually, Peruvians hoped that a government enterprise, founded during the administration of Oscar Benavides, would carry out exploration and development of a state-owned petroleum industry. To begin this enterprise, the Benavides government bought out several small petroleum companies with dubious petroleum reserves. In part, this move by Peru was prompted by the diplomatic proddings of the Mexican legation, which was actively advocating the emulation of Mexican nationalization elsewhere in Latin America.[9] The Peruvian company, the Empresa Petrolera Fiscal, became a viable entity, but by the middle 1940s it was evident that even when heavily favored by the government's fiscal and regulatory policies, the company could not really take on the task of rapidly expanding Peruvian oil industry.

The controversy over the concessions of the Sechura Desert, an area thought to contain rich petroleum deposits and contiguous to the

La Brea y Pariñas fields, well illustrated Peru's dilemma vis-à-vis economic development and the role of foreign capital in the economic progress of a nation. During the 1940s, this Sechura concession came to the forefront of Peruvian politics. The government decided to develop the deposits, for it was increasingly clear that with the rapidly expanding Peruvian consumption, the day when Peru would be forced to import oil was not far off. The government's first step was to order a feasibility study to find out if the state-owned company could develop the field, or if other Peruvian capitalists could do it. When the study was reported, it placed a price tag of S. 100 million for exploration alone. Neither the Peruvian treasury nor the Peruvian private capitalists could possibly raise such a sum.[10] Since I.P.C. had the drilling equipment and personnel in a location close to Sechura, it soon became obvious that if any foreign company became involved, it would be I.P.C.—no other company could afford to underbid it.

The question became how to strike a deal with the alleged "thief" responsible for the 1922 Laudo, how to develop the Sechura field while protecting Peru's interests from possible I.P.C. infringement. President of Peru José Luís Bustamente y Rivero reached an agreement with I.P.C. in 1946—the Sechura Contract. The contract became a subject for discussion first in the Aprista-dominated Peruvian Congress, but in a matter of days, the discussion became a cause célèbre, with every political group and both major Lima newspapers jumping into the fray to guard the national interest.

Luís Miró Quesada, chief editor of El Comercio, took up the cause of his fallen brother Antonio, who led the Civilista schism in 1918.[11] The contract came under scrutiny. With perhaps more pomp and circumstance than the occasion merited, El Comercio reminded its readers that "after the age of iron and coal, which were the determining factors of material power in the last century, in our time the basic factor of that power is petroleum . . ."[12] Miró Quesada at first simply demanded that Peruvians give a great deal of attention to the matter of this oil concession. He asked that final consideration be postponed pending this further discussion. The Peruvian Senate concurred, and within a week of his first editorial, Miró Quesada produced a list of specific objections. Recounting the fact that the proposed contract involved six provinces, two departments, two cities, several roads, etc., Miró Quesada demanded caution—as if Peru was about to relinquish part of its territory. He exhorted the citizenry to exercise "patriotic care," for the new concessions could affect Peru's commitments to hemispheric defense. Finally, he specifically demanded that the contract be limited to a specific period, after which the Peruvian government or local capitalists would step in and continue the development of these new oil fields.[13]

Miró Quesada rationally admitted that Sechura should be developed, and that only I.P.C. had the economic and technological resources to do so—however, he could not emotionally accept an agreement which delivered what he imagined to be Peru's 20th century version of the ancient Potosí mine to his hated enemy, the International Petroleum Company. I.P.C. was needed for the initial development but Peru deserved the fruits. Noting these objections raised against the contract, I.P.C.'s general manager H.A. Grimes forwarded a proposal to the Peruvian government declaring that I.P.C. would be willing to accept a time limit on the concession of no less than forty years, with a possible twenty-year extension. However, in exchange for this concession, the company demanded that the tax rate be fixed for the duration of the contract[14]—a provision which Miró Quesada and other critics of I.P.C. interpreted as an attempt to usurp the taxation powers of the Peruvian Congress.

As the battle over Sechura progressed, certain facts became clear. Echoing objections raised during the second decade of the century, Peruvian conservatives opposed the agreement even while recognizing that there was no viable alternative to an I.P.C. concession. At the same time, the government was in no position to stall in developing additional oil sources in Peru, for ignoring Sechura would only cause an eventual energy crisis. This battle of the 1940s was not a carbon copy of the controversy during the Pardo administration. One new factor was the Alianza Popular Revolucionaria Americana, a political party and movement which did not exist in the early 20th century but by the 1940s loomed as Peru's dominant political force. APRA was founded in 1924 by a young Peruvian student leader, Víctor Raúl Haya de la Torre. At its inception it was a radical movement— aiming for social reform in Latin America—however, its true strength was in Peru. By 1940, Apristas had eschewed their early radicalism, and developed a gradualist progressive political party. In addition to this new factor of Aprista political pressure, the Peruvian Armed Forces were invited to study the Sechura Contract and issue an opinion. Their report was confidential, but the word soon leaked out that the armed forces were not favorably disposed towards I.P.C. or the proposed contract.

No sooner had the question of Sechura and its potential exploitation by I.P.C. come to the fore as a clear political issue than the Apristas and the oligarchy began to maneuver to place responsibility for what was to be a necessary but an unpopular political act—the Sechura Contract—in each other's lap. Miró Quesada, who hated the Apristas for ideological and personal reasons, presented an ambivalent position. On the one hand he stated that the contract was of the gravest importance and should be given utmost consideration. On the other, he knew that if APRA used its congressional majority to railroad the contract through, El Comercio would acquire a major weapon against the then radical party—alleged collusion with Peru's number one "public enemy" and foremost representative of Yankee "imperialism," the I.P.C.

Manuel Seoane, the leader of APRA's congressional forces, was far too wise to make such a mistake. Besides, the Apristas' enemies jumped the gun by accusing the party of collusion before the Sechura Contract was even approved. An opposition senator argued that I.P.C. had "no moral responsibility whatsoever," and therefore any agreement with such a company would be immoral regardless of the conditions. Another senator ventured to recount previously disproved charges that I.P.C. had been defrauding Peru by carting off more oil than it declared and even put a price tag on the alleged fraud, S. 5 billion. Still another critic of the agreement declared that "it reminded one of the contract between Mephistopheles and Faust, in which the devil wanted to take the soul of the contracting party by all means."[15]

Taking note of the maneuvering of his enemies, and speaking for APRA's senatorial delegation, Manuel Seoane went on record stating that even though APRA could simply vote the Sechura Contract into law, it would not do so; rather, it would vote for tabling the contract as a sign of respect for public opinion and democratic procedures. Seoane also attempted to disassociate his party from the contract and from I.P.C., but with little success, for the opposition, now angered by APRA's tactical withdrawal, zeroed in on the party.

The political forces opposed to the contract noted that APRA had three cabinet members in the government including Minister of Development César Elias, the public official responsible for negotiating the contract. Time and again, APRA was pinned with "moral responsibility" for the contract; both conservative and leftist critics joined hands in an effort to embarrass the party. The attacks of course centered on I.P.C. and "yankee imperialism," though some of the conservative spokesmen carefully distinguished between the North American people and their political leaders on the one hand, and the imperialist trusts on the other hand.[16]

The intensive criticism carried on by both major Lima newspapers, El Comercio and La Prensa, as well as the negative attitude of the armed forces convinced the Apristas that the issue should be allowed to rest and perhaps to die in the forseeable future. The coup de grace came when the editor of La Prensa, Francisco Graña Garland, a prominent critic of the Sechura Contract and a relation of Don Luís Miró Quesada, was assassinated on January 7, 1947, barely three days after the bitter parliamentary debate over the contract.[17] The crime was eventually traced to APRA, but shortly after it occurred, several political figures implied that the assassination was the result of Graña Garland's opposition to the contract.

The controversy over the Sechura Contract had several unforeseen effects. According to Fredrick Pike, APRA's friendly attitude towards

International Petroleum Company brought about a change of attitude at the Department of State. From that point on, the United States regarded that party as its favorite Peruvian political group.[18] Furthermore, the issue of Peru's need for increased petroleum productivity got lost in the fray. The Sechura Desert remained as forlorn as it had been since Oscar Benavides declared it a national reserve during the previous decade. Domestic oil consumption continued to rise, while production continued its slow but consistent drop—foreshadowing the impending energy crisis all responsible Peruvians knew was inevitable.

APRA made its friends in the Department of State, but it abandoned the cause of I.P.C. when the political price rose to prohibitive levels. Peruvian conservatives and leftists alike counted the whole affair as a victory against APRA and I.P.C. The armed forces, for the first time, showed their hand, and it was commonly known that they did not approve of I.P.C.'s presence in Peru. Not all developments were equally as bad for I.P.C., for the assassination of Graña Garland brought a new editor to La Prensa, Pedro Beltrán, who charted a course for his newspaper which was diametrically opposed to Miró Quesada's El Comercio. La Prensa became International Petroleum's friend and Miró Quesada's enemy.[19]

The matter of petroleum development rested during the remainder of Bustamente's term in office. Having gauged the depth of animosity which many Peruvian harbored against I.P.C., the company once again attempted to project a low profile in Peru, hoping that better times would come again. The fate of the Sechura Contract illustrated the inability of the Peruvian Congress to reach a decision on the oil problem. While APRA had a clear majority, it hesitated to use its power regarding the contract. Consequently, APRA's power was negated by a small aristocratic group in the Senate under the leadership of Héctor Boza, who had the help of El Comercio, for a time La Prensa, and the political groups to the left of APRA.

After the assassination of Graña Garland, APRA's opposition became even more bitter. Knowing that the Senate could not function without an executive committee and that in order to elect the committee two-thirds of the senators had to be present, the anti-APRA minority—amounting to slightly over one-third of the Senate, did not attend the session on the constitutionally appointed day, July 28, and consequently, the Senate was forced to suspend its session. Since the Chamber of Deputies could not function unless the Senate did, the entire Congress was effectively de-activated, thus cancelling APRA's solid congressional majority and leaving Bustamente to rule by decree. APRA reacted to this situation by preparing a coup d'état with the aid of some junior military officers—an unsuccessful coup which took place October 3, 1948. In response, the Bustamente government repressed APRA and this action in turn created further unrest. Before the month was over, the military, under the leadership of General Manuel Odría, took over the government of Peru, justifying this action by declaring that Bustamente had been unable to deal effectively with APRA.[20]

Since Congress had effectively destroyed itself the year before the coup, Odría did not even have to go through the motions of dismissing it. He ruled by decree, and once more Peru moved ahead. The price controls which had divided Don Luis Miró Quesada and Pedro Beltrán were eliminated. El Comercio had to buy its newsprint at the unregulated higher price, unprotected by an artificially low rate of exchange.[21]

Manuel Odría, who ruled as dictator of Peru from 1948 to 1956, had much in common with Augusto Leguía, and his regime was dubbed the Ochenio (a period of eight years) in a manner reminiscent of the Oncenio, Leguía's eleven year rule. Like Leguía, Odría had a middle-class background, and was a firm believer in the laissez-faire principle. He succeeded where other men failed—he gained the confidence of foreign investors and the economic results of this confidence were impressive for Peru. The flow of capital from abroad quickly increased, and by the end of the Ochenio, foreign investment in Peru doubled. Industrial productivity grew between 1950 and 1955.[22] As with the rest of the economy, petroleum exploration and production also boomed. While the Korean War was partially responsible for Peru's growth, the Odría regime did take decisive action to encourage foreign investors to come to Peru.

Probably with the technical advice of I.P.C., the Odría government passed a new petroleum law, No. 11780, in 1952. Odría had himself elected president within the constitutional framework in 1950, but APRA—Peru's major political party, was outlawed. This fact, combined with Odría's military base of power, made it impossible for the sort of paralyzing obstructionism which had plagued prior administrations in their attempts to deal with the question of oil. However, the regime did embark on an after-the-fact public relations campaign which set out to make the new law acceptable to the country.[23] International Petroleum seconded this campaign with a public relations effort of its own. In one of its most influential publications, a magazine entitled FANAL, the company published several articles explaining and justifying the new legislation.

General Odría and his closest advisors, including the Minister of Development Carlos Salazar, accepted the arguments which I.P.C. had long pressed on the Peruvian government. The official administration argument was that while petroleum production had remained static at best, and had even declined since its peak during the 1930s, domestic consumption had greatly increased. Thus, while in 1940 domestic consumption amounted to only 27.7 percent of production, in 1952 the level was raised to 58.8 percent of production. The government noted that while in 1914 Peru accounted for 85 percent of all petroleum exports from the South American continent, in 1952 Peru only exported 2 percent of the total continental export of oil. The consequences of this stagnation were obvious—Peru would soon need to import oil. In addition, the country was losing out on much needed tax revenues by leaving potential oil lands unexploited. The Odría administration informed the Peruvian Congress that a "modest daily production of 2 million barrels" would net the treasury between 500,000 and 1 million soles per year in taxes.[24]

The facts were clear and I.P.C. and the Peruvian government concluded that Peru should enact legislation which would make exploration, development, and exploitation more attractive to foreign capital. This action would bring about a reversal on the petroleum scene. Odría was quoted as saying:

> The new law is inspired with the purpose of converting Peru into a great petroleum exporter. . . . We need to be exporters, so that great amounts of dollars will come into our country, dollars which will improve our currency on account of the abundance of foreign exchange in our markets; thus the wages of the worker and the salaries of the clerks will have greater purchasing power, and the government will be able to deal with the great national problems which up to this time have been put off.[25]

Manuel Odría, whose style of populist authoritarian rule has been compared to that of Juan Domingo Perón of Argentina,[26] definitely wanted to help the laboring classes. He was a firm believer in the role of the state as a stimulator of the economy—but not as a direct participator. He needed tax revenues to carry out his costly programs of public works. So, it did not take much effort on the part of the always influential management of I.P.C. to persuade Odría that a new promotional petroleum law was all that was needed to bring growth and tax money to Peru.

The law which was proclaimed on March 18, 1952 was indeed a piece of far-reaching and comprehensive legislation. Peru abandoned the system of royalties which had been the cornerstone of previous petroleum development. Instead, the state became a partner in all future petroleum development, with a 50 percent share of all profits. The law assured the state a minimum of 22 percent of the value of all petroleum exports, whether or not there was a profit. Peru also received a surface tax which varied with the extension of the land under exploitation. A depletion allowance of 25 percent was established for domestic companies; foreign companies received one of 15 percent.[27] The law provided that concessions in the coastal area of Peru were to be granted for a period of forty years, with a possible twenty year extension—a provision which closely paralleled the I.P.C.-proposed time limit during the Sechura Contract dispute.[28]

Of course, the law had no immediate effect on La Brea y Pariñas, which continued to operate under the rules set by the Laudo of 1922. Why then was I.P.C. so interested in a law which it knew would have no effect on its holdings? The answer was twofold. First, the company wanted more favorable petroleum legislation in Peru so that the Sechura Desert would be opened to all bidders, including I.P.C.—not under the provisions of a particular contract, such as the one which aroused so much controversy in 1946, but under a general law applicable to everyone. I.P.C. hoped to have an edge on its competition by virtue of its established position, and the company's critics could not very well argue against its entry into the development of the Sechura Desert as long as this was done under general law. I.P.C. also hoped that its special status under the Laudo of 1922 could eventually be eliminated by "adapting" the company to the general petroleum laws of Peru. Originally, the Laudo was quite profitable for the company, but as time passed, I.P.C. became a semiutility, supplying the domestic market at fixed prices. The Laudo was a guilded cage from which I.P.C. was anxious to escape.

The Odría plan worked as expected. Several oil companies applied for and obtained exploratory concessions in the Sechura Desert and in other parts of Peru. I.P.C. got sizeable rights in the Sechura Desert, and during 1954, the company feverishly drilled in the promising fields. However, an unpleasant surprise awaited I.P.C. and the Odría administration—the Sechura Desert was a barren wasteland for oil. I.P.C. spent over 120 million soles drilling six wells.[29]

The unforseeable futility of this venture had a number of very drastic effects. First, it dealt a severe blow to the rapport between I.P.C. and the Odría administration, for after all, I.P.C., the technical wizzard of petroleum, had assured Odría that if certain legislation was enacted, exploration and development would make Peru a second Venezuela. The first installment on that promise went on as expected, but the second proved impossible. Certainly, I.P.C. could not rationally be blamed for the lack of oil, but then, Mother Nature was not readily accessible for reproach. Consequently, many Peruvians who had been already predisposed to believe the worst of I.P.C. for historical reasons saw the latest development as one more trick foisted on Peru by the clever yankee capitalists.

Economically undermined, the Odría regime lost ground. Without new sources of revenues, the far-fetched public works program which had created a somewhat superficial sense of prosperity in the capital could not be continued. In 1956, Odría had to make good on his promise to hold elections. His own support dwindled, and a conservative former president, Manuel Prado, was elected to office.

Not only did the Sechura fiasco contribute to Odría's demise, it also forced I.P.C. and the Compañía Petrolera Lobitos into a merger which would prove as economically successful as politically disasterous. As stated earlier, Compania Petrolera Lobitos was a wholly-owned subsidiary of Lobitos Oil-Fields, Ltd., a London-based holding company. This company entered Peruvian business in 1902, and operated under Petroleum Law 4452 of 1922—the company had a concession to exploit oil in exchange for a 10 percent royalty of its crude oil production.

From the beginning, the Lobitos company had an interesting relationship with I.P.C. For instance, both firms were represented by the same agent in Lima—Milne and Cia., S.A. Lobitos Oil-Fields exploited what became known as Concesiones Lima, a property contiguous to La Brea y Pariñas. Even though Law 4452 required Lobitos to satisfy the internal needs of the Peruvian market before exporting any oil, the company exported its oil anyway, and left I.P.C. to deal with the domestic market. In 1950, Lobitos reversed its position and began marketing operations in Peru. It is possible that the Peruvian government pressured that company into carrying its share of the unprofitable domestic market. Since Compañía Petrolera Lobitos (C.P.L.) never had a refinery in Peru, all of its products for domestic consumption had to be refined by I.P.C. at the Talara refinery. And since at the beginning of its domestic operations Lobitos Oil had no service stations of its own, I.P.C. agreed to let that company use its own network of "Esso" stations to market its products.[30] For a pair of competitors, I.P.C. and C.P.L. certainly behaved in a surprisingly cooperative manner.

The cooperation of the two companies took a decisive turn, when in May 1957 the two consolidated operations. Diminishing returns in a market of frozen prices made it plausible for the two companies to consolidate to the point that Lobitos Oil itself became a holding company with a 50 percent interest in the Lima Concessions. I.P.C. acquired the other 50 percent interest, and assumed responsibility for the operations of the field. The working force of C.P.L. was simply absorbed by I.P.C. The two companies divided the crude oil coming from the Lima Concessions in half, but since C.P.L. did not have a refinery, all of the oil was refined by I.P.C.'s Talara plant. Milne and Cia. marketed Lobitos Oil products, and when all was said and done, C.P.L. was little more than a trade name—it had no personnel in Peru.

One of the immediate effects of the consolidation of International Petroleum Company and Compañía Petrolera Lobitos was that I.P.C.'s share of the petroleum business, which had been a substantial 65 percent, suddenly increased to approximately 90 percent. The irritation which Peruvian nationalists felt for I.P.C. increased commensurately. This deepening resentment had immediate and concrete consequences for I.P.C.

In August 1957, I.P.C. applied to the Peruvian Ministry of Development for an "adaptation" of La Brea y Pariñas to the Petroleum Law of 1952 (No. 11780). In its formal petition, the company stated:

> It is our belief that we should seek to exchange the special regime deriving from the . . . Arbitration Award for that of the . . . Law. . . . Apart from the several inconveniences which derive from operating under a special regime, the functioning of two different legal systems,—that of the Arbitration Award for La Brea y Pariñas and that of the Petroleum Law for concessions obtained under that Law,— will generate, as is evident, confusion and problems of a practical nature, both for the officials of the Government and for the Company.[31]

In a covering letter, Jack Ashworth, I.P.C.'s general manager, pointed out that the petition was accompanied by a tax comparison illustrating the differences between the old Laudo system and that of the new proposal. The company would pay slightly higher taxes under the new system, at least as of 1956. After nearly two months, the company received an answer in the form of a Supreme Resolution: "It is not in the best interest of the Nation to permit the adaptation requested . . . it is therefore resolved: To reject the petition presented by International Petroleum Co., Ltd . . ."[32] After its great efforts promoting a new petroleum law, I.P.C. was denied "adaptation" of its property to the new system.

The significance of this event cannot be exaggerated. For decades, the company fought to maintain its special status under the provisions of the 1922 Award and the original sale; now the company pleaded to leave the arbitration cocoon—to come out under Peru's general petroleum law. However, the Peruvian government denied this request, thus condemning the company to a languishing death under the Laudo. I.P.C.'s economic vitality was nullified by price controls, and the Peruvian government was not about to allow the company to rise like the mythical phoenix out of its own ashes.

Obviously, the political situation had changed considerably. In another day, the company would have enlisted the support of the Department of State and the American press to condemn these "confiscatory" policies. Or it might have gone farther—pulling its ships out of service between Talara and Callao. Perhaps I.P.C. might have influenced the New York financial circles, asking them to demand prompt payment on Peru's eternal foreign debt. The company did none of these things—the late 1950s were very different from the 1920s. For one reason, Standard Oil (New Jersey), while still the giant of international oils, did not loom as large in American political circles as it once had. The oil trusts, which during the 1920s were among the three or four major industrial concerns in the U.S., had become only one of the twenty or thirty major industries in the U.S. Now the petroleum industry competed with the auto makers, retailers, electronics firms, and many more in their demands for governmental attention. The growth and diversification of American industry dwarfed the importance of the international oils such as Standard Oil (New Jersey). Like the railroads which were once a dominant factor in the political economy of America and today are only a sub-group on the Dow Jones transportation index, so the international oils have become merely a part of the "oil group," sharing their influence with domestic oils and many other industries.

Another factor which diminished the bargaining power of I.P.C. in Peru was its conversion from an exporting industry to a supplier of domestic needs. Obviously, the international oil companies derive their bargaining strength from the fact that they are the intermediaries between oil-producing and oil-consuming countries. For example, if Venezuela nationalizes its oil industry, who will buy its oil? The Venezuelans can take over the wells, the pipes, the tanks, and even the refineries; but the tankers, gas stations and allied facilities which constitute the marketing end of the oil business are primarily on foreign soil and not subject to nationalization. The Venezuelans can and have pressured the oil companies with very good results without using their trump card—nationalization. Nationalization would be disastrous for the oil companies, but it would be even more disastrous for Venezuela. The oil companies derive a great deal of strength from the knowledge that nationalization would be mutually destructive.

When I.P.C. changed from an exporting to a domestic operation, it lost its most important lever. By the late 1950s and early 1960s, I.P.C.'s operations in Peru were self-contained. Oil was pumped out of La Brea y Pariñas and Lobitos, refined in Talara, and marketed throughout the country. The Peruvian government was in a position to take over the operations by merely severing the umbilical cord which connected I.P.C. to its parent company, Standard Oil—via Toronto and Esso Inter-America in Coral Gables. The Peruvians were not quick to grasp this radical alteration of the balance of power in their favor. However, it was only a matter of time before I.P.C. would be dragged out once more into the spotlight—this time divested of its traditional power.

International Petroleum Company did not stumble into the 1960s weakened by ignorance or self-abandon. The company was aware of its precarious position and took steps to counteract its unhealthy powerlessness. These steps were in two directions: the development of I.P.C. as a model employer, and the efforts by the company to win acceptance in the Peruvian oligarchy via a wide-ranging public relations program.

The beginning of I.P.C.'s effort to become the model employer reached back to 1937. In that year, Nelson Rockefeller visited Venezuela and went on an inspection of the properties of Creole Petroleum Corporation, a company which like I.P.C. was owned by Standard Oil and operated in Venezuela. Apparently appalled by the working conditions existing in Creole Petroleum's work camps, Rockefeller prodded Standard Oil and its subsidiaries into a policy of broader social responsibility. Out of his visit to Venezuela and the consequent social awakening, Rockefeller eventually founded the International Basic Economy Corporation, with the goal of bringing socioeconomic progress to the underdeveloped nations and additional profits to the family corporation.[33]

Rockefeller's new social awareness filtered into Peru, and signaled a turnaround in the personnel management at Talara. Up to the early 1940s the work force of La Brea y Pariñas had, for the most part, been housed in barracks. North American employees, mostly Canadian, had separate quarters. Native Peruvian workers led a generally bleak life of common meals in mess halls and little privacy in the barracks. There was little opportunity for advancement.

In 1940, John Oldfield, currently General Counsel for Esso Inter-America and Director of I.P.C., and Michael Wright, now Chairman of the Board of Humble Oil Company, Standard Oil's marketing arm, went to Peru to construct a new town in Talara. They brought in town planners, anthropologists, and other specialists. Streets were laid, and houses, hospitals, schools and parks were constructed. To avoid the creation of a "company town" in the more narrow sense of the term, I.P.C. added what it called a "free enterprise area" where Peruvian merchants were invited to set up shop. The company went beyond construction of a new town; I.P.C. improved its treatment of the Peruvian workers. Free nursing and medical care were extended to the working force, generous pension plans were established, salaries were raised to the point that they were the highest in Peru. For the first time in Peruvian history, collective bargaining was introduced. The company also made a conscious effort to diminish antiforeign sentiments by reducing foreign personnel to a minimum.[34]

By the early 1960's there were 4,990 workers in Talara. Their basic hourly wage was 6.12 soles, but with indirect payments such as overtime included, the average wage was 7.89 soles per hour. Industrial workers in Lima-Callao earned an average of 5.68 soles; therefore, I.P.C. workers received wages which were 39 percent higher than those of the best paid workers in Peru—those in the Lima-Callao area. According to the company, the workers received other benefits amounting to between 205 percent and 246 percent of their basic wages— a credible assertion considering that the company gave free benefits to virtually all of the relatives living with any Talara worker. The Latin American extended family frequently includes not only wives and children, but grandparents, brothers and sisters, and aunts and uncles. With 4,990 workers in Talara, there were 29,504 such relatives, making a total of 34,494 Peruvians receiving such benefits as free medical attention and medicines, and heavily subsidized housing. Workers in Talara paid 6.50 soles a month for a two bedroom house, the equivalent of less than one hour's wages, and 10.00 soles per month for a three bedroom house—about one and a half hours' wages. The company provided generous pensions and sickness compensation, and it built twelve schools for the children of its workers. I.P.C. paid the salaries of the teachers, who were supervised by the Peruvian Ministry of Education. The company even paid these teachers bonuses for their work in Talara.[35] The company's policy was clearly to go well beyond the benefits which, in theory, the Peruvian government required all employers to provide for their workers, and therefore by Peruvian standards, the workers of I.P.C. were a pampered elite.

Pampering, however, did not necessarily render the I.P.C. work force into a mindless and grateful herd. Approximately 85 percent of the workers belonged to one of two unions operating in Talara. One of the unions reflected the Aprista philosophy and was affiliated with the Confederation of Workers of Peru, the International Workers of Mexico, and the International Union of Petroleum Workers, a United States-based organization. This Aprista union had traditionally been strongest among the more educated refinery workers living in Talara. The other union, claiming a "socialist" philosophy although it opposed nationalization of the petroleum industry, originated with the field workers who were stationed at the various wells and supporting installations throughout La Brea y Pariñas. After World War II, the company was able to purchase vehicles and tires, and the field workers were gradually brought to Talara; however, they continued to support their separate union. Until 1957, the Aprista union was the largest, but in that year I.P.C. incorporated Lobitos into its operations, and these additional workers swung the balance and the "socialist" union became the largest. During the early 1960s, the Aprista union counted about 1,300 members, while the "socialist" union had a membership of 2,400. These unions often competed with each other in degree of militancy. Since I.P.C. was the largest petroleum producer in Peru, the company endured every strike which took place in the oil industry. The other petroleum companies merely followed the general outlines of the I.P.C. settlements. From the middle 1940s to 1968, I.P.C. was struck four times, for an average of eighteen days each time.[36]

The good treatment I.P.C. accorded its employees paid off, for during the times of crisis from 1959 to 1968, the working force supported the company's position and consistently opposed nationalization. However, the fact that the Peruvians who derived such great benefits were relatively few in number—less than 35,000, and lived in isolation at Talara, minimized their effect on the controversy. Therefore, the price which the company paid for its happy workers was high—its cash outlay was considerable. For instance, from 1952 to 1962, the cost of living went up by 100 percent in Peru; productivity in La Brea y Pariñas increased by 30 percent. Salaries for white collar employees, however, went up 300 percent and for the oil workers, the increase was about 250 percent. Since the I.P.C. personnel had excellent conditions and wages, they tended to stay with the company; by the early 1960s the company had 1,450 retired employees collecting the equivalent of 10 percent of their active payroll.[37]

In a broad political sense, the town of Talara was to Peru what West Berlin is to East Germany and the Soviet bloc—a living reminder within their own borders which illuminates by contrast their own poverty and underdevelopment. Talara was a glaring example to the poorly paid sugar workers, and even the workers in Lima, of how it would be possible to live if the affairs of Peru were administered as were the affairs at La Brea y Pariñas. To add insult to injury, the employees of the state-owned Empresa Petrolera Fiscal lived under far inferior conditions in the state oil fields right next door to La Brea y Pariñas.

To Don Luis Miró Quesada, who wrote his doctoral dissertation on labor at the University of San Marcos at the turn of the century—a man who considered himself an authority on labor, I.P.C.'s labor policies must have seemed nothing short of blasphemy.[38] The same was true for many upper class employers in Peru, who saw I.P.C. as a dangerous spoiler of their labor supply. In time the company's management realized that they had gone "too fast, too soon" in improving the lot of their workers. John Oldfield confessed that the labor policies of I.P.C. lost it friends in the oligarchy, to the point that the 10 percent of the population which comprised the social and political power base in Peru decidedly opposed the company.[39]

In public relations the company proved to be quite proficient. Its efforts ran the gamut of Madison Avenue advertising techniques adapted to suit the particular circumstances in Peru. International Petroleum published a hefty magazine and a widely-circulated newsletter. The magazine, FANAL, was an expensive, high quality, and fairly large publication devised to appeal to Peru's intellectual elite. The articles in FANAL were timely and of high literary quality; the subjects were of historic or literary importance and usually stressed Peruvian themes. Occasionally, the company did press its point of view in an article. Even then, the article was well informed and well written. Through FANAL, I.P.C. tried to reach the influential elements of Peruvian society. In 1954, for example, on the occasion of the fiftieth anniversary of the Superior War College, FANAL carried an article tracing the history of the institution, listing its contributions to the Peruvian nation, and relating the merits of various directors of the college and distinguished alumni.[40]

FANAL was not merely a vehicle for the company to praise military institutions and leaders. Given the difficulties that Peruvian intellectuals faced in getting their work published in a country of limited resources, FANAL provided a place for Peru's most distinguished writers to appear in print, and to do so at a profit. Articles by Peru's leading intellectuals appeared in this publication during the 1950s and into the 1960s. In fact, in 1955, the publication carried articles by two members of the Miró Quesada family—their more serious work did not fit into the casual format of El Comercio's Sunday supplement.[41] The anniversary of FANAL's publication prompted I.P.C. to collect testimonials for its publication. The list was most impressive—the head of the Lima Bar Association, a prominent army general, the chief librarian at the Lima National Library, the senior professor of the Liberal Arts Faculty at the University of San Marcos, publisher Pedro Beltrán—the editor of La Prensa, Aurelio Miró Quesada, Raúl Porras Barrenechea, President of the Peruvian Senate, and a score of prominent writers, poets, and clergy. In short, the intellectual elite of Peru was called upon to express in writing its gratitude for a publication dedicated to them and sponsored by I.P.C.—they responded generously.[42]

Less than ten years later the company was badly in need of support, and called for similar testimonials. This time there were none from the Miró Quesada family or from Pedro Beltrán, and while prominent Peruvians still lavished their praises on FANAL, the truly influential testimonials of 1957 were missing. However, the company gained considerable support from an intellectual elite which would otherwise have been at the forefront of the anti-I.P.C. campaigns. Instead of the customary acrimony with which Latin American intellectuals often shower American companies, a Peruvian journalist was moved to write: "If other powerful enterprises did what I.P.C. does, editing magazines without aim of profit, the Peruvian culture would be greatly benefited."[43]

International Petroleum Company also published a monthly newsletter, Noticias de Petróleo. The purpose of this more widely circulated publication was to inform the public about technical developments in the oil industry and more importantly, to promote relentlessly I.P.C.'s point of view regarding the role of private companies in the oil industry and more specifically its own role in the Peruvian economy. The publication reminded its readers that the Russians, for instance, paid three times as much for their gasoline as did the Peruvians.[44] I.P.C. made it a policy to harp constantly on the shortcomings of state-owned petroleum enterprises in Mexico, Bolivia, Brazil, and Argentina. For example, Noticias de Petróleo reported that "under the state monopoly" Mexico produced half as much petroleum in 1959 as it had back in 1921 and 1922 under private initiative.[45] Positive news dealing with private enterprises always appeared in Noticias, as if such reports tended to prove the contention that state-owned companies were failures by contrast. On at least one occasion, Noticias de Petróleo carried a reprint of an article which was extremely critical of Petrobras, the Brazilian oil enterprise, accusing it of gross mismanagement and of pro-communist dealings.[46]

One constant theme in both of International Petroleum's publications, as well as in countless special editions ranging from pamphlets to book length treatises, was the justice of the company's position vis-à-vis ownership of La Brea y Pariñas, petroleum prices, and other touchy subjects.

I.P.C. did not limit itself to publishing in its attempt to influence that powerful 10 percent of the Peruvian populace. Periodically, the company sponsored literary competitions, providing prizes for the best compositions on a certain theme. The company sponsored one such competition in 1953, when Peruvians were invited to compose a poem extolling Ramón Castilla, a 19th century military hero and former president of Peru. Presiding over the selection jury was Aurelio Miró Quesada. In 1955, I.P.C. sponsored a similar contest—this time with the objective to write an essay on "the independence of Peru and the Peruvian contribution to the freedom of the Spanish colonies in America." In 1965, the "Esso competition of young artists" was held. All painters and sculptors under forty were invited to participate.

International Petroleum Company also aided the Peruvian government in its quest for international prestige and recognition by providing financial support for the Peruvian exhibition in Paris in 1958. In recognition for that help, the Prado administration bestowed the Order of Merit for Distinguished Service on Jack Ashworth, I.P.C.'s general manager.[47]

The company was sensitive to Peru's Catholic traditions. All religious holidays were observed in Talara, where the company had built the churches. Management saw to it that every new I.P.C. facility, including every gas station in the country, was duly blessed by the competent ecclesiastical authority in the community.

I.P.C. provided speakers for groups such as the chamber of commerce and labor unions, for these meetings provided a forum for the company to explain its position on various issues. The importance of these efforts was clear, considering that the lecturers were often the company's highest executives in Peru, including the general manager. One particularly important group to which these lectures were given regularly was the student body and staff of the Center for Higher Military Studies (CAEM). This military school eventually proved very important in reshaping the social philosophy of the Peruvian armed forces.

Evaluating the effectiveness of I.P.C.'s public relations efforts and more particularly its courting of the Peruvian intellectual elite is difficult, for it is impossible to know how the population at large and the intellectuals in particular would have acted had there been no FANAL, Noticias de Petróleo, and no literary and artistic competitions. However, it does seem fair to state that the company succeeded in at least blunting a potentially leading adversary, a fact which might help to account for the prolonged stay of I.P.C. in Peru throughout the 1960s, in spite of official and popular hostility.

International Petroleum Company did not play the role of "ugly American" in Peru. Quite the contrary, while the company made tactical errors such as its radical labor policies, beginning with the 1950s it showed a great deal of sensitivity to Peru's customs, institutions and national pride. If anything, the company can be criticized for going too far in its efforts to cater to Peruvian nationalism, as for example, when I.P.C. decided to change its name to Petróleos Viru—Viru was the Inca word from which the name "Peru" is presumed to have evolved.[48] Harries Peterson and Tomas Unger put it well when they remarked:

> In spite that in recent years I.P.C. has carried out an impressive job of public relations, we feel they have omitted giving the country a true image of itself. La Brea y Pariñas, the low export prices, the high taxes, the price controls, the growing costs of production, etc.—many of these factors beyond the control of the Company—have led I.P.C. to take an apologetic position, frequently giving irritating apologies which were never requested.[49]

Would it have been better for I.P.C. to state clearly that its reason for existence was to produce profits for its parent company, Standard Oil (New Jersey)? By portraying itself as a sort of philanthropic organization with a side interest in the production and distribution of oil, the company generated more mistrust than it really deserved. However, while the company engaged in wide-ranging efforts to soothe Peruvian nationalism, I.P.C. stubbornly held on to its own form of nationalism—corporatism, in areas which would eventually render compromise an unreachable goal.

NOTES

1. Max E. Crawford, "Los Problemas de la Industria Petrolera en el Peru," FANAL, VIII, No. 37 (1953), pp. 21-22.

2. Calculated from data in: U.S., Department of State, Annual Petroleum Report—1967—Peru, Department of State Document No. A-592 (Washington: U.S. Government Printing Office, 1969), Enclosure No. 1.

3. James Fred Rippy, British Investment in Latin America, 1822-1949—A Case Study in the Operations of Private Enterprise in Retarded Regions (2nd. ed.; Hamden, Connecticut: Archon Books, 1966), pp. 131-132.

4. Harries C. Peterson and Tomas Unger, Petróleo: Hora Cero (Lima: n.p., 1964), p. 301.

5. Ibid., pp. 126-146.

6. Ibid., p. 305.

7. Ibid., p. 130.

8. Ibid., pp. 137-141.

9. Laurence A. Steinhardt, American Ambassador to Lima to the Department of State, March 28, 1938, U.S. Department of State Decimal Files, No. 812.6363/3380; February 2, 1939, No. 823.6363/196; March 20, 1939, No. 823.6363/200.

10. For reports of parliamentary action on this matter, see "Cámara de Senadores," El Comercio, December 27, 1946, p. 2.

11. Luis's brother, Antonio Miró Quesada and his wife were assassinated by Carlos Steer, an Aprista fanatic on May 15, 1935. Luis Miró Quesada then became family patriarch and editor of El Comercio. Naturally, the ideological animosity the Miró Quesadas felt for APRA before the crime was afterwards magnified a thousand-fold into a feud which knew no truce.

12. Luis Miró Quesada, "El Contrato sobre la zona petrolífera de Sechura," El Comercio, December 27, 1946, p. 7. This quotation and all others taken from Spanish materials in this thesis were translated by this author unless otherwise noted.

13. See the editorial "El contrato sobre el petróleo de Sechura," El Comercio, December 30, 1946, p. 2.

14. The text of this company demand is reproduced in: "Documentos Parlamentarios," El Comercio, January 4, 1947, p. 4.

15. See the record of the Congressional debates as reproduced in: "Cámara de Senadores," El Comercio, January 3, 1947, p. 4.

16. Ibid.

17. Sir Robert Marett, Peru (New York: Praeger, 1969), pp. 172-173; See the editorial in El Comercio, January 8, 1947, p. 2.

18. Fredrick B. Pike, The Modern History of Peru (New York: Praeger, 1967), p. 285.

19. Miró Quesada's feud with Pedro Beltrán reportedly originated shortly after the latter assumed the editorship of La Prensa, and publically favored an end to price controls. Miró Quesada, whose newspaper benefited from such controls, opposed eliminating this system. Beltran, on the other hand, was a businessman with varied financial interests, and he considered price controls detrimental to business. Confidential Interview with I.P.C. executive, Coral Gables, Florida, May 26, 1971.

20. Pike, Modern Peru, pp. 286-290.

21. Since the official rate of exchange was S. 6.50 to the dollar and the unofficial rate was S. 13.00 to the dollar, this single act of the Odría regime caused the price of newsprint to double, a change which El Comercio felt severely and Beltrán in contrast applauded. Confidential source.

22. Pike, Modern Peru, p. 176.

23. In 1954, for example, the government published a colorful pamphlet with the caption "deeds, not words" across the cover. It included several tables of facts and figures. Peru, Dirección General de Información del Peru, Petróleo (Lima: n.p., 1955).

24. José Pareja Paz Soldan, "Nacionalismo Constructivo," FANAL, VII, No. 35 (1953), p. 30.

25. Odría's remarks are extensively quoted in: International Petroleum Company, "Petróleo en el Peru," FANAL, VII, No. 35 (1953).

26. Pike, Modern Peru, pp. 291-292; Torcuato S. DiTella, "Populism and Reform in Latin America," Obstacles to Change in Latin America, ed. Claudio Veliz (New York: Oxford University Press, 1965), p. 67.

27. The depletion allowance is a tax deduction which oil companies are commonly granted to permit them to build up cash reserves which offset their diminishing oil supplies. If company "X" makes a net profit of $1, million, it will be taxed on a net profit of $750,000 assuming a 25 percent depletion allowance. In the U.S., the depletion allowance for oil companies was 27 percent for many years, and in recent years it was reduced to 24 percent. In Canada, the allowance has traditionally been 25 percent, but the government, anxious to promote oil development, is planning to increase the allowance to 33 1/3 percent. In comparison, then, the Peruvian law was not particularly generous with domestic companies and rather conservative with foreign enterprises.

28. For a detailed description of the law, see: Soldan, FANAL, VII, No. 35, pp. 30-35.

29. Peterson and Unger, Petróleo: Hora Cero, p. 17; "100 Años de Industria Petrolera en el Peru," FANAL, XVIII, No. 68 (1963), p. 29.

30. Ibid., pp. 56-63.

31. The La Brea y Pariñas Controversy, Vol. I (International Petroleum Company, February, 1969), Exhibit 3.

32. Ibid.

33. The company still exists and in 1971 it had assets of nearly $200 million dollars. The Rockefeller family still holds a 60 percent interest in the enterprise, and its present chief is Rodman C. Rockefeller, reputed top businessman among John D. Rockefeller's seven great-grandsons. See: Joseph Engelhof, "Profit Necessary in Social

Activity Too: Rockefeller," Chicago Tribune, October 4, 1971, Section 3, p. 7.

34. Interview with John Oldfield at Esso Inter-America, Coral Gables, Florida, May 24, 1971.

35. This information was supplied by an issue of the company's newsletter dealing with its working force. International Petroleum Company, Noticias de Petróleo, XII, No. 115 (February, 1960).

36. This information was provided in a confidential interview with an I.P.C. executive, Coral Gables, Florida, May 25, 1971. See also: Peterson and Unger, Petróleo: Hora Cero, pp. 230-232.

37. Peterson and Unger, Petróleo: Hora Cero, pp. 234-235.

38. Luis Miró Quesada considered himself a pioneer in the field of labor, but his attitude was extremely paternalistic. Until the military junta headed by current Peruvian President Juan Velasco Alvarado ordered a union for the workers of El Comercio, they had been unable to form one. Miró Quesada's dissertation and other philosophical writings appear in: Luis Miró Quesada, Albores de la Reforma Social en el Peru (Lima: Talleres Graficos P.L. Villanueva, 1965).

39. Interview with John Oldfield, Coral Gables, Florida, May 27, 1971.

40. "La Escuela Superior de Guerra—Cincuenta años al servicio del Ejército," FANAL, VIII, No. 38 (1954), pp. 36-38.

41. Aurelio Miró Quesada, "El Inca Garcilaso, ejemplo de síntesis," FANAL, X, No. 43 (1955), pp. 28-31; Luis Miró Quesada Garland, "Evolución de la Arquitectura Peruana," FANAL, X, No. 45 (1955), pp. 28-31.

42. "'Fanal' Alcanza Cincuenta Ediciones," FANAL, XII, No. 50 (1957).

43. Elsa Arana Freire, "Testimonio sobre FANAL," FANAL, XX, No. 26 (1965), pp. 22-25.

44. "Los sovieticos pagan por la gasolina más del triple que los peruanos," Noticias de Petróleo, XII, No. 113 (September, 1959).

45. "Bajo el Monopolio estatal México produce hoy solo la mitad del petróleo que producia en 1921 y 1922," Noticias de Petróleo, XIII, No. 117 (May, 1960).

46. The article was originally published by O Globo. Eugenio Gudin, "Petrobras: desperdicio e incapacidad," Noticias de Petróleo, XIV, No. 123 (August, 1961).

47. See "El Gerente de International Petroleum Co. condecorado con la orden 'Al Mérito por Servicios Distinguidos,'" FANAL, XIV, No. 55 (1959).

48. The project was dropped when El Comercio got wind of the story and ridiculed it. Interview with John Oldfield, Coral Gables, Florida, May 27, 1971.

49. Peterson and Unger, Petróleo: Hora Cero, pp. 54-55.

CHAPTER

4

A MULTINATIONAL CORPORATION PLAYS LATIN AMERICAN POLITICIAN

Three candidates presented themselves to the people during the Peruvian presidential election of 1956, and since President Odría outlawed the Alianza Popular Revolucionaria Americana (APRA), all the candidates were drawn from either the more traditional political elements of Peru or from a new breed of young, moderate reformers, usually Catholics, inspired by the liberal Papal Encyclicals of John XXIII calling for social justice. In Peru, these reformers organized a party, the National Front for Democratic Youth, which was led by a Texas educated architect, Fernando Belaúnde Terry. The other candidates for election in 1956 were Manuel Prado, a former president (1939-45) who appeared as the standard bearer for a hastily organized political party called the National Coalition, and Hernando de Lavalle, President Odría's personal choice, leading the Unión Nacional.

Prado and Lavalle had no substantial political organization, and the recently formed National Front of Democratic Youth had not been tested in a national election. The unknown election factor was the only Peruvian mass political party, APRA, and its leader Víctor Raúl Haya de la Torre. The Apristas wanted to play a legal role in Peruvian politics, and the party leaders contacted all the presidential candidates in order to discover their postelection intentions towards APRA. Prado promised to legalize APRA as his first official act, and he subsequently won the election by a substantial margin. He immediately carried out his promise.

What won Prado his election—the deal with APRA—also won him a most persistent enemy, Don Luis Miró Quesada and his newspaper El Comercio. Miró Quesada, whose personal feud with APRA was a notorious factor in Peruvian politics, considered any compromise with that party immoral—a personal affront to his dignity. Henceforth, the Prado administration did nothing well in the eyes of

CORPORATION PLAYS POLITICIAN   65

El Comercio, and even further, Prado soon became the primary target of the old Lima sage.

Manuel Prado inherited Odría's Peru, but without Odría's good fortune. The Korean War and its consequent boom for Peruvian exports had long since been terminated. The Sechura Desert had proved an economic fiasco. The International Petroleum Company, which had given advance money to the government of Peru in consideration for future taxes beginning with the Sanchez Cerro administration, discontinued this practice during Odría's rule.[1] Manuel Prado faced a shortage of government revenues and deteriorating economic conditions. Many difficult decisions confronted him. Prado's first Minister of Finance, Juan Pardo, the grandson of Peru's first Civilista president, insisted on sustaining the sol at a fixed rate of exchange, 19 soles to one dollar. Since this rate was quite unrealistic given the actual economic condition of Peru, this policy caused a run on the sol, and consequently a sharp drop in Peru's foreign exchange reserves. By early 1958 the situation was desperate, for the Central Bank was nearing the end of its dollar reserves, and the government was under daily attack not only by El Comercio, but by Pedro Beltrán's La Prensa.[2] Both of Lima's prominent newspapers criticized Manuel Prado.

Once more, the old arguments concerning price controls which had first been taken up during the Bustamante administration were dusted off and brought to the fore. Miró Quesada benefited from a fixed exchange rate—he could purchase dollars to buy newsprint abroad, and he opposed devaluation. Pedro Beltrán, with his multiple business interests involving exports, favored a more realistic rate of exchange. On January 22, 1958, the Prado government suspended the sale of foreign exchange by the Central Bank, in effect floating the sol.[3] During the month of January, El Comercio published several editorials attacking the Prado government for its failure to "defend" the currency. El Comercio also attacked "the official organ of the exporters," La Prensa.[4]

Not only were the old arguments on government controls revived, but the problems of the petroleum industry once again haunted the Peruvian president. During the twenty years preceding 1958, production of crude petroleum had grown 10 percent while consumption had grown 400 percent. Petroleum and it derivatives accounted for 75 percent of the energy consumed in Peru, and given the government-imposed low prices for oil products, there was virtually no chance of altering this proportion.[5] I.P.C. obtained and published testimony from coal industry executives and technicians stating that the artificially low prices of petroleum derivatives precluded any meaningful growth of the coal industry, for the latter could not compete with the controlled prices of petroleum.[6] Low prices, I.P.C. maintained, prevented the company from making heavy investments in development and improvements, thus guaranteeing a rapid decline in productivity at La Brea y Pariñas.

Mindful of the critical situation, Prado devised a clever scheme to raise the price of gas and also to raise taxes. Knowing that an increase in the cost of petroleum derivatives would be hard to sell to the Peruvian people, the Ministry of Development started a publicity campaign aimed at explaining the reasons for the hike well in advance of the actual increases. The advertisement placed in various Lima newspapers attempted to explain how the new prices would affect transportation. For example, the increases in the bus fare from Lima to Trujillo were tentatively posted. The increase was justified in terms of the highway construction program. This advertisement specifically promised the construction of nine highways in the easternmost Selva section of the country, ten in the Sierra, and the completion of the Pan-American highway, which ran down the coast of Peru. It ended with a patriotic plea: "the progress of Peru is well worth a few pennies."[7] Within one week following the opening of the publicity campaign, people began to hoard gasoline in anticipation of the price increase. Long lines were reported at gas stations. By January 14, there was a severe scarcity of gasoline in the city of Cuzco, and I.P.C. was reported to be speeding shipments to the area.

Organized opposition to the gasoline price hike and the gasoline tax increase was quick to react. The Teamsters Union met January 13, 1958, and their first meeting ended in a brawl when a delegate from Chulucanas accused the more moderate Union of Public Service Drivers of Lima of being an institution in the service of Standard Oil.[8] With the teamsters apparently divided, the administration moved quickly. On January 23, the Chamber of Deputies passed the gasoline price increase, with only the Christian Democrats making a significant effort to stop it. However, the Teamsters Union managed to pull together and publish a paid announcement carried by the Lima dailies denouncing the price increase on gasoline.

The Teamsters argued that since 70 percent of all passengers and cargo were carried by car, bus, or truck in Peru, a gasoline price increase would have a very deleterious effect on the general welfare of the population. More specifically, the union noted that while the Prado administration was asking the Congress for an increase in taxes amounting to between 25 and 30 cents per gallon, the Ministry of Development was announcing price increases of 65 to 70 cents per gallon. To whom was the difference going? The union argued that the petroleum companies, primarily I.P.C., would pocket the difference, and in passing they charged I.P.C. with being a "virtual monopoly" since its acquisition of the Lobitos fields.[9]

Miró Quesada immediately recognized the union's argument as a potential source of embarrassment for the Prado administration. In the afternoon edition of El Comercio that same day, the gasoline issue was moved to the first page—with a prominent headline: "Increases of taxes and prices of gasoline." The following day, January 26, 1958, El Comercio carried an editorial which to a large extent incorporated the arguments put forth by the union. It also added its own interpretation—the government's proposal would in effect open the doors to price increases at I.P.C. discretion. This was an inaccurate interpretation unless the assumption was made that the government would order higher prices as per I.P.C. demand. The editorial also emphasized that I.P.C.'s profits were re-invested not in Peru but in distant lands and that the price increase of gasoline would have a drastic effect on the cost of living index in so far as food and clothing prices would reflect the new increase.[10]

By now in hot pursuit of what was shaping up as a major weakness in the Prado administration, El Comercio dug deeper into the government's argument that a tax increase was necessary to carry on the construction of highways. In the January 27 editorial, Miró Quesada noted that since the Peruvian government had previously borrowed large amounts of money, including $10 million from I.P.C., and had pledged the revenues from the gasoline tax to serve this debt, the future gasoline tax revenues would have to be used for the most part for debt payments. More specifically, out of 1.5 billion soles in estimated gasoline tax revenues, over 800 million soles would have to be used to serve the pre-existing debt, thus leaving some 722 million soles to be used in the highway construction program.[11] In a succeeding editorial, Miró Quesada warned the Senate against passing the government's bill.

With the intensified heat generated by the opposition, APRA did what it had done before—the party attempted to disassociate itself from the price increase. Almost as a test of APRA's intention, the Christian Democrats tried to resurrect the issue in the Chamber of Deputies, only to be rebuffed by the APRA majority. In spite of its verbal retreat, APRA wanted to stick by Prado on the gasoline issue. On January 28, the Senate passed the government's bill, and almost immediately, Miró Quesada lambasted the government editorially.[12]

But Miró Quesada was merely playing the issue; the real confrontation came between the government and the Teamsters Union. On January 30, after the government's bill had been passed by both the Chamber of Deputies and the Senate, the Federación de Choferes del Peru (Teamsters Union) published a communique calling for a meeting to consider the "grave situation" created by the passage of the bill. With the absence of the more moderate Drivers of the Public Service of Lima, the Teamsters Union issued an ultimatum stating that they would go on an indefinite strike the day after the price increase was enacted into law.[13]

The threat of a strike was enough to cause the Prado government to delay proclamation of the price increases. Prado opted for a cooling off period hoping to diffuse unionist anger. But El Comercio kept up its campaign. In articles and editorials, the paper denounced the impending price increase. Two months went by from the time the bill was approved by Congress to its enactment. In early April the price increase was finally officially approved by Prado, and as announced, the Teamsters Union began a strike.[14]

The strike was particularly effective in the south of Peru, especially in Arequipa and Cuzco, that area's two major cities. It soon became clear that the severity of the teamsters' walkout would complicate the lives of Peruvians, since other workers joined the boycott. On April 9, the vendors of the Central Market of Cuzco held a rally to decide whether to go on strike in support of the Teamsters Union. The local police attempted to disperse the rally and violence erupted. A twelve-year-old boy was killed, and there was ominous threat of widespread rioting. The army and the police began patrolling the streets. In Arequipa, the strike spread to blue- and white-collar workers, but order was maintained.

In Cuzco the situation was different—conditions worsened to a point little understood in Peru, and for the most part unreported anywhere else. Of all the recent works on Peruvian history or politics, the 1958 events at Cuzco remain unmentioned with the exception of a book by British scholar and former British Ambassador to Peru Sir Robert Marett, who dedicates a whole sentence to the crisis.[15] The management of I.P.C. and the Prado administration, however, recognized the significance of the crisis.[16] According to I.P.C. management personnel, the city of Cuzco was in the hands of rebel militia composed of Teamster Union members and other radicals for three days; the Peruvian government was able to retake the city only because the rebels failed to occupy the airport, and loyal troops were rushed in by air.[17] Even Miró Quesada must have become alarmed by the events, for El Comercio failed to carry news stories on the Cuzco uprising. Only in an editorial published days later did that paper hint at the urgency of the Cuzco events. According to El Comercio, the Cuzco rebels formed a "popular Committee" to rule the city, and only the desperate appeals from high clerics and other respected leaders prevented a bloody confrontation.[18] The Prado government strengthened its hand when troops arrived in Cuzco, and consequently the government was able to bargain successfully for an end to the revolt. However, the rebels won concessions. Teamster Union leaders were granted safe conduct to fly to Lima to negotiate with the government on the price increase. The end result of the uprising was that Prado backed down. Gasoline taxes were increased by 25 cents for regular and 30 cents for premium; but the 40 cents per gallon price increase for the companies was cancelled, thus creating a critical situation for I.P.C.

This brief uprising in Cuzco is of utmost significance, for it tends to undermine a whole body of scholarly literature about Peru and about Latin America in general. First there is a common notion that Latin American oligarchies function as the agents of international capitalism. A good example of this thesis comes from Irving Louis Horowitz:

> In terms of an international stratification system the masses are those portions of the underdeveloped society that are exploited by the very national classes—the bourgeoisie and the proletariat alike—that are in turn subject to the severe pressures from an international cosmopolitan "center." The pecking order enriches the national "class" sectors at the expense of the internal "mass" sectors, while it weakens the nationalist's resolve to seek revolutionary methods for pressing economic and social demands.[19]

How does this statement apply to Peru? Peru is a rather "typical" Latin American nation—it has a large concentration of Indians, high illiteracy, and a low participation ratio in politics. I.P.C. is a subsidiary of the actual prototype of international capitalist institutions—Standard Oil (New Jersey). According to Horowitz's thesis, the organized workers of Peru should have supported or at least acquiesced to the price increase in deference to the "cosmopolitan center" (Standard Oil). In the "pecking order," the unions enriched themselves at the expense of the "internal 'mass' sector." Yet in Peru it was a labor union which disregarded this "pecking order" and nearly unseated the government of the "national 'class' sector," pressures from the "cosmopolitan center" notwithstanding.

Scholar Julio Cotler notes that labor unions "have fallen into new patterns of dependence as their demands for improvement and benefits are directed exclusively toward the unionized—without taking into consideration the national context."[20] However, the Teamsters Union in Peru opposed the price increase and had a rather sophisticated and well-developed argument which involved a definite conception of the national interest. Both the opinions of Horowitz and Cotler do not fit the context of Peru.

Of the Prado administration, John Gerassi said that for six years they "ruled the country as they wanted because the Apristas in Congress backed them."[21] However, the supposed Aprista influence on labor must have fizzled out; the Prado government was powerless to effect a gasoline price increase—an Aprista-backed program. Even moderate students of Peruvian politics are prone to refer to the "forty families" which ruled Peru, and which presumably in 1958 were still in charge even if that country was in a "transitional" stage.[22]

The management of I.P.C. emulated scholarly opinion by continuing to think fallaciously that it was the upper 10 percent which "counted." Yet, the evidence suggests that in the 1950s, Peru was not a country where a tiny oligarchy ruled. The oligarchy was in fact a deeply divided group—it was deeply divided in 1918, and it was divided forty years later over which policies Peru should follow regarding foreign—particularly American—capital. To advance the notion that the oligarchy ruled does not take into account the veto power that organized labor had by now achieved over certain policies, unless the definition of oligarchy included truck drivers and market vendors.

Although the rebellion in Cuzco was hushed up with a surprising degree of effectiveness, the fact that the government was forced to back down, and perhaps of equal importance, the fact that the military was forced to bargain with rebel leaders was deeply humiliating for both the Prado administration and for the military. El Comercio could draw only limited comfort from the knowledge that I.P.C. had been foiled. The lessons of Cuzco went unheeded, and neither the pro-I.P.C. factions nor the anti-I.P.C. factions of the old oligarchy realized that a protracted struggle over the petroleum issue endangered the structure of Peruvian society.

The International Petroleum Company's position, which until then had been very difficult, became critical during 1958. Costs rose while prices remained fixed in soles, which meant that prices actually declined rapidly. The company reversed its tactics from quiet persuasion of the government's top executives to a broad campaign aimed at influencing Peruvian public opinion. Both FANAL and Noticias de Petróleo, the two company publications, began to carry articles which clearly and unequivocally had one message: prices must be raised or the Peruvian petroleum industry would collapse. The facts were the same—the rapid rise in domestic consumption and stagnant production—but the arguments were strengthened. Since the 1901 discovery of the Lobitos fields, no significant new oil fields had been developed in Peru. To hope for new fields in eastern Peru as a solution to the immediate supply problems was unrealistic, for a trans-Andean oil pipeline would cost at least $100 million—money which Peru did not have. The only way to keep production from falling at La Brea y Pariñas was to employ costly methods of "secondary recovery,"[23] Faced with low prices, the company found it increasingly difficult to justify the investments required in order to keep up production. In the past, petroleum exports had in effect subsidized domestic consumption, but in 1957 I.P.C. was able to export only one-third the oil it exported in 1937. With Chile, Bolivia, and Ecuador developing oil of their own, the company's profitable exports to these countries were doomed in any case, and I.P.C. would now have to compete in distant markets, where transportation costs diminished their profit margins. The company argued that since the last price increase in 1954, the costs of its operations had gone up 60 percent. The sol drifted lower and lower in relation to the dollar, and nearly all of their equipment had to be purchased in dollars. According to the company, I.P.C. received only 93 cents of the 2.23 soles per gallon of regular gasoline—the price people paid at the stations. Ninety-six cents went toward payment of various taxes, 14 cents paid for transportation from Talara to Callao, and 20 cents went to the local gasoline dealer. International Petroleum argued that it could not produce, refine, store and distribute gasoline at the rate of 93 cents per gallon.[24]

One of I.P.C.'s worst years was 1958. By early fall it was evident that the company would be able to export only 2.5 million barrels of oil, in contrast to the well-over 4 million barrels it exported in 1957. With rapidly dropping profit margins, the company was ever more anxious to impress its point of view on the Peruvian public. During the previous five years (1953-57), I.P.C. invested $64 million on new drilling and secondary recovery just to maintain production levels. I.P.C. argued that it would have to invest $8.6 million in production; since the company could allocate only $6 million in its budget, the difference would have to come from $3.3 million of the year's estimated profits—leaving only $1.2 million profit. This sum represented a return of less than one percent on the company's $180 million investment.[25] Thus, I.P.C. laid its cards on the table. Even questioning various aspects of I.P.C.'s argument, the fact remains clear. Peruvians paid the lowest prices in the world for gasoline. Even Venezuelans paid the equivalent of 3.00 soles per gallon while Peruvians paid only 2.23 soles. North Americans and Chileans paid the equivalent of 7.50 and 8.10 soles respectively.[26] Furthermore, the company calculated that the small profit of 1958 would turn into a deficit within the next two years. By 1961, I.P.C. anticipated an annual loss of $2 million per year—a loss which would grow rapidly if a price increase was not allowed.[27] To deal with this situation, the company adopted a new policy. Beginning in 1959, I.P.C. ceased all new drilling, and relied on the output of La Brea y Pariñas and Lobitos regardless of the total production-consumption ratio.

Manuel Prado's second term in office reached its lowest level of political credibility in late 1958 and early 1959. Numerous labor strikes, an economic crisis of major proportions, and attacks by both major Lima newspapers were more than the government could endure. Boxed in by the Teamsters Union on the one side and I.P.C.'s no drilling policy on the other, Prado desperately searched for an imaginative solution to his multiple political woes. In the middle of 1959 he struck upon what must be considered a most innovative course of action: he invited Pedro Beltrán, the editor of La Prensa and an arch-critic of his administration, to take the reins of government as Prime Minister of Peru. At first Beltrán balked at the offer, but assured by Prado of a free hand in dealing with the problems of Peru, he yielded and became Prime Minister in July 1959. It was as if Lyndon Johnson had picked the editor of The New York Times or the Washington Post or NBC News to become his Chief of Staff at the height of the Vietnam War protests. Now Beltrán had to cease attacking the government—this in itself was a significant relief to the beleaguered Prado, and begin to think in more positive terms about possible and practical solutions to Peru's problems.

Since the petroleum controversy had a very high priority on the list of problems faced by the government, one of the first official acts of Prime Minister Beltrán was to order a committee to study the petroleum crisis. Article 208R of the Petroleum Law of 1952 (No. 11780) established that the government would determine petroleum prices by adding up the costs of production, transportation, storage, refining, distribution, sales, and taxes, plus "adequate" profit margins commensurate with the investment.[28] The International Petroleum Company had long ago ceased to receive an "adequate" return on its investment, but neither El Comercio nor the Teamsters Union were sympathetic to the plight of the American company. Their ability to veto any upward price adjustments in favor of the company had been demonstrated as recently as 1958.

Pedro Beltrán proved as imaginative in dealing with the problem as his nominal boss Manuel Prado had been in making him Prime Minister. In consultation with the committee, Beltrán determined that an "adequate" return for the company would have to be in the area of 6.6 percent even though in most countries the oil industry had yields closer to twice that rate. Even instituting a 6.6 percent return for I.P.C., however, would require a very substantial price increase. How could this be made acceptable to the Peruvian workers, especially the teamsters, a consideration which obviated the thesis that the workers do not "count" or participate in the political process of Peru?

Beltrán decided to destroy the traditional hierarchy of prices for petroleum products. Prices were not to be raised across the board, but selectively so as to minimize the impact on the neediest Peruvians. By a decree dated July 25, 1959, Beltrán dramatically increased the prices of petroleum products. The price of regular gasoline was increased by 146 percent; premium gasoline was raised

CORPORATION PLAYS POLITICIAN 73

205 percent. Kerosene was to be distributed under two prices. Domestic kerosene, the important source of energy in cooking and heating for the lower classes of Peru, was raised only 15 percent. On the other hand, kerosene used in indistry was increased a large 248 percent.[29] Reaction to the price increase was swift. As they had done in 1958, the teamsters went on strike. El Comercio once more could be counted on to attack Beltrán's decision. Unlike the strike in 1958, however, this one in 1959 failed to arouse widespread sympathies. Beltrán suspended constitutional guarantees and arrested several labor union leaders. In a matter of days, the situation was completely under control, and the price increases were an accepted fact of daily life in Peru.

Beltrán's ability to deal with the petroleum crisis stabilized the political situation considerably, but it also angered the government's opposition, which had grown accustomed to using the petroleum issue as a major source of embarassment to the government. Furthermore, the price increase provided ammunition for Miró Quesada, who now embarked on a crusade against what he perceived as an unholy alliance of Manuel Prado, APRA, I.P.C., and El Comercio's prime competitor, La Prensa. To the aging Don Luis, it must have seemed as if all of his enemies had joined hands to ruin him and Peru.

One of the developments which most angered the opposition was Beltrán's effort to open up the door of "adaptation" for I.P.C. In 1957, the company petitioned the Odría administration for adaptation or inclusion of La Brea y Pariñas under the general Petroleum Law of 1952; that petition was denied. In Article 6 of the July 25, 1959 decree, Prime Minister Beltrán established his intention of granting I.P.C. adaptation, for he was not satisfied with a mere solution to the immediate crisis. Beltrán wanted to solve the problem of La Brea y Pariñas once and for all. Accordingly, on August 8, 1959, I.P.C.'s general manager Jack Ashworth submitted a formal document to the Ministry of Development agreeing to pass its rights over the subsoil of La Brea y Pariñas to the Peruvian state, as soon as the law authorizing the adaptation of the property had been promulgated.[30]

In the opinion of Augusto Zimmermann, a protégé of Don Luis Miró Quesada and the only nonmember of the family to hold an important position with El Comercio, the decree of July 25 signaled the beginning of the final battle over La Brea y Pariñas. He stated:

> At the instant in which the Decree was first known by the public, the act of recuperation of La Brea y Pariñas commenced. Without surmising the consequences, without imagining the long chain of events which would follow, the President of the Council of Ministers opened the door so that the country would begin to form a clear consciousness of the importance and significance of La Brea y Pariñas.[31]

That July 25 decree brought together an unlikely coalition of radical leftists, conservative nationalists, and the armed forces.

The leftists were members of several parties, including some radicals from within the ranks of Fernando Belaúnde's Acción Popular. In fact, the initial offensive in the Peruvian Congress was carried out by an Acción Popular senator from Belaúnde's home town of Arequipa, Alfonso Montesinos. In the Chamber of Deputies, the anti-I.P.C. campaign was spearheaded by a deputy from Lima, Alfonso Benavides Correa. The July 25 decree prompted Benavides Correa to take the floor of the Chamber of Deputies and recount the long history of I.P.C.'s activities in Peru. As might be expected, he projected I.P.C. in the worst possible light. The company's detractors, however, really presented no factual information concerning I.P.C.'s actions from 1917 to 1939.

On August 27, Alfonso Montesinos initiated a similar campaign in the Peruvian Senate, recounting the diplomatic interventions of Britain and the United States in Peru's affairs. He questioned the company's presentation of the facts, and alledged that the value of I.P.C.'s investment in Peru was between $98 and $103 million and not $217 million, as I.P.C. had claimed of late.[32] According to his calculation, the company would be receiving a return a 26.7 percent profit over the value of the investment under the decree of July 25.[33] Clearly, Montesinos hoped to confuse the issue as far as possible. By using the "book value" of the company's investment, he hoped to create the impression that the company was doing in 1959 what in fact it had done during the 1920s and 1930s—squeezing a very large profit out of Peru. Montesinos availed himself of the company's past record in hopes of demolishing I.P.C.'s arguments one by one, from the most technical figures on the cost of drilling wells to the more general matters of return on an investment. More importantly, citing a forum on petroleum held at the University of San Marcos in Lima, Montesinos claimed that I.P.C. took 1,000 million soles out of Peru under the aegis of an illegal international award, and that by "adapting" the company to the general petroleum law, the Prado administration wanted to grant the company the right to take 60 billion soles more.[34] Both Montesinos and Benavides Correa contended that the reason I.P.C. and the government were in a hurry to reach an "adaptation" agreement was that the 1922 Laudo had a fifty-year life span set to expire in 1972. At that point, ownership of La Brea y Pariñas would revert to the Peruvian state. Soon after the initial congressional offensives of August 1959, the price issue was dropped as the primary point of dispute and the legitimacy of the company's title over La Brea y Pariñas became the target of the anti-I.P.C. campaign.

On September 7, 1959, Beltrán sent his Minister of Foreign Affairs to face a parliamentary inquiry. Minister Raúl Porras Barrenechea, in an effort to placate the opposition, made a statement which would henceforth represent the position of the Prado-Beltrán government:

> Although Peru has vigorous moral reasons which we all know and share to invoke the intrinsic invalidity of acts which have affected the national interest, the acts precisely for their international character are of a definitive nature. International life would be unstable and hazardous if unilateral action in international matters were to be permitted.[35]

In his own obscure way, Porras Barrenechea meant to state that the 1922 award was invalid but that its unilateral abrogation would set a dangerous precedent. Instead of calming the opposition, the government's statement merely encouraged it to intensify the assault. Answering the arguments of Porras Barrenechea, Benavides Correa stated that the 1922 award was null ipso jure, and hence did not bind the Peruvian state. Taking off on a very imaginative tangent, the deputy for Lima surprised the government and I.P.C. by stating that the Laudo did not in fact exist, wherewith he challenged the government to come up with a copy of the agreement. Upon a search of its archives, the Peruvian government found no trace of the celebrated document. Concerned with the absence of the Laudo of 1922, personnel from I.P.C. travelled to London. They contacted the appropriate officials at the British Foreign Office and they produced the originals of the signed documents. The Peruvian Consul was asked to verify the authenticity of the documents and copies were promptly forwarded to Lima. This clarification, however, came weeks after the original allegation had taken its toll in public distrust.[36] Porras Barrenechea's statement illustrated serious weaknesses in the government's position, and Benavides Correa's attack showed the ability of I.P.C. opponents to capitalize on those weaknesses and to go further in their attempts to shock Peru into a drastic solution to the La Brea y Pariñas controversy.

During the remaining months of 1959 and in early 1960 the battle raged. El Comercio magnified every attack on I.P.C., and the government and La Prensa counterattacked, suggesting that Benavides Correa should have failed his first year of law school if he could not recognize the validity of the Laudo. I.P.C. was quick to react to these attacks. Responding to Benavides Correa's charge that the company had taken 1,000 million soles out of Peru, I.P.C. suggested that "the fantastic figure" "was born of some heated mind; that it had sprouted, like Minerva from the head of Jupiter, definitive and round." But, after ridiculing the charge, I.P.C. presented a detailed argument loaded with facts and figures and stated that the company had taken only 145 million soles, an amount which it believed quite reasonable considering the investment it had in Peru.[37] I.P.C. was very disturbed by the assertion that in 1972 La Brea y Pariñas would revert back to the state, and it began a public relations campaign designed to counteract this assertion. In articles and pamphlets, the company contended that the Laudo of 1922 merely covered the matter of taxes, and that after 1972, if no adaptation had taken place, I.P.C. would continue to own both the subsoil and the surface property of La Brea y Pariñas, and would continue extracting oil subject to whatever general legislation was in effect at that time.[38]

In a way the company overreacted to the attack. The publicity campaign stating that the end of the Laudo would have virtually no effect on its ownership or modus operandi was a tactical error of major proportions, for it was undoubtedly interpreted as a hardening of the company's position, and a blatant statement of its intention of continuing operations regardless of the Laudo's termination. Peruvians who might have hoped to avoid a confrontation with the company during the 1960s on the assumption that 1972 would bring an automatic solution to their problems, had those hopes dashed. International Petroleum Company was not merely a fifty year guest. It was a self-proclaimed permanent resident.

During January 1960, the acrimony rose to unbelievable levels. The more radical parliamentarians, particularly those belonging to the small but militant Movimiento Social Progresista, joined hands with Benavides Correa and Montesinos in their attacks on I.P.C. and the government. In late January, Benavides Correa introduced a bill declaring the 1922 Laudo invalid, and therefore not binding on Peru. This was but the first of a series of ten similar bills submitted by various combinations of radicals with the same intent.

At first the Prado-Beltrán government remained calm. After all, these were the desperate efforts of radicals who were a very small minority in a parliament dominated by what they called the apro-pradismo-beltranismo—a coalition of APRA, Prado's supporters, and Beltrán's friends. Beltrán's calm, however, came to a sudden end on February 2, 1960, when a commission of army chiefs issued a document stating that the 1922 Laudo was null and void on various legal grounds, principally that Law 3016 had not authorized the Laudo of 1922, and that no Peruvian representative had been instructed to cede rights over the subsoil to I.P.C. Therefore, the Army officers recommended that the Laudo be excluded from the Peruvian registry, and that "International Petroleum Company pay the exact total of taxes due from the 1st of January of 1915."[39]

The army's stand came as a shock to all involved in the controversy except the Social Progresistas and some of the more radical members of Acción Popular. Both parties had been courting the military during the preceding years. On the day following the army announcement, Prime Minister Beltrán went to army headquarters to request an interview with the commanding general, Alfredo Rodríguez Martínez. He tried to persuade the general that Benavides Correa and his allies were political agitators in the service of the international Communist movement. However, he failed to do so. He then sent various Cabinet members on the same mission on several occasions during early February. February 5, General Rodríguez Martínez issued a second communique, this time in the name of the Joint Chiefs of Staff, condemning the 1922 Laudo as injurious to the national sovereignty. This communique ominously demanded that in keeping with Article 213 of the Peruvian Constitution, the Joint Chiefs expected to have any proposed solutions to the La Brea y Pariñas controversy submitted to them for study so that they could issue an opinion on the matter.[40]

Prado and Beltrán needed no further word. The hand-writing was on the wall. Obviously the army would veto adaptation unless the International Petroleum Company paid the back taxes which Benavides Correa and Montesinos claimed the company owed Peru. Furthermore, a mere continuation of the Laudo was not acceptable to the army chiefs, for they saw it as injurious to the national interest.

Clearly then, Beltrán had overreached himself. While his attempt to put through a price increase was clever enough, the army simply would not tolerate any further concessions to I.P.C. Pedro Beltrán, however, had an amazing capacity of finding his way out of blind alleys. His first step was to effect a tactical withdrawal from the planned adaptation, thus avoiding a confrontation with the army. He then embarked on a two-fold policy designed to produce a compromise acceptable to the army, and also to discredit Miró Quesada, El Comercio, and its radical allies. The war between La Prensa and El Comercio was destined to escalate to previously unimagined levels.

On January 21, just prior to the Army communique on the Laudo, the Chamber of Deputies called for yet another study of the La Brea y Pariñas controversy—this time by the Advisory Commission of Foreign Affairs—a group composed of distinguished Peruvians—former presidents and ministers of foreign affairs. On May 10 the commission issued its report. It concluded that even though the Laudo was essentially defective, it could not be ignored after it had been in effect for thirty-eight years. The commission rejected the possibility of taking the matter to some international judicial body, and instead suggested that the President should study the matter and then propose a new law to the legislature which "would establish a new regime in replacement of the present one." The commission also rejected the alternative of nationalization, but it specifically said that whatever the solution arrived at, Peru should contemplate "obtaining compensation for the small yield the country has received."[41] The idea of compensation—first suggested by the radicals—began to gain respectability in Peruvian circles.

On August 30, Prime Minister Beltrán sent a bill to Congress incorporating the recommendation of the Advisory Commission. In essence, the bill proposed that from that point on, I.P.C. would hold La Brea y Pariñas as a concession for thirty years. This term might be extendable to forty. A complicated system of taxes and royalties was promulgated. In practice, the company would be subject to a regime very similar to that established by the General Petroleum Law of 1952; however, the taxes would be higher, and the company would pay certain annual bonuses to the government. No doubt these provisions were designed to comply with the judgment of the army and the Advisory Commission, which declared that I.P.C. should make restitution to Peru for their previous oil exploitation under the "defective" Laudo.[42]

The reactions to Beltrán's proposals were predictable. The Prime Minister's own newspaper La Prensa greeted the bill with jubilant front page headlines: "Government sends Parliament a bill that puts an end to the Laudo. Immediate vindication* of the subsoil of Brea, Pariñas and Lobitos. Concession to I.P.C. for 30 years and nationalization without payment at the end. I.P.C. will pay the State 300 million in cash [soles] immediately and 950 [soles] in term payments; the State to receive 60 percent of the profits. Concessions limited to 100,000 hectares. 66,000 will go, without payment to Compañia Petrolera Fiscal [Peru's state-owned oil enterprise] with its wells and installations."[43] This headline was in itself a good summary of the government's bill, except for the fact that the bill referred to "nationalization" only in the loosest sense of the word. Extensive articles in the same issue of La Prensa argued in detail that indeed this was a highly favorable solution for Peru; that it went beyond what the Advisory Commission had recommended in its May 10 report, and that I.P.C. would be paying some of the highest oil industry taxes in the world.[44] The editorial from the following day's [September 2] issue further emphasized that I.P.C.'s profits would be split on a 60-40 basis, with Peru receiving 60 percent of the profits.

---

*The word "vindicate" is used throughout the manuscript in the sense of the Spanish verb "vindicar." More specifically, in connection with the La Brea y Pariñas case, Peruvians used the word to indicate that they wished not only to liberate, or claim La Brea y Pariñas, but to mete out just retribution to those they believed guilty of misappropriation.

CORPORATION PLAYS POLITICIAN 79

La Prensa stated that nationalization was inevitable and, in short, the proposal was highly favorable to Peru.[45]

The reaction of the congressional opposition was as predictable as that of La Prensa. It was as negative as La Prensa's was positive. Once again, Deputy Alfonso Benavides Correa led the anti-I.P.C. campaign. He charged that the Beltrán bill was nothing more than covert "adaptation." He based his allegation on the fact that the bill merely outlined a contract to be concluded between the government and the company. In other words, passage of the bill did not mean that its provisions were automatically put into effect, but that they awaited I.P.C.'s approval. Benavides Correa went on to state that the government put forth the proposal because I.P.C. had already agreed to the terms of the contract, and that the bill represented nothing but a "bilateral" contract.[46] In addition, he argued that the proposal merely brought I.P.C. under the provisions of the General Petroleum Law of 1952—a solution which I.P.C. had long sought. He noted:

> ... it turns out that the great and extraordinary conquest which Sr. Beltrán proposed to vindicate Peru's inalienable, imprescriptible and sovereign rights over the mineral subsoil of La Brea y Pariñas, had already been proposed by none other than I.P.C. itself in August of 1957, before Sr. Beltrán became the Minister of Development and Commerce and premier.[47]

For Benavides Correa and his allies in Congress, the real dilemma was simple: "to collect, or not to collect the debt" which I.P.C. owed Peru for all past exploitation of La Brea y Pariñas.[48] Benavides Correa did not limit himself to an attack on I.P.C. alone. He identified the culprits as a "clan," a "union of banking capital with industrial and commercial capital, and union of both parties with the country's government." And, as the axis of this supposedly monolithic lobby, this clan, the radical deputy identified Felipe Thorndike Beltrán, nephew of the Prime Minister—a man with multiple interests in the petroleum business and in the newspaper business. More specifically, Benavides Correa identified Felipe Thorndike Beltrán as a first cousin of the editor of Ultima Hora—a Lima newspaper which like La Prensa supported the government, as a former manager of Petrolera Peruana—an oil company recently purchased by American interests, as a member of the Board of Directors of the Compañía Petrolera Lobitos, and as a member of the Superior Council of Petroleum—a private group of oil entrepreneurs. Benavides Correa charged that Thorndike Beltrán acted as a link between all these organizations and Prime Minister Beltrán, and since he was the

Prime Minister's only nephew and Beltrán had no children of his own, he charged that Felipe was Beltrán's heir apparent. In a book which he published after the congressional debates, Benavides Correa expanded his charges, and included long lists of the enterprises to which Beltrán's nephew was connected.[49]

Similar charges were made in the Senate by Acción Popular Senator Alfonso Montesinos, and of course, El Comercio could be counted on to provide a forum for opposition to the government's policy. In sharp contrast to La Prensa's headlines for September 1st, El Comercio's front page proclaimed: "Senator Montesinos accused the Beltrán Cabinet of plotting with International Petroleum. The Cabinet is called responsible for recognizing $100 million more than I.P.C. had invested in the country." Another headline read: "The Executive proposes that I.P.C. continue to exploit La Brea y Pariñas for 40 more years."[50] In the editorial section, El Comercio argued that for a monopoly to exist, a company did not have to control 100 percent of the business. By virtue of its 90 percent control of the crude oil production in the country, International Petroleum Company was a monopoly. It charged that I.P.C. illegally exploited the fields while paying miniscule taxes, that the company threatened and coerced Peru in order to obtain price increases, that I.P.C. spent millions in public relations—purposefully trying to confuse public opinion, and that the company threatened the security and sovereignty of Peru.[51] This September 1st attack merely presaged what was to be a daily barrage in the following months. In a subsequent editorial, El Comercio's battle cry centered on the point that if the state did gain control of La Brea y Pariñas in forty years, by then there would be no petroleum left.[52] As a policy, El Comercio identified anti-I.P.C. forces as "patriotic"—those who deviated from the Miró Quesada hard line were dubbed the "entreguistas."

In an attempt to secure the balance of power in their favor, the anti-I.P.C. parliamentarians and El Comercio deliberately attempted once again to involve the army in the dispute. On September 2, Benavides Correa stated that the Joint Chiefs of Staff were opposed to the Beltrán bill. The army, which had experienced some changes in command since the incident in February 1960 when it had first issued a statement on the matter, denied having any opinion on the controversy. El Comercio knew, however, that the armed forces were generally sympathetic to its position in spite of the changes in top leadership, and played the army officers to its advantage. The paper reminded the army of the "elevated mission" assigned to it by the Peruvian constitution. That "elevated mission" required the army to stand in eternal vigilance protecting the country from a bill which "seriously compromised the sovereignty and security of the Fatherland." El Comercio warned that the "Armed Forces will not permit the progress of bills which are damaging to the country and threatening to its rights and high national interests."[53]

Here again was an interesting twist. The radical left and a conservative newspaper joined in calling for unconstitutional military intervention necessary to save Peru from what they interpreted as a treacherous coalition of foreign and domestic capitalists bent on defrauding the country. Obviously, El Comercio and its radical allies were engaged in a "no-holds-barred" offensive designed to ruin Prime Minister Beltrán and International Petroleum Company. Their goals, however, were not identical—a conclusion which will be examined later.

Recognizing the attack on the jugular vein of his government, Pedro Beltrán reacted immediately. As a connoisseur of Peruvian oligarchical intrigue he had several dramatic options which he could play against his enemies. The first such move came on September 6 during a television appearance by Eudocio Ravines, an associate of Beltrán and a writer for La Prensa. Ravines had been a Communist in the 1920s and an associate of Haya de la Torre—founder of APRA, and of José Carlos Mariátegui—Peru's foremost Marxist intellectual. Ravines stayed on good terms with Moscow until the Nazi-Soviet pact. He then abandoned international Communism and became an outspoken critic of the Communist movement in Peru. This background as a former high Communist Party official in Peru promised to be useful to Pedro Beltrán. Ravines put his knowledge to use in the television broadcast. He declared that Senator Alfonso Montesinos was a Communist. When the surprised interviewer asked how he knew, Ravines stated that he had personally issued Montesinos his membership years ago. Associates of Montesinos, who were watching the live television broadcast, marched over to the studio and tried to attack Ravines.[54]

During the momentous first week of September events moved quickly. Senator Carlos A. Miñao, a former Army general, introduced legislation calling for the nationalization of La Brea y Pariñas. Instead of taking any action the Chamber of Deputies once more dumped the issue in the lap of a study group, but the Special Commission of the Chamber of Deputies passed the problem on to the army by formally requesting its opinion on the matter of La Brea y Pariñas. The Social Progressist Party issued a statement calling on the Peruvian people and the army to stand united, and warning the army against becoming involved in aiding the government.

El Comercio played up statements by retired general Alejandro Barco López, Senator from Lima, who sided with Senator Montesinos. The paper published a series of articles by another retired general, César A. Pando, who took a very decided position against I.P.C. In a September 8 editorial, El Comercio noted the position of the three retired generals, stating that their points of view reflected well upon the armed forces. Once more, El Comercio encouraged the army to overthrow the government.[55] In fact, it seemed as if the paper would stop short of nothing in its effort to discredit Beltrán and I.P.C. For example, when an unfortunate young boy fell into a service station underground tank and died, El Comercio mentioned that it was an Esso station connected with I.P.C., as if the company were responsible, and not the local dealer.[56]

It was during this period that an organization was formed for the specific purpose of fighting I.P.C.—the National Front for the Defense of Petroleum. The Front's president was retired General César A. Pando; its executive vice-president was Alberto Ruíz Eldredge, a Castro sympathizer and Political Secretary of the Movimiento Social Progresista. Other members included Senator Alfonso Montesinos and Deputies Alfonso Benavides Correa and Fernando Noriega Calmet, an avowed enemy of I.P.C.[57] The Front organized anti-I.P.C. demonstrations and published a series of public statements in several Lima newspapers denouncing the company. The Front for the Defense of Petroleum also published a pamphlet attacking I.P.C. Of greatest importance, this group sought the backing of individuals and other groups in its anti-I.P.C. crusade. While it got support from the Society of Retired Personnel of the Armed Forces of Peru, and did manage to attract several labor leaders to a meeting, the Front failed to gather support from any major group or organization.

International Petroleum Company attempted to counter the Front's efforts by gathering its own allies. The company got the backing of a group of forty retired military officers, but, in general, most Peruvians were unwilling to become involved in the controversy, let alone in the entreguista cause which had been so maligned by El Comercio. I.P.C.'s most significant support came from its own workers, who in early October travelled in great numbers to Lima to protest the attacks on the company. Even though El Comercio tried to discredit these workers by suggesting that they had been sent by the company, it seems clear that they came on their own, from genuine concern for their future should nationalization take place.[58]

The La Brea y Pariñas controversy, which had virtually destroyed the Civilista Party and made possible the 1919 Leguía coup, came close to having the same effect on Belaúnde's Acción Popular. Senator Alfonso Montesinos was a member of Acción Popular—one of the most important men in that party. It was general knowledge in Lima's political circles that Montesinos would be chosen to run in the number two position on the Belaundista ticket in the 1962 election.

During the first two weeks of September 1960, however, while La Prensa was trying to sell Beltrán's petroleum bill to the Peruvian people and El Comercio was doing its best to make sure the bill failed, Belaúnde reached an important decision. He decided to accede to the general principles of the government's petroleum bill, but to demand that the time span of the new concession be reduced from thirty to five years. In accordance with his decision and in keeping with his role as party leader, he sent a message to Montesinos on September 19 explaining his reasoning and asking that Montesinos conform to this more conciliatory position. Montesinos reacted with anger and announced that if the party took the Belaúnde position, he would immediately repudiate Acción Popular in public. Efforts to placate Montesinos failed, and finally Belaúnde had to accept the senator's point of view to avoid a split in the party. Acción Popular was virtually forced to introduce a bill in Congress ordering the immediate confiscation of La Brea y Pariñas without compensation. Despite Belaúnde's concession to party unity, Montesinos's star dimmed considerably following Ravines's television appearance. During 1961, it became apparent that Belaúnde would not choose Montesinos as his running mate, or even as a senator for another term. After the election of 1962, Montesinos was forced out of politics.[59]

November 1960 brought still another dramatic move on the part of the very resourceful Prime Minister and his associate Eudocio Ravines. On November 16, a group of Cuban exiles, allegedly guided by Ravines, conducted a raid on the Cuban embassy in Lima. They came away with several suitcases filled with confidential papers from the embassy files. In time, selected documents were passed on to the Peruvian military and the press. These included several communications from the Cuban Ambassador to Peru, Luis R. Alonso, to the Ministry of Foreign Relations and the Ministry of the Revolutionary Armed Forces in Havana. In a report dated October 4, 1960, the Cuban ambassador gave a detailed account of "political expenditures" and noted:

> In accordance with the instructions received from the Armed Forces Minister, Commander Raúl Castro, I have directly concerned myself with the organization of insurgent groups in cooperation with the Communist Party and Apra Rebelde [a radical spinoff from APRA], as well as with the other friends of the left who are ready to go all out, in case the announced imperialist invasion of Cuba should take place.[60]

Funds were passed directly by the ambassador through the Peruvian Communist Party to individuals in responsible positions in every political party and in numerous labor unions, newspapers, and other organizations, including one publisher. From the list of "political expenditures," it soon became clear that Havana was underwriting the publication of pamphlets and books in defense of the Cuban regime, that it had friends on nearly every newspaper, and that it provided heavy subsidies for the Social Progressist Movement, particularly for its leader Alberto Ruíz Eldredge, the man who distinguished himself as an advocate of the Cuban Revolution in the Peruvian Congress, and as the organizing element behind the National Front for the Defense of Petroleum.

The Prado-Beltrán government chose to delay release of the Cuban documents, probably because they were sure to evoke embarrassment not to the radical left alone, but to many more prominent Peruvians. On January 4, 1961, however, all hell broke loose in the Peruvian Senate when the War Minister, General Alejandro Cuadra Rabínez read the list of recipients of Cuban funds. In a sense, the disclosure of the Cuban papers brought this stage of the controversy to an end.

The elections which were scheduled for 1962 began to loom larger and larger in everyone's mind. For El Comercio the issue was once more how to prevent APRA from taking control of the government. For APRA the problem was how to become acceptable to the armed forces so that it could take over if it won an election. Thus, as 1961 progressed, APRA and Pedro Beltrán, who had presidential ambitions of his own, dropped the thorny issue of La Brea y Pariñas, and declared an unofficial moratorium on the problem until after the election.

The period from July 1959 to the end of 1960 proved singularly important in the La Brea y Pariñas controversy. I.P.C. entered this stage of its history as a troubled entity, but there was no question then concerning its legitimacy in Peru's petroleum industry. When the battle was over, I.P.C.'s legitimate existence had been severely undermined. The question was not whether I.P.C. should be removed from Peru, but how soon it could be ejected. Yet, in spite of the overall political deterioration in the company's position, the score was not completely negative.

The price increases of July 1959 gave the company a new lease on life, and despite opposition from the political left, El Comercio, and even from the armed forces, I.P.C. endured. It outlived the presidency of Manuel Prado and even the premiership of Pedro Beltrán. Politically weakened, with its reputation in tatters, Standard Oil's Peruvian affiliate navigated the stormy waters of the early 1960s and made ready for the final battle.

NOTES

1. According to a company executive, the last loan advanced to the Peruvian government was made in 1953. Confidential interview, Coral Gables, Florida, May 25, 1971.

2. Pedro Beltrán received his training at the London School of Economics. He is reportedly a firm follower of Adam Smith, and consequently a strong upholder of sound finances and laissez-faire. Sir Robert Marett, Peru (New York: Praeger, 1969), pp. 181-182.

3. "El Banco Central de Reserva suspende la Venta de Certificados de Divisas," El Comercio, January 23, 1958, p. 3.

4. See El Comercio articles entitled "Defender nuestra moneda," and "Nueva maniobra del organo de los exportadores," January 24, 1958 and February 2, 1958 respectively.

5. "El Petroleo: o alza de precios o crisis," Noticias de Petróleo, XI, No. 107 (1958).

6. "La industria carbonara del país no puede progresar—se lo impiden los bajos precios artificiales de los productes de petróleo," FANAL, XIV, No. 54 (1958), p. 22.

7. El Comercio, January 10, 1958, p. 9.

8. "En gran desorden terminó la Primera Reunión Nacional de Sindicatos de Choferes," El Comercio, January 15, 1958, p. 3.

9. See the paid advertisement, "La Federación de choferes del Peru, a todo el Gremio y al Pueblo," El Comercio, January 26, 1958, p. 2.

10. "El proyecto sobre el alza del precio de la gasolina," El Comercio, January 26, 1958, p. 2.

11. "El Plan Nacional de Carreteras," El Comercio, January 27, 1958, p. 2.

12. See the articles: "Después de agitado lo debate se aprobo alza de la gasolina," El Comercio, January 29, 1958, p. 4; "Alza lesiva para nuestro pueblo," El Comercio, January 30, 1958, p. 2.

13. "Choferes de todo el país señalan plazo de huelga," El Comercio, January 31, 1958, p. 3.

14. "Choferes inician huelga mañana por alto de gasolina," El Comercio, April 10, 1958, p. 1.

15. Marett stated: "In April 1958 the city of Cuzco, in the heart of the Northern Andes, was taken over by what were probably communist-inspired rebels, their cause being supported by Belaúnde's Acción Popular, as also by the normally right-wing El Comercio." Marett, p. 181.

16. I.P.C. management brought these events to the attention of this researcher. Virtually nothing was written at the time of the uprising, but it is not clear whether the Peruvian government intended to keep this crisis out of the public eye.

17. Confidential interview with I.P.C. executive, Coral Gables, Florida, May 26, 1971.

18. "El deber del Gobierno en hora actual," El Comercio, April 13, 1958, p. 2.

19. Horowitz writes this in his own introductory chapter of his edited work. Irving Louis Horowitz, ed., Masses in Latin America (New York: Oxford University Press, 1970), p. 13.
20. Julio Cotler, "Internal Domination and Social Change in Peru," Horowitz, p. 429.
21. John Gerassi, The Great Fear in Latin America (London: Collier-MacMillan, Ltd., 1965), p. 136.
22. Rosendo A. Gomez, "Peru: The Politics of Military Guardianship," Political Systems of Latin America, ed. Martin Needler (Princeton, N.J.: D. Van Nostrand, 1964), pp. 291-316.
23. "Secondary recovery" or "technical rejuvenation" of an oil field involves artificial stimulation of the oil flow. Various means can be used to accomplish this end: water flooding, gas injection or repressurization, steam stimulation, or "in situ combustion"—fire flooding. Repressurization with water or gas involves a fairly simple but costly process whereby water or gas is forced into the underground deposits so as to force the oil out, much like liquids are forced out of an aerosol can. Steam or fire flooding involves heating the oil-saturated rock so that oil will flow out and into underground reservoirs from where it can be piped. The latter is the more costly method.
24. "La verdad sobre la situación de la industria petrolera peruana," FANAL, XIV, No. 54 (1958), pp. 17-21.
25. "La industria petrolera necesita un sistema de precios adecuado," FANAL, XIV, No. 55 (1958), pp. 19-22. This same article was reproduced in Noticias de Petróleo, XI, No. 107 (October, 1958).
26. Ibid., p. 20.
27. Ibid., p. 22.
28. Harries Peterson and Tomas Unger, Petróleo: Hora Cero (Lima: n.p., 1964), pp. 301-302.
29. Ibid., p. 305.
30. Augusto Zimmermann Zavala, La Historia Secreta del Petróleo (Lima: Editorial Grafica Labor, 1968), p. 22.
31. Ibid., p. 21.
32. Montesinos claimed that his figures came out of U.S. Department of Commerce publications. His opponents noted that these figures reflected the value of the property and equipment when purchased and did not take into account the current values or costs. The refinery might have cost $5 million to build early in the century; in 1959 it would have cost several times that. In figuring the value of the investment Montesinos used the first figure, and the company used the second. For a transcript of Montesinos's congressional presentation and the various interruptions, see: Ibid., pp. 56-59.
33. Ibid., p. 66.
34. Ibid., pp. 74-76.

35. Ibid., p. 78.
36. Interview with John Oldfield, Coral Gables, Florida, May 24, 1971.
37. "El Mito de los Mil Millones," Noticias de Petróleo, XII, No. 113 (September, 1959).
38. "La Brea y Pariñas revertirá al estado en 1972?" Noticias de Petróleo, XII, No. 114 (November, 1959).
39. The text of this "internal" communication is reproduced by Augusto Zimmermann. See: Zimmermann, Historia Secreta del Petróleo, pp. 81-82.
40. For a photostatic copy of the document, see: ibid., p. 85.
41. The full report is included in" The La Brea y Pariñas Controversy, Vol. I (International Petroleum Company, February, 1969), Exhibit 4.
42. Ibid., Exhibit 5.
43. La Prensa, September 1, 1960, p. 1.
44. "El Proyecto va aún mas Lejos de lo que Planteó la Consultiva," and "Ahora IPC Pagará Una de la Tributaciones mas altas del mundo," La Prensa, September 1, 1960, pp. 6, 7.
45. "La Revindicación del Petroleo," La Prensa, September 2, 1960, p. 2.
46. Most of Benavides Correa's speech is reproduced in Zimmermann, Historio Secreta, pp. 110-135.
47. Ibid., p. 124.
48. Ibid., p. 126.
49. Ibid., pp. 129-131; Alfonso Benavides Correa, El Petróleo Peruano, ó "la autopsia de un clan" (Lima: Papel Grafica Editora, 1961), pp. 152-165.
50. El Comercio, September 1, 1960, p. 1.
51. "El Monopolio del Petróleo," ibid., p. 2.
52. "Proyecto entreguista sobre el Petróleo," El Comercio, September 4, 1960, p. 2.
53. "La Fuerza Armada y la reivindicación del Petróleo," El Comercio, September 4, 1960, p. 2.
54. Information from: Confidential interview with I.P.C. executive, Coral Gables, Florida, May 26, 1971; "Veneno de Ravines causó indignación general," El Comercio, September 6, 1960, p. 1 (Afternoon edition).
55. "El Ejército y la reivindicación del petróleo," El Comercio, September 8, 1960, p. 2.
56. "Por negligencia punible murió en niño Marco Antonio Salazar," El Comercio, September 8, 1960, p. 5.
57. Frente Nacional de Defensa del Petróleo, Declaración de Principios y Exposición de Motivos (Lima: Technograf, S.A., 1960), p. 199.

58. "Asalariados de la IPC llegaron ayer a Lima; Han sido traidos para manifestar su apoyo al proyecto petrolero del Ejecutivo," El Comercio, October 11, 1960, p. 3.

59. Zimmermann, Historia Secreta, pp. 99-106.

60. Photostatic copies of the documents were provided by I.P.C. While the authenticity of the papers has been denied by the Cuban government and the alleged recipients of the funds, it has on the other hand been upheld by defecting employees of the Embassy. The fact that a raid did take place, and that the exposé reached into the ranks of La Prensa as much as El Comercio tends to support the authenticity of the papers. The fact that anti-I.P.C. forces seemed to come up with money to publish pamphlets and books on the petroleum issue in a country where writers have to absorb the initial costs of publication also suggests some outside financing.

CHAPTER 5

ANATOMY OF THE ANTAGONISTS

EL COMERCIO

One of the most important participants in the controversy surrounding La Brea y Pariñas, and in the general political process of Peru was El Comercio, and the family that has owned it since the 19th century, the Miro Quesadas. Like The New York Times in the United States or Le Monde in France, El Comercio was, and still is, a very influential publication in Peru—a gate-keeper to the minds of many people. This newspaper is more important to Peru than The New York Times is to the United States because has little competition from other news media. American papers compete with television and radio for the attention of the public. In a relatively poor society like Peru such competition is minimized by the small number of TV and radio receivers.[1] Given the relative concentration of political and economic power as well as population in the Lima-Callao area. El Comercio had even greater impact.[2] There were other dailies in Peru, but Peruvians considered only two of them "great" newspapers, El Comercio and La Prensa. The other newspapers were generally categorized as prensa chica, or small press.

Of the two important newspapers in Lima, only El Comercio had a continuous existence under two generations of the same family.[3] Indeed, considering the countless coups, dictatorships, wars, and constitutions since El Comercio's original edition, the newspaper endured with remarkable stability in a country where governments, ideologies, and even constitutions come and go frequently. El Comercio has been an intensely political institution, and outlived most of its targets, including the International Petroleum Company—another old institution in the economic and political life of Peru.

What prompted one enterprise to become the archenemy of
another? Why did El Comercio engage I.P.C. in mortal combat with
disastrous effects for the company and nearly disastrous effects for
the newspaper? The answer to this question is in the background of
this extraordinary family running El Comercio. The current generation
of Miró Quesadas took over control of the paper when their father,
the first Antonio Miró Quesada, died in 1905. The editorship went to
this eldest son, Antonio, who ran the paper with the help of his brothers
until he was assassinated in 1935. The position of editor-in-chief and
head of the family then went to Luis Miró Quesada, the oldest surviving
brother who has been editor of the paper, and family patriarch to this
day.

While information about the affairs of the family is scanty, several important factors must be considered. First, the family's only
source of wealth and prestige is the newspaper. They have made it a
matter of pride that their positions are not influenced by any extraneous business considerations. The family has grown large over the
years. Even though customarily they would carry only the Miro of their
last name, they have retained the two last names of the family founder—
Miró Quesada—with great pride. Since this family is a sort of institution in itself, its interests are carefully guarded against the changing
winds of Peruvian politics—a feat usually accomplished by having
important family members in nearly every political party in Peru.
Thus, no matter what group or political movement wins in Peru, there
is sure to be a Miró Quesada in its leadership. The one important
exception to this practice which cannot be ignored is the Aprista Party,
a group which the Miró Quesadas have engaged in an unparalleled
vendetta during the last 40 years.

To illustrate the uncanny flexibility of this family, one can draw
many examples from the political literature of Peru. During the 1930s,
when fascism was overrunning Europe, one of the Miró Quesada
brothers, Carlos, travelled to Italy. Convinced of the virtues of
fascism, he wrote a series of very favorable articles for El Comercio.
The Italians were so pleased with his statements that they compiled
and published the articles in book form in Italian.[4] By 1940, the
situation had changed enough to prompt Carlos Miró Quesada to
change his view. His reason was: "The Third Reich has sacrificed
its principles and has permitted Communism—a barbaric Asian
phenomenon—to dictate the law in Poland and the Baltic."[5] It was not
long before Peru's Communist Party returned fire. In one of their
resolutions passed at the Party Congress of 1942, the Communists
denounced the Miró Quesadas as part of a native pro-nazi fifth column.[6]

In 1959, under the impact of sputnik and the Cuban revolution,
the Miró Quesadas began to take a second look at the Communist
movement. In that year, Francisco Miró Quesada Cantuarias, more

commonly known as Paco, took an extensive trip to the Soviet bloc nations, including visits to Moscow and even to Peking. Francisco was a nephew of Don Luis, and as the intellectual and philosopher of the family he was very influential with his uncle.

After his return from the Communist world, Francisco Miró Quesada wrote several articles for the Sunday supplement of El Comercio, and his articles in turn were compiled and published in book form. While Francisco did not engage in outright praise of the Communist regimes of the Soviet Union and China, he shocked many family friends with his participation in an officially sponsored tour and the subsequent publication of his friendly account of Soviet society. In the book preface, Francisco Miró Quesada related this conversation with a friend who had read the articles in El Comercio:

> Whoever reads them realizes that you have been impartial, understands that you have not gone to the Communist countries to criticize or to praise them, but rather to observe them. One realizes that you have returned to tell the truth. But, at the end of the reading, one is left with a feeling of sympathy. The reality you describe through your pen has defects. But the final impression is that one is dealing with a sympathetic reality.[7]

Francisco Miró Quesada was clearly impressed with the Soviet arguments, and even more interestingly, with Chinese arguments.

In Peking, he was told that there had been two kinds of bourgeoisie in China, the national and the bureaucratic. The latter was allied with Chiang Kai-shek and was exiled to Formosa, but the national bourgeoisie was told that despite their destined disappearance, they would be allowed to keep the means of production for awhile. The regime merely took over the means of distribution. Francisco Miró Quesada was told that the Chinese government actually allowed this national bourgeoisie to exploit the workers during the first stage of the reordering of Chinese life. The Chinese hosts assured him that the national bourgeoisie would be re-educated and would take up management positions in the nationalized industry. But even if they were not ready, additional time would be allowed for them to make the transition. Miró Quesada was so impressed by the Chinese presentation that he entitled the chapter dealing with China, "About capitalism in China."[8] The Chinese went so far as to tell Miró Quesada that there were several political parties in China. He was even introduced to the leaders of some of these parties—the Kuomintang and the Association for the Construction of Democracy of China, a political party supposedly composed of bourgeoisie and many capitalists, small and large.[9]

Francisco Miró Quesada returned to Moscow from Peking in a state of bewilderment. He never quite understood that what the Chinese described as political parties were nothing more than various state-sponsored associations or groupings along occupational lines. He continued to attack Marxism, but concluded that the Soviet Union was not really a Marxist state. Through what he called "a supermarxist analysis of jazz" he decided that since art reflects the conditions of production in Marxist theory, and the Soviets enjoy jazz—a capitalist art form, the Soviet Union was turning into a bourgeois, capitalist, and exploiting society.[10]

Coinciding with Francisco Miró Quesada's pilgrimage to the Soviet Union and China, El Comercio began to include articles by a great number of leftist writers in its Sunday supplement. A new humorous column entitled "Behind the Nylon Curtain" and authored by someone with the pen-name "Sofocleto" began to appear regularly. This column ridiculed the life style of people in the United States.

It was after Paco's return from Moscow that El Comercio began its most extensive campaign against the International Petroleum Company. I.P.C. executives saw a definite trend in the chain of events involving their company. The management of I.P.C. believed that Don Luis Miró Quesada feared a violent swing to the left similar to the one which had taken place in Cuba. The only way to preserve the family's status and its livelihood in such an eventuality was to make their position more compatible with the Peruvian left by reflecting an increasingly anti-American point of view.[11] Naturally, I.P.C. acted as a lightning rod in the subsequent storm.

Of course, neither the company nor Pedro Beltrán let Miró Quesada's challenge go unanswered. Augusto Zimmermann Zavala, a loyal employee of the Miró Quesadas, claimed that I.P.C. joined hands with foreign capital to destroy El Comercio. He states that Beltrán and I.P.C. management contacted various industrialists and advertisers and tried to persuade them that El Comercio was anti-American, anti-free enterprise, and an ally of international Communism. As a result of this pressure during the early 1960s, National Broadcasting Company (N.B.C.) cancelled an agreement to operate a television station in Lima jointly with El Comercio. The Miró Quesada family had to sell the station at a loss of several million soles. A similar fate befell a radio station operated by El Comercio.[12] I.P.C. management candidly admitted that they suggested to other American businesses that El Comercio had taken an anti-American tone, and that it would be wise not to advertise in the newspaper.

Not all exchanges between I.P.C. and El Comercio were acrimonious. In late 1959 and early 1960, the company tried to convince the Miró Quesada family to ease the I.P.C. issue out of the

headlines. El Comercio, however, continued the attack on I.P.C., and
the Miró Quesadas explained this action as an attempt to put down
Pedro Beltrán. The editor of La Prensa reportedly sent letters to
various firms in the United States, including advertising agencies,
and suggested that they cease doing business with El Comercio because
of its anti-American attitude.[13]

Even though the company management did not accept Francisco's
explanation as the complete truth, it is probably correct to assume
that the elder Miró Quesada, Don Luis, perceived both I.P.C. and
La Prensa as his enemies. The events of July 1959 provided him with
a good opportunity to launch a simultaneous attack on both. This
animosity for Beltrán was to a large extent the result of normal
competition between the two leading newspaper entrepreneurs. This
competition, however, did not prevent the two men from having social
relations before Beltrán became Prime Minister.[14] Don Luis Miró
Quesada felt personally offended at Beltrán's rise to power. For
decades he had viewed El Comercio as a source of political power.
Now La Prensa's editor Pedro Beltrán had outmaneuvered him at his
own game.

It was unfortunate that I.P.C. had to request a price raise from
Miró Quesada's archcompetitor, for the company automatically
became involved in a quarrel from which it had little to gain. By 1962,
Beltrán and I.P.C. had ceased to deal with the Miró Quesadas socially.
In a sense, they broke diplomatic relations. Since in Peruvian politics,
most of the problem solving takes place on a personal level,
this social break between Beltrán and I.P.C.'s management and the
Miró Quesadas precluded face-to-face confrontation, and thus eliminated a major bargaining medium.

THE SOCIAL PROGRESSIST MOVEMENT

Another group prominently involved in the campaign against
I.P.C. was a relatively small political party, the Movimiento Social
Progresista. The Social Progresistas, as members of this group
were called, claimed to be "socialist humanists" and "revolutionary,"
men opposed to capitalist society's failures and human exploitation.
They were "revolutionary" because they believed that "the great
national problems can only be solved through a profound change in the
social and economic structure of the country." Unlike the radical
fringe of the Aprista party, however, which broke ranks and launched
a guerrilla movement in 1965, the Social Progressists by and large
operated within Peru's political framework. Among their basic
objectives were the socialization of Peruvian agriculture and the
suppression of the feudal system which they claimed existed in Peru,

the nationalization of natural resources and the means of production, and the reform of the credit or banking system so that financial resources would no longer be in the hands of the privileged, but rather in the service of the entire country for development. Peru's development and improvements in the standard of living required a planned economy, according to the Social Progressists. The 1959 Cuban Revolution heavily influenced this Peruvian political movement, as much of its rhetoric on "socialist humanism" reflected. No concession to "the economy of free enterprise and the imperialist interests which are the beneficiaries of the country's dependence . . ." would be allowed. The movement urged its followers "to eradicate the capitalist system" and to "deliver to the people the political and economic power."[15] Members of the Social Progressist Movement in the Chamber of Deputies went on record as sponsors of a resolution censuring the Beltrán Cabinet for supporting the United States's O.A.S. moves against the Cuban government in 1960.[16] When the documents allegedly stolen from the Cuban Embassy in Lima were made public, the leader of the MSP, Alberto Ruíz Eldredge was listed as one of the recipients of the largest Cuban revolutionary welfare payments.[17]

The Social Progresistas were the product of Peruvian higher education and social structure. Many were trained as lawyers, doctors, and other professionals, but their upward social mobility was thwarted by their lack of connections with the Peruvian oligarchs. I.P.C.'s management admitted that these radicals were intelligent and well-educated; however, given their lack of contacts, they would never occupy a place in Peruvian society commensurate with their professional capabilities. Like the young reformers of Acción Popular who had been inspired by Papal encyclicals, the radical MSP members wanted to reform Peru. However, unlike the men of Acción Popular, most Social Progressists did not have the family pedigree of a Fernando Belaúnde whose ancestors had been prominent in Peruvian politics, diplomacy, and literature for several generations. The young radicals formed the Movimiento Social Progresista in 1955, but it was not until the Cuban Revolution that they developed their own pedigree, couched in the language of Cuban Marxism.

The Social Progressists despised the Alianza Popular Revolucionaria Americana (APRA) vehemently, in the same manner that Lenin had despised the socialist, gradualist, and other nonviolent reformers. For them, APRA had become "the defender of the oligarchy and the large foreign enterprises . . . the submissive servant of the interests of imperialism."[18] The MSP had long despaired what its members saw as the collusion of the wire services and the newspapers with United States imperialism. When the Miró Quesada's El Comercio, APRA's ancestral foe, launched the 1959 offensive against I.P.C.,

MSP quickly grasped a golden opportunity. El Comercio was an institution of the establishment but it shared common enemies with MSP. Out of this mutual hatred grew an unlikely alliance of one of Peru's foremost oligarchs and one of its militant revolutionary groups. The ultimate objectives of El Comercio and the Social Progressist Movement were quite different, however. The first wanted to keep APRA out of power and I.P.C. out of Peru, but basically it had no quarrel with the sociopolitical structure of which it was a beneficiary. The Movimiento Social Progresista, on the other hand, merely wanted to use the I.P.C. issue as a first step in what it hoped would be the eventual destruction of Peru's entire sociopolitical system.

THE MILITARY

The Social Progressists knew that in order to make a real impact on Peruvian politics they needed more than El Comercio's cooperation. Their credibility was greatly enhanced by the Cuban Revolution. What had happened in Cuba could happen in Peru. El Comercio's daily coverage of their congressional speeches added an aura of respectability to a group which five years earlier was dismissed as an inconsequential fringe of the Peruvian left. MSP now needed to convince Peru's ultimate power brokers, the military, that it was their movement which was best tuned to the temper of the times.

The opportunity to mingle with the military came when MSP's leader, Alberto Ruíz Eldredge, was invited to speak to the students and staff of the Center for Higher Military Studies (CAEM). Ruiz Eldredge used this opportunity to the fullest. He developed close relationships with several CAEM officers—much to the annoyance of I.P.C. management, which had for years sponsored an annual four-hour review of the Peruivan petroleum industry at the Center for Higher Military Services (CAEM). Eventually, an officer friendly to I.P.C. attempted to alert the armed forces command of the close relationship between Social Progressist activists and CAEM officers, only to be told that the CAEM curriculum called for the officers to be exposed to all types of philosophical orientations, including Marxism. By the middle 1960s, even though I.P.C. continued to send lecturers to the Center, the officers began to react more and more belligerently towards the company's general manager and his staff, thus indicating that to a very large extent, the Social Progressists were able to persuade CAEM officers that their position was valid.

Several scholars have written about the Peruvian military in general and about the Center for Higher Military Studies in particular.[19] According to Luigi Einaudi and Carlos Astiz, among others, CAEM's curriculum during the late 1950s and early 1960s evolved from the traditional and technical fare to a far more comprehensive program including a heavy dosage of social science. The officers ceased to concern themselves exclusively with the specifications of weapons systems or Prussian battle plans, and began to look into the socio-economic problems of Peru. By 1962, CAEM officers predicted that in less than twenty years Peru's population would be twenty-one million; seven million people would have to be incorporated into a productive modern economy, and at Peru's current rate of growth that goal would never be achieved.[20]

It was at the Center for Higher Military Studies that I.P.C. was found wanting as a corporate citizen of Peru. This inquisitive body of officers CAEM's faculty—a truly new breed of soldier, judged that I.P.C.'s role in the Peruvian economy was damaging to the national interest. It was from this forum that radicals such as Ruíz Eldredge, Montesinos, and Benavides Correa persuaded the Army that I.P.C. owed Peru large amounts of money, and that the national honor demanded not only the expropriation of the company but its complete humiliation. In other words, a mutual agreement between the government and the company for even a token compensation was out of the question for the radical anti-I.P.C. forces—the company had to be unceremoniously routed from Peru.

International Petroleum lost its cause even though for years it had courted the favor of the armed forces. In 1946, the company gave the Air Force a substantial amount of land in La Brea y Pariñas for the construction of the air base "El Pato." In 1954, I.P.C. gave a building to the Air Force for use housing officers, and it also gave houses to the Army. In this and in every case where I.P.C. ceded land to the Armed Forces or the government, it required the receivers to acknowledge legally its claims to the subsoil under the land or property ceded.[21] I.P.C. supplied its neighboring military installations with electricity and water. How could the military overlook the company's generous efforts and side with the radicals?

The answer to this question must be sought in the military's hatred for APRA. On July 7, 1932, the Apristas carried out a revolt in the city of Trujillo. After a bloody assault on the garrison of that city, they captured it and about sixty military officers and enlisted men. The Apristas held the city during that day, but by night it became apparent that the government forces would soon reclaim the garrison. The Aprista leaders fled before the government troops launched their massive attack, but not before they ordered the death of the officers they had captured earlier in the day. The Aprista mob even reportedly mutilated some of the officers' corpses. When the Army recaptured Trujillo, the officers in charge summarily executed any man suspected of having participated in the uprising.[22] Henceforth, the Army commemorated July 7 every year as the day of the Trujillo massacre. The military held APRA responsible. Although some army officers were working with APRA during the 1932 uprising, and others have secretly worked with that party since the massacre, the Army as a whole kept alive an undying hatred for the Aprista party. It made a well known commitment to the principle that APRA would never win the presidency of Peru.

ALIANZA POPULAR REVOLUCIONARIA AMERICANA

The Trujillo massacre did not entirely explain the army's antagonism for APRA. As the military became more involved in socioeconomic engineering, and offered more radical proposals to deal with national problems. APRA moved in the opposite direction. According to Luigi Einaudi,

> It could be said that having started, APRA on the left, and the army on the right, the two have moved toward and perhaps passed each other in opposite directions until today many military officers may be more favorable toward social innovation than the Aprista leadership, which lives increasingly in the past.[23]

After the unsuccessful coup of 1948 and the long period of repression during the Ochenio of Odria, APRA acquired legal recognition only by throwing its support to one of Peru's most traditional leaders, Manuel Prado. During the Prado administration, APRA joined in what became known as the convivencia, a political association which included APRA and such notable representatives of the Peruvian establishment as Pedro Beltrán.[24] In the words of former British Ambassador to Peru, Sir Robert Marett,

> At long last, and largely thanks to Manuel Prado, the Aprista lion and the Establishment lamb lay down together.[25]

Later, in 1962, APRA made a political deal with its former enemy General Manuel Odria. These alliances clearly illustrated APRA's realization that it was no longer Peru's only popular mass party, but had instead become one party among many. Haya de la Torre's willingness to deal with the traditional political leadership indicated that the Apristas and the Army indeed crossed each other's paths on the political spectrum sometime during the late 1950s, and by the early 1960s the military had come to look upon APRA as part of the inept establishment which, in their view, was keeping Peru stagnant. This conception had some validity, considering APRA's turnabout on the petroleum issue. In 1931, an Aprista leader wrote denouncing "imperialism" and partially defined it thus:

> Imperialist is the Standard Oil Company (yankee company) which in the United States pays 4 and 5 dollars to its workers for a day of work of 7 or 8 hours, while in Peru it pays two soles and 53 cents for a work day of 10 or 8 hours.[26]

According to the Aprista leadership, the answer to this imperialism was nationalization.[27] By 1946, however, APRA changed its position on the petroleum question. Manuel Seoane, Haya de la Torre's second in command, delivered a speech pointing out that unlike countries such as Argentina, Peru produced more petroleum than it consumed, and thus it needed the exporting and technical expertise which foreign capital provided. APRA's solution to the oil problem was to increase Peru's share of the petroleum industry's profits.[28] As the party's position developed over the years, several questions became crucial. If Peru expropriated La Brea y Pariñas, would Standard Oil allow Peruvian oil to enter the international markets? Where could Peru get the tankers to transport its oil if it could be sold? As an alternative to an unfeasible nationalization, APRA preferred their "most practical program," to force I.P.C. to pay higher wages and higher taxes. The resulting revenues would be used to create other industries.[29] The problem with APRA's reasoning was that as time went on it became less and less valid. Domestic consumption in Peru increased astronomically while exports dropped. In 1962 Peru became a net importer of oil. APRA forgot the reasons for its 1946 position and stuck to its conclusions. Sir Robert Marett observed that: "Among liberals in the U.S.A., the conviction grew that APRA represented the true forces of democracy in a country which for too long had groaned under the heel of a rich oligarchy.[30] Perhaps the Apristas preferred to safeguard these North American sympathies by keeping their favorable attitude towards the American oil company even in the face of changes which rendered their previous reasoning obsolete.

APRA's support in Congress for Beltrán's I.P.C. programs led the Peruvian military to conclude that indeed I.P.C. and APRA were closely tied. Therefore, the Army's aversion for APRA was automatically translated into an aversion for International Petroleum Company. This dislike was then reinforced by the military's traditional fear that foreigners controlled their fuel supply. By allowing I.P.C. to control the production and distribution of oil in Peru, they felt that the destiny of their country was too much in the hands of foreigners— this was a rather traditional view of defense policy.[31]

PÉDRO BELTRÁN AND LA PRENSA

Another major participant in the controversy over La Brea y Pariñas was Pedro Beltrán—editor and owner of La Prensa and a very wealthy man with many commercial and agricultural interests. Beltrán was described by an I.P.C. manager as Wall Street's ideal of the South American businessman, newspaperman, and statesman, and he was proud of the esteem in which American businessmen and government officials held him. La Prensa regularly reported his many commendations from the United States. An article in the February 1962 issue of Fortune magazine hailed Pedro Beltrán as the Peruvian statesman who could very well become his country's next president. La Prensa greeted the Fortune article with a front page headline. "Beltrán an exceptional statesman considers Fortune magazine."[32] Americans were generally impressed with the results achieved by the Beltrán Cabinet. Peru's gross national product grew at an annual rate of 4.5 percent, and the country's foreign exchange reserves were replenished.[33] A United States commercial mission which visited Peru in late 1960 found that country much improved in stability, and ruled that Peru's investment climate was most favorable for U.S. capital.[34]

Originally, La Prensa was strongly antagonistic to APRA, for the 1947 assassination of La Prensa's editor Francisco Graña Garland was linked to that party. When Pedro Beltrán succeeded Graña Garland as editor, he reportedly swore eternal hatred for APRA on Graña Garland's grave. By the late 1950s, however, Beltrán's animosity for APRA was wearing thin. Like many other Peruvians with political ambitions, Beltrán knew that it would be difficult to govern Peru without the cooperation or at least the acquiescence of APRA. Don Luis Miró Quesada, Beltrán's competitor, seldom missed a chance to reproach this accomodation with the Apristas, and as early as February 1958 he editorially condemned Beltrán for shaming the memory of Graña Garland by associating La Prensa with the APRA-Prado coalition.[35]

As the 1962 elections approached, Beltrán began to maneuver for his own presidential nomination. He resigned from the Cabinet, but it soon became apparent that he did not have the popular support he needed, even if Fortune and the U.S. Department of Commerce endorsed his fiscal accomplishments. He withdrew from the presidential race, and by early 1962 it was clear that he would support the Aprista leader Víctor Raúl Haya de la Torre for the office of president. La Prensa's support for Haya de la Torre took two forms. The large front page headlines depicted Haya de la Torre as the triumphant leader making the final bid for the long-denied presidency. APRA supported Prado in 1956 because of his promise to legalize the party.

The Apristas regarded Prado as a transitional ruler who would make it possible for Haya de la Torre to assume the leadership of Peru in 1962. But one institution blocking APRA's probable success was the Army. Would the Army use its veto-power in 1962 as it had done before in order to dash Haya de la Torre's presidential ambitions?

Clearly, the Apristas hoped that the Army would acquiesce. After all, APRA had long ago renounced its revolutionary tactics. The party had ceased to advocate socialism in any meaningful form, and it had in general become a political grouping acceptable to the Peruvian oligarchy. Even Washington looked with favor on Haya de la Torre. His support for I.P.C. did not go unnoticed. Beltrán called on his Army friends to assure the country that Haya de la Torre would be an acceptable president of Peru. On January 5, 1962, General Alejandro Cuadra Rabínez, Beltrán's Minister of War, declared that the Armed Forces would not only abide by the results of the elections, but would in fact guarantee their "purity."[36] Here was La Prensa's second task—to publicize positive commitments to free elections—elections which would determine the next president of Peru. Although Cuadra Rabínez's position within the armed forces was not a strong one, on January 12 he again declared that "whoever the people elect will occupy the chair."[37] To press this point of view further, La Prensa carried an article by another general, arguing that the Armed Forces were "essentially obedient and hence could not engage in political deliberation."[38]

THE OLIGARCHY

During most of the 19th century, Peru, like other Latin American nations, was dominated by an oligarchy composed of the Roman Catholic Church, the Armed Forces and the landed elite. At that time land was the trademark of wealth and high social status. As Peru entered into the world markets, the resulting demand for particular products made some types of land more valuable than others. Since there was a demand for sugar and cotton, large plantations along Peru's coastal strip were developed to meet it. This emphasis on agriculture had an impact on the nature of the Peruvian oligarchy. The aristocrats of the sierra, the gamonales, retained their vast holdings—their self-sufficient haciendas; however, they lost much of their power and influence to the prominent coastal families. This coastal oligarchy differed from the sierra oligarchy because they were export-oriented. Theirs were the crops that generated most of Peru's foreign exchange, and consequently they tended to dominate the import market as well. As a direct result of their strength in the foreign trade of the country, the landed coastal oligarchy dominated Peru's

ANATOMY OF THE ANTAGONISTS 101

credit institutions. Through their control of the banks, they, in turn, controlled most of Peru's commercial and industrial ventures. French scholar François Bourricaud wrote:

> There is . . . a Peruvian oligarchy, in the sense of a nucleus of powerful families who control the nation's wealth. Its members are not mere consumers, and while they may not themselves be producers or organize production, they determine its scope and direction. Is this plutocracy a governing class? The question is hard to answer. The power of a governing class is always difficult to define; the fact that such a class exists, however manifestly, does not mean that it governs everything. And in Peru, the problem of measuring the extent of the oligarchy's power is especially baffling.[39]

The "oligarchy" which Beltrán and Prado represented was an entity difficult to categorize, and this difficulty stemmed from the fact that the oligarchy closely guarded its affairs, since many Peruvian businesses functioned as family-owned enterprises rather than publically-owned corporations, disclosures of ownership and operations were far less prevalent than those in the United States. It was the banking system of Peru which many Peruvians, including the military, regarded as one of the chief culprits of the inequitable social structure. The Social Progressist Movement wanted to reform the credit system so that it would be available to the population at large and not only to a few privileged elements of Peruvian society. The large Peruvian banks were used as holding companies (companies that own other businesses) for the oligarchy or for foreign business interests. For instance, the Banco Internacional was in fact owned by the Bunge Born firm, an agricultural conglomerate based in Argentina, but also operating in Peru. This bank accepted the public's money, but it lent money almost exclusively to Bunge Born ventures.[40]

The Prado family controlled not only the presidency through Manuel Prado, but it also controlled a vast financial empire through the Banco Popular. The lending policy of this bank was to give funds for a venture only if the bank got a substantial share of the business. If the venture failed and the loan was defaulted, the bank simply took over. If the business succeeded, the Banco Popular had a share in the success. The Prado family bank owned the newspaper La Cronica, and a radio station of the same name. They also had a 20 percent interest in APSA, the Peruvian airlines.[41]

While the Peruvian oligarchy was not homogeneous on an economic or political level, it was quite homogeneous and cohesive on a social level. Therefore such institutions as the Jockey Club and more importantly, the Club Nacional were significant. Membership lists for these groups are secret. However, Phillip Gillette, a sociologist at the University of California, Los Angeles, obtained Club Nacional membership lists going back to the 19th century. He found that during the 20th century the proportion of high political office holders belonging to the Club Nacional progressively declined, except during the Prado administration, when this trend was temporarily reversed.[42] This temporary upswing in the political fortunes of the oligarchy perhaps caused a kind of overconfidence. The oligarchy was now brave enough to carry out a public internal struggle over the petroleum problem. Peru's military officers, especially those steeped in social science at CAEM, probably perceived this increase in oligarchical power as a direct threat to the preeminent role of the military, with its middle class and rural background.

THE PRESIDENTIAL CAMPAIGN OF 1962

Seven candidates sought the office of president in the 1962 election campaign in Peru, but only four were running in earnest, and only three had realistic possibilities of winning the election. General Odría's followers, who had backed Hernando LaValle in 1956, now supported the general himself—under the banner of the Unión Nacional Odriista (U.N.O.). Haya de la Torre once more was the standard-bearer of the Alianza Popular Revolucionaria Americana, and Fernando Belaúnde Terry was the candidate of Acción Popular. The fourth candidate was Héctor Cornejo Chávez, the leader of the Christian Democratic Party, a political grouping which closely paralleled Acción Popular in its ideology. The Christian Democrats appealed to the same young, reformist Catholic constituency that Acción Popular attracted. However, Fernando Belaúnde Terry was a far more charismatic candidate than Cornejo Chávez, and therefore Acción Popular got the bulk of the votes of this constituency.

While Cuadra Rabínez and other senior officers had attempted to commit the army to support whoever won the election of 1962, the younger officers were definitely unhappy with the possibility of either Haya de la Torre or even General Odría assuming the presidency. Their favorite candidate was Belaúnde.[43] The oligarchy divided its sympathies among Odría, Belaúnde, and Haya de la Torre. However, Beltrán and the very large financial interests with which he was associated decided to support Haya de la Torre. This group was impressed by APRA's "good" behavior during the Prado administration, and they were now willing to let APRA have a try at the presidency.

The coming of the election offered a breathing spell for I.P.C. In a report covering 1962, the American embassy staff in Lima commented:

> The Government of Peru was occupied with politics during the first half of 1962 so that the La Brea-Pariñas controversy remained in the background. Six of the presidential candidates running for office . . . expressed themselves as being in favor of immediate nationalization of the La Brea-Pariñas and Lobitos concessions and one candidate identified himself with progressive nationalization.[44]

While the single candidate was not identified in the report, there was little doubt to his identity. Belaúnde and Cornejo Chávez were both committed to nationalization in principle. The minor candidates were all radical leftists. The only traditional conservative, General Odria, vaguely pledged his party to:

> Defend the national resources, while promoting their exploitation in accordance with the Constitution and Laws of the nation; demanding the immediate and definitive solution to the problem of La Brea y Pariñas.[45]

Victor Raúl Haya de la Torre was the only candidate committed to "progressive nationalization," or "covert adaptation," as the enemies of I.P.C. preferred to call it—the alternative which Pedro Beltrán and APRA had supported since 1961.

While I.P.C. attempted to project a low profile during the election, its sympathies for Haya de la Torre could hardly be concealed. Early in the campaign, the Aprista leader traveled to Talara, where I.P.C. personnel gave him a tumultuous reception. Speaking to what was reported to be the greatest crowd ever assembled in Talara, Haya de la Torre once more pledged his support to "progressive nationalization," a statement which won him warm support from the I.P.C. workers. After the speeches, the Aprista leader was treated to dinner at the workers' Esso Club.[46]

Of the minor candidates for election in 1962, only one was running almost exclusively on the petroleum issue. That candidate was César Pando, a retired general and the head of the Front for the Defense of Petroleum. The other radical candidates were Luciano Castillo, of the miniscule Socialist Party, and Alberto Ruíz Eldredge, head of the Movimiento Social Progresista. The elections were held as scheduled on June 10, and the vote-counting process began immediately. However, vote-counting took weeks in Peru, and the candidates were condemned to a long wait. There was usually a considerable amount of speculation between the election and the announcement of the results. The Lima papers published a daily count of the votes processed up to that point, and tension built up as time passed. For reasons known only to him, Fernando Belaúnde Terry chose to claim victory on the basis of the votes counted during the first few days. El Comercio, which had favored his candidacy, echoed Belaúnde's enthusiasm. As time went on, however, it became increasingly clear that Belaúnde would not receive the minimum one-third of the vote required for the presidency. Claims of victory gave way to accusations of fraud in the pages of El Comercio, and soon the Armed Forces began an investigation.

When the results of the election were finally announced, Haya de la Torre had the highest number of votes (557,047), followed closely by Belaúnde (544,180) and Odría (480,798). The other candidates received between nine and fifty thousand votes apiece. César Pando ran fifth, ahead of Castillo and Ruiz Eldredge, who came in last.[47] In order to win the election a candidate had to have at least one-third of the vote, and since the closest candidate missed the mark by a fraction of a percentage point (Haya de la Torre received 33.0 percent of the vote), it was clear that the contest would have to be decided by the Peruvian Congress. In the Congressional elections, APRA won 114 seats out of a total 241, just short of an absolute majority, but with a very definite edge over the runner-up parties. Furthermore, since the Odriistas were far more compatible with Haya de la Torre than with Belaúnde, it seemed as if the APRA leader's victory was a foregone conclusion.[48]

With Haya de la Torre on the verge of achieving the presidency, the Belaúndistas and El Comercio launched a shrill fusillade of accusations, all the time appealing to the Army to correct what they claimed was an Aprista fraud. Realizing that the Army would not stand for the election of Haya de la Torre, the Apristas compromised. They agreed to support their former enemy, General Odría, for a second term, with the understanding that they would have an even larger role in the new administration than they had had with Prado. Their compromise came too late, for the Army had already set up a coup d'état. In the early hours of the morning of July 18, 1962, a mere ten days before the change of governments, a crack unit of Peruvian Rangers surrounded and then captured the Presidential Palace and placed Manuel Prado under arrest. El Comercio probably had advance notice of the coup, for its photographers were there as a tank crashed through the iron gates of the executive mansion. That very day the Lima newspaper gave profuse coverage to what must have been Peru's best photographed military coup.[49] During the next few hours, and in front of the cameras of El Comercio reporters, an officer asked the leaders of the Peruvian Congress to clear the congressional building.

The military's announced intention in carrying out the coup was to annul the results of the 1962 election. They promised, as the military usually does on such occasions in Latin American countries, new "clean" elections. But, unlike previous coups in Peru, the Armed Forces did not install a strong man in power. Instead, the officers insisted on calling their take-over an "institutional" coup, meaning that no single man was responsible—the military as a whole engineered the governmental take-over. A junta was established to rule Peru in the interim, with members of all three military services participating. The junta insisted on maintaining collective leadership, and when its chairman General Ricardo Pérez Godoy showed caudillistic tendencies, he was promptly dismissed and replaced by General Nicolás Lindley. The junta surprised the country when it announced that it would not merely preside over a new electoral process, but that it also intended to work toward solving Peru's most urgent problems in the interim. This task fell to the colonels and the majors at the Center for Higher Military Studies (CAEM), who then searched their files for answers to Peru's dilemmas.[50]

The junta proceeded to create a Planning Institute, with the task of formulating a comprehensive plan for national development over a period of several years. This institute eventually produced a national plan of economic and social development to span 1962-71.[51] The junta also created a Housing Bank (Banco de la Vivienda), with the purpose of by-passing the oligarchically-controlled credit institutions in providing low interest loans to would-be home owners. The generals started several pilot land reform projects. Their most well-known effort was in the La Convención valley, where peasants appropriated lands illegally. The junta even declared 1963 as Literacy Year, and made plans for a massive effort to teach the Peruvian illiterates how to read and write.[52] There was talk of annulling the concessions of La Brea y Pariñas, a move apparently advocated by General Bossio, the junta government's minister most directly associated with the Center for Higher Military Studies.[53]

However, the junta's reformist zeal lasted only from July to December 1962. In early 1963, the government took a more moderate course—many of its radical projects were forgotten, and the military leaders accepted La Prensa's pressing argument that there was a grave danger of a communistic take-over by the labor unions and peasant movements. During the first week of 1963, some 2,000 persons were arrested in Peru—many of them leftist leaders. General Bossio was apparently forced to resign by his fellow officers as early as October 1962, and with him went any hopes which the radicals might have entertained concerning the nationalization of I.P.C. With Bossio out of the way and the junta engaging in anti-communist campaigns, the United States was quick to warm up diplomatic relations which had been cool since the coup.[54] I.P.C. was relieved by the more conciliatory attitude on the part of the military. Before the junta handed over the reins of government to a civilian president, I.P.C. was forced by the government to make a substantial purchase of government bonds—bonds which were not specifically issued for I.P.C. but which were definitely a way for private entrepreneurs to show their support for the junta.[55]

Even though the military junta mellowed in terms of many of its original plans, it did pursue one of its goals to the very end. The military supported the election of Fernando Belaúnde Terry. Belaúnde was the kind of reformer with whom the CAEM officers could identify— he seemed to have the vision and the charisma to make major changes in Peruvian society. The question became: how to assure Belaúnde's victory?

With many of the radicals out of the picture, the Armed Forces believed that Belaúnde would easily catch the votes which had been cast for them in the 1962 election. Just to be on the safe side, Belaúnde reached an agreement with the Christian Democrats. In exchange for some Congressional seats in safe districts, the Christian Democrats backed his candidacy. When the election was over, Belaúnde had received 39.0 percent of the vote. Haya de la Torre got 34.0 percent and Odría got 25.5 percent. Peru's military junta handed the reins of power to Fernando Belaúnde Terry on July 28, 1963, in what can only be described as an atmosphere of general euphoria over what appeared to be a new age in Peruvian politics.

NOTES

1. In fact, television serves only the Lima area. For the 2.1 million radios in Peru, there are 150 radio stations. U.S. Department of Commerce, Overseas Business Reports: Basic Data on the Economy of Peru (Washington: U.S. Government Printing Office, 1969), p. 17.

2. Ibid., p. 2.

3. La Prensa was taken over by the Leguía government and turned into an official publication during the Oncenio. In 1947, its editor Francisco Graña Garland was assassinated, and there was then another change in ownership and editorial policy.

4. Carlos Miró Quesada Laos, Intorno Agli Scritti e Discorsi di Mussolini (Milan: Fratelli Treves Editori, 1937).

5. Carlos Miró Quesada Laos, Lo que he visto en Europa (Lima: Imprenta Torres Aguirre, 1940), p. 197

6. Partido Comunista Peruano, Congreso Nacional, Resoluciones del Primer Congreso del Partido Comunista del Perú (Lima: n.p., 1942), p. 8.

7. Francisco Miró Quesada Cantuarias, La Otra Midad del Mundo, Vol. 1. (Lima: Tipografía Santa Rosa, S.A., 1959), p. 9.

8. Ibid., pp. 97-100.

9. Ibid., pp. 101-103.

10. Ibid., p. 136.

11. Confidential interviews with I.P.C. executives, Coral Gables, Florida, May 23-28, 1971.

12. Augusto Zimmermann Zavala, La Historia Secreta del Petróleo (Lima: Editorial Gráfica Labor, 1968), pp. 167-170.

13. Confidential source.

14. Up to the time when Beltrán became Prime Minister, he used to send Don Luis complimentary watermelons from his hacienda. Zimmermann, p. 167.

15. See the ideological statement of the Movimiento Social Progresista in S. Martinez, Ideario v Plan de Gobierno de los Partidos Políticos (Lima, n.p., 1962), pp. 130-140.

16. Peru, Cámara de Diputados, Diario de los Debates, Tomo I, Legislatura Ordinaria de 1960 (Lima: Publicación Oficial, 1960), pp. 210-213.

17. See the report on political expenditures. Luis Ricardo Alonso Fernandez to Carlos Olivares Sanchez, Department of Latin American Affairs, Havana, October 4, 1960.

18. Martinez, Ideario y Plan de Gobierno, p. 135.

19. See Luigi R. Einaudi, Peruvian Military Relations with the United States (Santa Monica, Cal.: Rand Corporation, June, 1970); Luigi Einaudi, Revolution from Within? Military Rule in Peru since 1968. See also: Carlos A. Astiz, "The Peruvian Armed Forces as a Political Elite: Can They Develop a New Developmental Model?" Paper delivered at the 1969 Round Table of the International Political Science Association, Rio de Janeiro, Brazil, October 27-31, 1969; Victor Villanueva, El Militarismo en el Perú (Lima: Empresa Grafica T. Scheuch, S.A., 1962.

20. Villanueva, El Militarismo, p. 176.

21. Noticias de Petróleo, XIII, No. 116 (April, 1960).

22. Fredrick B. Pike, The Modern History of Peru (New York: Praeger, 1967), pp. 264-266.

23. Luigi Einaudi, Peruvian Military Relations with the United States, p. 15.

24. Carlos Astiz, Pressure Groups and Power Elites in Peruvian Politics (Ithaca, N.Y.: Cornell University Press, 1969), pp. 99-100; François Bourricaud, Power and Society in Contemporary Peru (New York: Praeger, 1970), p. 185.

25. Sir Robert Marett, Peru (New York: Praeger, 1969), p. 178.
26. Luis E. Heysen, El ABC de la Peruanización (Lima: Editorial APRA, 1931), p. 16.
27. Ibid., p. 17.
28. Manuel Seoane, Crédito Externo y Justicia Social—Un discurso polémico (Lima: Editorial Atahualpa, 1946), p. 54.
29. Harry Kantor, The Ideology and Program of the Peruvian Aprista Movement (New York: Octagon Books, 1966), p. 78.
30. Marett, Peru, p. 168
31. Luigi Einaudi, Oral Presentation at the 67th Annual Convention, American Political Science Association, Chicago, Illinois, September 7, 1971. (Panel: Comparative Military Regimes in Developing Societies).
32. La Prensa, January 29, 1962, p. 1.
33. Pike, Modern Peru, p. 298.
34. "Estabilidad en el Peru," La Prensa, January 7, 1962, p. 14.
35. "Nueva maniobra del organo de los exportadores," El Comercio, February 2, 1958, p. 2.
36. "Las Fuerzas Armadas Garantizarán Sufragio," La Prensa, January 6, 1962, p. 2.
37. "Quien Elija el Pueblo ocupará la Silla—Fuerzas Armadas Garantizan Pureza del Proceso Electoral," La Prensa, January 13, 1962, p. 2.
38. General Pedro A. Herida, "Ortodoxia Institucional del Ejército," La Prensa, January 18, 1962, p. 8.
39. Bourricaud, Contemporary Peru, p. 48.
40. Confidential interview with I.P.C. executive, Coral Gables, Florida, May 27, 1971.
41. Ibid.
42. Interview with Phillip D.S. Gillette, Washington, D.C., May 18, 1971.
43. Marett, Peru, p. 185; Astiz, "The Peruvian Armed Forces as a Political Elite," p. 20.
44. U.S., Department of State, Supplement to Annual Petroleum Report—1962—Peru, U.S. Department of State Document No. A-717, April 10, 1963, p. 1.
45. See the official statement of the Unión Nacional Odriista in Manual del Elector (Lima: J. Mejia Baca, 1962), p. 241
46. Entusiasta Recepción Tuvo Haya en Talara," La Prensa, January 28, 1962, p. 2.
47. See "Cuadro del Resultado Final con las Cifras Oficiales del J.N.E. de 1962," Humberto Ugolotti Dansay, Las Elecciones de 1963 y la Elección del 62 (Lima: n.p., 1963), p. 181.
48. Marett, Peru, pp. 185-186.
49. El Comercio, July 18-19, 1962.

50. Astiz, "The Peruvian Armed Forces as a Political Elite," pp. 24-26.
51. Banco Central de Reserva del Peru, Plan Nacional de Desarrollo Economico y Social del Peru, 1962-71 (Lima: Banco Central, 1961).
52. Pike, Modern Peru, pp. 301-302; Astiz, "The Peruvian Armed Forces as a Political Elite," p. 26.
53. Astiz, ibid.
54. Ibid., pp. 26-29.
55. Confidential interview with I.P.C. executive, Coral Gables, Florida, May 25, 1971.

CHAPTER

6

**INTERNATIONAL PETROLEUM
COMPANY
AND BELAUNDE
FACE EACH OTHER**

THE FIRST ROUND

    Neither in the campaign of 1962 nor in that of 1963 did La Brea y Pariñas figure as a major issue. Most of the political parties avoided the thorny question in their formal platforms. Candidate Belaúnde did promise that he would solve the problem, but he did not specify how he would. Fernando Belaúnde Terry was inaugurated as President of Peru on July 28, 1963, in the midst of general euphoria. He had the support of many Peruvians, including the Armed Forces and El Comercio. During his inaugural address, Belaúnde promised to settle the La Brea y Pariñas controversy within ninety days. Soon after he was installed in office, negotiations between Peru's President and the management of International Petroleum Company began.

    All during the month of August and well into October 1963, I.P.C. and the government negotiated. I.P.C. was willing to exchange its rights over the subsoil of La Brea y Pariñas for a contract to operate that property for a period of at least two or three decades, a plan which company management had advocated since the early 1950s. According to the company, considerable progress toward "adaptation" was made during this period. On October 17, 1963, however, the government came up with a proposal which surprised the company. That proposal included an exchange of I.P.C.'s property rights for a twenty-year operation contract, but it also set forth a "tax debt" payment of $50 million over a five year period, and a tax regimen which according to the company would have exceeded 100 percent of the profits.[1]

    While Belaúnde and his party, Acción Popular, had always maintained a strongly nationalistic position on the I.P.C. issue, their campaign rhetoric had probably gone far beyond what they were

I.P.C. AND BELAÚNDE FACE EACH OTHER

actually willing to do with the large American company. In 1960 Belaúnde had given qualified support to Pedro Beltrán's "progressive nationalization" plan, but Alfonso Montesinos's threat to split the party had forced Acción Popular leadership to introduce a nationalization bill in the Peruvian congress. By 1963, however, Montesinos was out of the party, and in fact out of politics, and Benavides Correa, another vocal I.P.C. critic, had also made a tactful withdrawal from politics. Even the Social Progressists had done very poorly in the 1962 and 1963 elections. Despite his relative freedom from pressures of the extreme left, Belaúnde adopted a "get tough" policy with I.P.C.

Several reasons can be given for the President's strong position. Of course, El Comercio was as committed as ever to I.P.C.'s speedy demise, and Belaúnde was quite aware of the power of that newspaper. In fact, after his presidential inauguration, Belaúnde noted that Luis Miró Quesada had not dropped by to congratulate him as many of his supporters had done. He decided to visit Miró Quesada at his office at El Comercio headquarters, and a time was prearranged for the presidential visit. As Belaúnde entered the building which houses the newspaper, he was received in several lobbies by progressively more prominent members of the Miró Quesada family. Finally he was escorted to a great staircase, and at the top stood Don Luis himself. The patriarch of the family descended but a few steps to meet the president of Peru. This reception was widely interpreted as a snub in Lima circles. The incident illustrated well the power of the Miró Quesadas, and the willingness of even the president of the "supremo gobierno" to humble himself before the power of this one newspaper.[2] With La Prensa allied with APRA and the Unión Nacional Odriista (U.N.O.), Belaúnde feared losing the support of El Comercio, a consideration which made a compromise with I.P.C. very difficult.

Another factor which appeared to have strengthened the hand of Belaúnde was the election of John F. Kennedy as President of the United States. Kennedy had been in the White House since 1961, but Peruvians had been busy with internal politics and there had been no major confrontations with I.P.C. since the Democratic administration had taken over in the United States. Peruvians knew enough about American politics to discern that the Democratic Party was not nearly as sympathetic to big business as the Republican Party. They were well aware of the fact that Presidents Franklin Roosevelt and Harry Truman had had several confrontations with big business, and they knew of Kennedy's confrontation with the steel industry. Peruvian leaders watched intently how the young American president handled the situation concerning the unilateral abrogation of certain contracts between the Argentine government and several American oil companies, and they concluded that without a doubt, Kennedy would not stand behind Standard Oil (New Jersey) in a confrontation between its subsidiary, I.P.C. and the government of Peru.[3]

Fernando Belaúnde, a relatively young Catholic reformer, probably derived some comfort from knowing that his counterpart in Washington was, like himself, a young Catholic president. This feeling was reinforced when Kennedy ordered Teodoro Moscoso, the Coordinator for the Alliance for Progress, to fly to Lima immediately after Belaúnde's inauguration with an offer of substantial American aid. There are differing accounts of Moscoso's aid mission. According to Richard Goodwin, announcement of the aid grant was withheld pending a compromise between the Peruvian government and I.P.C., so that Belaúnde could then use the announcement of American aid to blunt any opposition to the compromise over La Brea y Pariñas.[4] The company's management suspected that Moscoso was annoyed by Belaúnde's suggestion that the announcement of aid be used in such a manner.[5] In any case, Belaúnde was assured of American aid regardless of the outcome of the dispute with International Petroleum, provided, of course, that no outright confiscation without compensation took place. In conversations between Moscoso and Belaúnde, the American envoy made it clear that the 1962 coup had delayed American aid, but now that the country was back on a constitutional course, more aid would be forthcoming.[6]

The Alliance for Progress itself had a very dramatic effect on both I.P.C.'s antagonists as well as on its Peruvian allies. The development plan set forth by the Planning Institute in 1962 included a provision that future foreign investment in Peru would change from private corporate sources to U.S. government aid through the Alliance for Progress.[7] Hence, there would be no need to be particularly careful with foreign capital as such, since the incoming capital would be public rather than private.

The reaction of I.P.C.'s Peruvian allies was to resent very deeply what they saw as Kennedy's policy of promoting reform in Latin America through the Alliance for Progress at the expense of private enterprise. Peru's oligarchs had long ago recognized the United States as an international ally in the defense of property rights. They sided with I.P.C. on many occasions, probably reasoning that if I.P.C. could be deprived of its property, there was no guarantee that their property would not be eventually taken from them. The Peruvian oligarchy observed an inconsistency in the U.S. position. Many U.S. citizens vigorously protested any attempts to tamper with the property of American companies abroad, while at the same time approving various agrarian reform schemes that included the confiscation of Peruvian lands long held by families of the oligarchy. In an article which accused the Kennedy administration of promoting two kinds of property, United States and Peruvian, with the latter wide open for confiscation, Enrique Chirinos Soto, an important Aprista, wrote for <u>La Prensa</u>:

I.P.C. AND BELAÚNDE FACE EACH OTHER

> If the Alliance for Progress were an invitation to confiscations and socialism, . . . it could not be at the same time, a carefully delineated invitation so as to exclude American investments from the confiscatory free-for-all.
>
> The American investors will have to go also into the pot of confiscations. . . .[8]

This belief that the United States government was interested only in protecting U.S. property while sacrificing Peruvian private property on the altar of reform was reinforced by the fact that throughout 1963, a very limited number of peasants organized and appropriated private haciendas located in the La Convención Valley. The Peruvian government did not prove very effective in dealing with this problem, and the liberal U.S. press reported these invasions in a very favorable light. If Washington was willing to promote reform at their expense, the Peruvian oligarchy could play the same game. Why not reform Peru at the expense of Standard Oil (New Jersey)?

What the Peruvian oligarchy could not see was that Kennedy himself was wavering in the defense of U.S. capital in Peru. They interpreted the Alliance for Progress as a betrayal, and promptly withdrew whatever support they had given previously to I.P.C. Belaúnde decided to take full advantage of the situation. He pressed the company to secure concessions to the very end. As the deadline he had set for himself approached with the company not yielding substantially, Belaúnde prepared a bill to send to Congress on the appointed day. On October 28, 1963, three months after his inauguration as president, Belaúnde sent a proposal outlining two alternative courses of action. The President wanted Congress to authorize him either to impose his solution on I.P.C. in the form he had made known to the company on October 17, or else to transfer La Brea y Pariñas to Peru's Empresa Petrolera Fiscal (E.P.F.).[9]

Belaúnde's proposal was awkward in the sense that it solved nothing. It merely served notice on the company that it would have to accept the government's terms or face confiscation. Belaúnde probably introduced this measure to save face, for October 28 was his deadline to solve the La Brea y Pariñas dispute and some dramatic announcement had to be made on the appointed day.

It was at that point that I.P.C. began to fight back energetically. Up to then, I.P.C. was scrupulous in its discretion on the negotiations with Belaúnde. Even when the Peruvian government leaked information, thus arousing the curiosity of the Lima press, the company limited itself to declaring that negotiations were under way but that a solution was yet to be found. Upon the introduction of the government's bill in the Peruvian Senate on October 28, however, I.P.C. issued a strongly worded press release stating that Belaúnde's proposal amounted

to "economic confiscation." I.P.C.'s president, M.M. Brisco, issued
a simultaneous statement in New York indicating that I.P.C. had for
the first time heard from the Peruvian government that the company
had a "debt" for back taxes. He denied the debt and charged the
Peruvian executive with promoting "economic confiscation" of I.P.C.'s
operations in Peru. In what must be considered a significant diplomatic
blunder, Brisco suggested that the Peruvian Congress would not approve
the Belaúnde's proposal.[10]

President Belaúnde was so angered by I.P.C.'s press release
and by Brisco's New York statement that he "admonished" I.P.C.'s
general manager Loren Smith. The government then issued an official
communique saying that Smith had been officially rebuked for issuing
a press release which contained "false and tendencious affirmations"
which the government naturally denied. The communique also noted
that Smith was reprimanded for trying to create impressions favorable
to the company abroad by lying about the nature of the Peruvian
government's bill.[11]

The management of I.P.C. remained undaunted by Belaúnde's
reprimand, and the following day the company took a full page ad in
nearly all of Lima's newspapers (with the exception of El Comercio)
to present its point of view. Under a large title reading, "The Executive's bill implies Confiscation," the company said in part that:

> Due to the overwhelming taxes and the other requirements
> which the bill establishes, it would imply that the Company
> would have to operate at a loss; therefore, the bill proposes
> ECONOMIC CONFISCATION.[12]

On October 31, another full page announcement appeared in the Lima
papers. In this one I.P.C. intended to show with facts and figures
that Belaúnde's proposed solution would tax more than 100 percent of
the company's profits. According to I.P.C., its net income before
taxes for the year 1963 would be $70 million; from this sum the company subtracted $47 million in operating and producing costs, thus
leaving a net income before taxes of $23 million. From that $23 million,
I.P.C. subtracted $7.8 million in proposed debt payments, duties and
taxes, thus leaving a profit of $15.2 million. In theory, the government
demanded 60 percent of the profit. Since the government did not allow
$10.9 million as legitimate costs, the total profit from which the
government wanted its 60 percent was $26.1 million—an amount which
would be $15.66 million, or $460,000 more than the total profit calculated by I.P.C. This discrepancy stemmed from the fact that the
Peruvian government considered I.P.C.'s payment to its employee
retirement fund excessive. It also did not allow the costs of producing
the oil which the company gave the government as a royalty as a tax

deductible expense. Furthermore Peru did not consider the payments on the alleged $50 million debt deductible from taxable income.[13] What just a few days before had been highly secret information discussed only in the privacy of the Presidential Palace was now spread over the pages of the Lima paper. International Petroleum Company was determined to take its case to the public, an eventuality which President Belaúnde probably did not forsee.

Not only did I.P.C.'s general manager Loren Smith speak up on October 29, but on the following day he made additional statements. He reasserted that the government's bill was confiscatory, and declared that he had been "admonished" for expressing an incontrovertible truth.[14] To underline the solidarity of the workers with the management of the company, I.P.C. personnel in Lima held a large luncheon for Loren Smith. There, they made speeches and read a "public" letter to Belaúnde. In that letter, the employees and workers of International Petroleun protested the "admonishment" of the general manager, and asserted that they would continue to press their point of view regarding the negative aspects of the president's bill. The only conciliatory note came from Smith himself, who suggested that negotiations between the company and the Peruvian government be initiated once more.[15]

Another strong reaction which Belaúnde did not foresee came from the American embassy, which actually circulated a communique to the Lima press expressing its "disillusionment" with the course of action taken by the Peruvian executive. Spokesmen for the American embassy stated that it hoped for an agreement between the company and President Belaúnde prior to the submission of a bill to the Peruvian Congress.[16] In Washington, a spokesman for the U.S. Department of State described official reaction as one of surprise and wonderment as to what might have brought about such a course of action by the Peruvian president. The Associated Press cable to Peru covering the State Department's reaction noted that just a few months earlier, President Kennedy sent "warm congratulations" to Belaúnde upon his election, and Under-Secretary of State Edwin Martin had recently described the Belaúnde government as the most progressive Peru had ever had. If nationalization of I.P.C. property was carried out without compensation, American aid would be suspended, and such a suspension would have a very negative effect on Belaúnde's announced plans of economic and social development.[17] How much of the report from Washington was actually planted by the Department of State and how much was pure embellishment by the Associated Press remains uncertain. But in any case, the message was clear. Washington encouraged Peru to solve the I.P.C. problem, but the solution envisaged by the U.S. government did not include any form of unilateral nationalization. Belaúnde misunderstood Washington, for he assumed that the

Kennedy administration had given him carte blanche to deal with the company in whatever manner he deemed necessary. He also overestimated the weight which Kennedy's personal sympathies would carry within the complex forces which actually shape American foreign policy.

From London came word that unidentified sources were questioning the effects of the Belaúnde bill on future foreign investment in Peru. From Coral Gables, Florida—the corporate headquarters of Esso Inter-America, came some additional saber-rattling remarks. Brisco once more repeated his charges for the eager Associated Press, and, in effect, he identified Belaúnde's position as one held by "some Peruvian extremists."[18]

This clamor from abroad and from I.P.C.'s management backfired on the company. While Washington, London and Coral Gables produced ominous sounding statements, the Peruvian congressional factions tried to outmaneuver President Belaúnde in what became a highly popular anti-foreign campaign. In the Chamber of Deputies, an Aprista spokesman took the floor to claim credit for Belaúnde's action. He said that APRA had been struggling to recover La Brea y Pariñas since 1929, and he also claimed that Belaúnde's proposal was patterned after the earlier Beltrán-APRA proposal. This Aprista deputy, Armando Villanueva, added that his party would support President Belaúnde's stand.[19] Instead of actually supporting the president's bill, however, APRA and the Unión Nacional Odriista, which had formed a congressional coalition, introduced and passed two bills of their own, and Belaúnde signed them into law on November 6, 1963. The first, Law No. 14695, revoked the law which in 1918 had authorized the executive to settle the La Brea y Pariñas controversy by international arbitration; the second, Law No. 14696, declared the Arbitration Agreement of 1922 "null ipso jure" for "having violated the pertinent legal requirements. . . ."[20] By passing its own bills, the opposition coalition hoped to steal the thunder from Belaúnde, his party Acción Popular, and his allies, the Christian Democrats. Both the opposition and the government coalitions had their eyes on an impending election which would determine who would be the mayor of Lima.

During the debate over the bills which were introduced by the APRA-U.N.O. coalition, a curious development occurred in the Chamber of Deputies. A deputy from Belaúnde's party, Acción Popular, took the floor to claim that the impending solution of the La Brea y Pariñas problem was "a patriotic act of the present government." Realizing that the Belaúndistas, with the help of El Comercio, were not about to let the Apristas and Odriistas cash in on Belaúnde's hard fought battle, APRA once more returned to the floor. Speaking for that party, Armando Villanueva remarked that his party had always favored the vindication of La Brea y Pariñas, and accused El Comercio of trying to confuse the issue. He went so far as to say that when Luis Miró Quesada was Secretary of State in 1931, he failed to do anything about the Laudo of 1922. Villanueva was answered by Sandro Mariategui, an Acción Popular deputy, who attacked APRA for claiming credit. He declared that APRA had in fact never been in favor of vindicating La Brea y Pariñas.[21] Some Communist Party deputies proposed that the American ambassador, John Wesley Jones, and I.P.C.'s general manager, Loren Smith, be declared persona non grata in Peru, but their motion was rejected. An Acción Popular senator, Juan Cravero, characterized the I.P.C. employees who wrote the public letter to Belaúnde protesting his policies as "traitors" and demanded that they be investigated by the police. However, his demands were not considered seriously.[22] A dissident U.N.O. senator who was later dropped from the party proposed that the government use military force to occupy I.P.C. installations—to prevent any disruption of the oil supply.[23] When this rush to capitalize on the popular anti-I.P.C. sentiment was over, it was Belaúnde who came out on top. For mayor of Lima, the APRA-U.N.O. coalition nominated General Odría's wife, María Delgado de Odría. Acción Popular and the Christian Democrats nominated Luis Bedoya Reyes, a man who had the personal support of Belaúnde. In December 1963 Bedoya Reyes became mayor of Lima.

Even though Belaúnde managed to increase his already great popularity in Peru by taking a tough position against I.P.C. in the La Brea y Pariñas controversy, by early November it was clear that his position was not without serious risks. On November 7, the National Federation of Petroleum Workers announced that they would proclaim an indefinite strike if the government nationalized I.P.C.[24] Ignoring this threat, Belaúnde pressed on in Congress, and asked that his bill of October 28 be passed quickly. Despite his efforts, some radical senators began to criticize the president for not going far enough.[25] Realizing the political dangers of a petroleum strike, a suspension of U.S. aid, and radical criticism, Belaúnde decided to chart a more conciliatory course.

In a November 12 interview with an Associated Press correspondent, the president declared that he was not in favor of the creation of a state monopoly over the petroleum industry. Clearly, since the nationalization alternative of his own bill would result in a state monopoly, Belaúnde's statement indicated that he would prefer a settlement whereby International Petroleum Company would continue to operate La Brea y Pariñas.[26] Belaúnde's statements worried the more extreme anti-I.P.C. elements in Peru, for he preferred I.P.C. to continue to operate La Brea y Pariñas. In the words of Augusto Zimmermann:

> The danger of this alternative was not that, for the first
> time, there appeared in the mind of the Chief Executive
> the idea of keeping I.P.C., but rather that the articles in
> the bill were written in such a way, that one could per-
> ceive with clarity an absolute identity of concepts between
> the so-called Beltrán bill and alternative "a" in the pro-
> posal of President Belaúnde.[27]

Zimmermann forgot that in his own account of the events of 1960, Belaúnde was basically in favor of the Beltrán solution, except for the fact that he wanted a shorter period of time for the operating contract.

In the same November 12 press interview, Belaúnde also stated that Peru's relations with the United States government "had not suffered alteration." Either the president wanted to minimize the impact of his decision on his relations with Washington—intending to calm Peruvian domestic tempers, or he believed that Washington was merely going through the motions of protest in order to satisfy the American petroleum lobby. Did Belaúnde have assurances from Kennedy that the United States would merely stage a standard diplomatic protest while backing Belaúnde in his encounter with I.P.C.?

The answer to this question lies hidden in the files of the Department of State—files which are inaccessible to scholarly researchers for at least until 1980. The issue was certainly confused during the first half of November 1963, for Belaúnde did not expect the American embassy to react as it did. Either the embassy played its part in a meaningless staged protest, or Washington was genuinely surprised, and Belaúnde's understanding was nothing more than a misunderstanding of Washington's intention.

President Kennedy was assassinated on November 22, 1963, and Lyndon B. Johnson assumed the presidency of the United States. The fact of Kennedy's assassination in Dallas, a city which Peruvians perceived as the heartland of Texas, "the richest oil emporium of the United States," was a bad omen.[28] Almost as if to confirm Peruvian fears, Lyndon Johnson immediately changed the Department of State's Latin America head, bringing in fellow Texan Thomas Mann. Belaúnde had great misgivings about this appointment. He knew that Mann had a long association with Texas oil interests, and he believed that Mann was an attorney for several American petroleum companies.[29] He expected a much tougher fight, for I.P.C. would surely have the solid backing of the U.S. Department of State.

In Belaúnde's view, the balance of power between his government and I.P.C. changed in favor of the company at this point. With Brisco in charge of I.P.C. and Thomas Mann in charge of U.S. Latin American policy, Peru would run into trouble, for the two men constituted a formidable team bent on forcing his country to accept I.P.C.'s terms.

Instead of negotiation the company assumed a position of stubborn insistence on its terms of settlement.[30] The Department of State suspended all foreign aid to Peru. Journalist and one time Kennedy staff member Richard Goodwin quoted a State Department official as saying:

> The idea was to put on a freeze, talk about red tape and bureaucracy, and they'd soon get the message. Unfortunately, they believed we were as inefficient as we said, and it took about a year for them to get the message.[31]

Goodwin stated that the Department of State acted on its own, without I.P.C. pressure for a suspension of U.S. aid; I.P.C. management claimed that they put no pressure on the U.S. government.[32] President Belaúnde, however, saw the situation in quite a different light. As far as the Peruvian chief of state was concerned, Standard Oil was behaving in its traditional way. Belaúnde believed that through its powerful lobbies in Washington and New York, I.P.C. secured the suspension of American aid. The company did technically bully various credit institutions into stalling action on several loans for which Peru had contracted. Without aid and without credit, Belaúnde saw his development programs come to a grinding halt. To this day, the Peruvian leader places full responsibility for the slow development of his country during the middle 1960s on Standard Oil (New Jersey), and claims that the Peruvian people concur.[33]

Whether I.P.C. was instrumental in bringing about the suspension of aid or not, the fact remains that aid was suspended pending a solution of the controversy. The British soon joined hands with the U.S. government in exerting pressure on Belaúnde. On January 3, 1964, the British government sent a diplomatic note to the Belaúnde government advising it that Britain considered the Arbitration Award of 1922 completely valid, and that it did not recognize Peru's right unilaterally to disavow the international agreement. This note was most likely sent at the urging of the U.S. Department of State, since the British had virtually no interest in the La Brea y Pariñas controversy.[34]

In early 1964, Belaúnde's bill was finally shelved, and in its place the Peruvian Congress passed Law No. 14863. President Belaúnde put his signature on it on February 12, 1964. It authorized the executive to "make suitable arrangements to resolve the pending matters on 'La Brea y Pariñas.'" Congress established no significant guidelines on the nature of the future arrangements. It merely stated that the petroleum deposits in question should be exploited in a manner "which best benefits the interests of the country." There was only one important requirement in this otherwise wide grant of discretionary powers to the Peruvian president—whatever solution was considered would have to be submitted to Congress for ratification.[35] Was this new law a Congressional booby trap set for President Belaúnde? By its passage, the APRA-U.N.O. coalition avoided the issue by making it Belaúnde's responsibility to find a solution. At the same time, however, the legislature reserved the right to crucify Belaúnde politically should the solution be unacceptable to it. Since APRA had managed to shroud its own position in vague contradictions, the party could simply wait. If the president arrived at a compromise with I.P.C., APRA could accuse him of selling out to American pressures. If Belaúnde took a hard line towards the company, APRA could attack him for damaging Peru's international standing and foreign credit.

In April 1964, a new round of negotiations between International Petroleum Company and the Peruvian government was initiated. In order "to clarify basic concepts and set the stage for active negotiations," Michael M. Brisco, I.P.C.'s president, and Michael Haider, Standard Oil's president travelled to Lima and held conversations with President Belaúnde.[36] Since personal relations between Loren Smith, I.P.C.'s general manager in Lima, and President Belaúnde had grown considerably worse during the first year of Belaúnde's term in office, a new general manager was appointed. This was Fernando Espinosa, an I.P.C. executive of Cuban origin, a man particularly suited for the job. He was the company's manager in Colombia just prior to his assignment in Lima, and while in that country, had successfully mediated a potentially disastrous crisis for the company.[37] Espinosa was the opposite of what many Latin Americans perceive as the typical North American businessman—cold, blunt and calculating. Very urbane and well educated, Fernando Espinosa was more a diplomat than a business executive. His task was to reach an agreement acceptable both to the Peruvian political leaders, and to the company. In addition, the new I.P.C. general manager found himself acting as intermediary between Belaúnde and his political rivals. Not since the 1930s was I.P.C. so deeply involved in the politics of Peru.

From May to July 1964, the company negotiated with the government. Fernando Espinosa visited President Belaúnde frequently, and the two developed a personal friendship which went beyond business negotiation.[38] By the end of July, an unofficial agreement was achieved. The company would cede its property rights over La Brea y Pariñas in exchange for a release from all claims for back taxes. As payment for operating the oil fields, the company would receive 20 percent of the sales of petroleum products from La Brea y Pariñas—that fee was to cover production costs. Any funds remaining after the company had been paid its production fee would be split on a 50-50 basis between I.P.C. and the Peruvian government. Both the basic and the contingent fees received by the company would be subject to a 50 percent

I.P.C. AND BELAÚNDE FACE EACH OTHER

income tax. It was calculated that this arrangement would result in a 65-35 percent split of overall profits in favor of the Peruvian government. I.P.C. gained a greater measure of control over the operation of its refinery, but at the end of a 25-year period, ownership of the refinery would revert to Peru. "Suitable provisions" were made so that pricing of petroleum products would cease to be a political issue of major proportions.[39]

Now that a private verbal agreement had been worked out, President Belaúnde faced the problem of whether it would be acceptable to APRA, La Prensa, and El Comercio. In his conversations with Espinosa, Belaúnde is reported to have asked repeatedly, "What would El Comercio say?"[40] Even though President Belaúnde placed some fourteen members of the Miró Quesada family in various government jobs—including some top choice diplomatic posts—and even though Don Luis's nephew Francisco Miró Quesada was Minister of Education—a Cabinet position, President Belaúnde related that he could not count on Luis Miró Quesada to support him in anything short of nationalization of I.P.C.[41]

There was little that Espinosa could do in regard to the position of El Comercio. The last effort at personal persuasion was made by company manager Jack Ashworth in late 1959. He flew from Lima to New York on the same plane as Luis Miró Quesada. Ashworth attempted to convince Don Luis of the error of his anti-I.P.C. position, only to be rebuffed by the editor of El Comercio, who was quoted as saying:

> Please do not try to persuade me. You are the General Manager of I.P.C. and you do well to defend your Company. I am the Editor of El Comercio, and I do well to defend my country. You have to be responsible to your share-holders. I have to be responsible to my readers.[42]

Fernando Espinosa, I.P.C.'s general manager during most of the Belaúnde administration, was so angered by the policies of El Comercio that he called in the company's legal staff with the intention of instituting a libel suit against that newspaper. However, I.P.C.'s Peruvian lawyers persuaded him to abandon this idea. They argued that it would be difficult to win against Miró Quesada, and that even if the company were to win, Don Luis could have a sudden heart attack or stroke and die—thus providing the anti-I.P.C. forces with a formidable martyr.[43]

I.P.C.'s unsuccessful bid for a change in El Comercio's policy did not daunt the company from approaching Belaúnde's chief political adversary, Víctor Raúl Haya de la Torre. Soon after the president expressed his fears of APRA to Espinosa, the latter got in touch with APRA's high command. He explained the nature of the agreement he had reached with Belaúnde and asked whether it would be acceptable to APRA. After a brief consideration of the details, the Aprista leadership expressed its willingness to accept the terms. Espinosa communicated APRA's assurances to Belaúnde, but the Peruvian executive declared that he could not put his trust in such private assurances. Espinosa returned to the APRA leadership, and persuaded them to make a public commitment. An unidentified Aprista leader was instructed to endorse a solution to the I.P.C. controversy in a public address—a solution which matched the agreement already arrived at between the president and the company. Espinosa pointed out this public commitment to Belaúnde, only to be told once more that APRA was not to be trusted.[44]

Seeking a way of convincing Belaúnde of APRA's honorable intentions, Espinosa insisted on talking to Haya de la Torre personally. "El Jefe," as the Aprista leader is known to his APRA associates, had just returned from his 1964 stay in Europe, and agreed to see Espinosa. I.P.C.'s general manager had several interviews with Haya de la Torre and managed to convince him that Belaúnde required his personal assurance of agreement, and that APRA would not try to capitalize on it once Belaúnde sent it on to the Peruvian Congress. When Espinosa met again with Belaúnde, however, and referred to Haya de la Torre's personal assurances, Belaúnde snapped: "That is a banana peel!"—a reference to the fact that the president interpreted the Aprista leader's assurances as part of a great political trap.[45]

Since President Belaunde had a Miró Quesada in the Cabinet, and a score of family members in other government jobs, he should have been able to secure at least silent acquiescence from El Comercio regarding any policy he wished to pursue, and since he had the personal assurances of Haya de la Torre, he should have been able to proceed with the La Brea y Pariñas agreement. There did not seem to be any thing APRA could do, however, to convince him.

Was Belaúnde really afraid of political repercussions from APRA and El Comercio? While Fernando Espinosa accepted the president's explanation for not sending the agreement to the Peruvian Congress for ratification, there is an alternative explanation. Perhaps Belaúnde did not want to solve the La Brea y Pariñas problem during 1964. After all, although American aid was suspended, Peru had been told that there was no suspension—merely a delay due to red tape in Washington. President Belaúnde might have been playing his own red tape game with the company. If Thomas Mann, Assistant Secretary of State for Latin American Affairs, had decided to suspend aid until the I.P.C. issue was settled without ever informing Peru of U.S. policy, Belaúnde might have been waiting for aid to resume before settling the I.P.C. issue without ever informing Washington of his intentions.

This conclusion is supported by the impressions of the general manger, Fernando Espinosa, who noted that the Peruvian president

I.P.C. AND BELAÚNDE FACE EACH OTHER

seemed to operate under the assumption that the United States government was very much under the influence of American business, particularly Standard Oil (New Jersey). During the conversations between Belaúnde and Espinosa, Belaúnde brought up the question of American aid several times. Espinosa got the impression that Belaúnde actually thought that the only thing needed for a resumption of aid was a telephone call from Standard Oil's president to Lyndon Johnson. However, as Espinosa pointed out in an interview May 28, 1971, if Standard Oil (New Jersey) had that kind of influence, it would certainly have put it to better use by having the U.S. government drop the pending anti-trust suits against the company, or make slight adjustments in the U.S. oil imports quota. Either action would have represented a greater dollar gain for the company than the entire Peruvian operation was worth.[46]

Fernando Espinosa met with Belaúnde on some sixty occasions, and if his interpretation was correct then his conclusion is quite valid. I.P.C.'s oil operations in Peru represented only an infinitesimal part of Standard Oil's assets—reported in 1968 as nearly $17 billion "book value." Standard Oil (New Jersey), the world's largest corporation, could not be easily swayed by Peru's pressure on what was at best a remote and almost forgotten province of its immense financial empire.[47]

Nevertheless, President Belaúnde might have thought that he was holding an important hostage within the borders of Peru, and that if he waited long enough, Standard Oil would order Lyndon Johnson to ransom I.P.C. with a bountiful aid grant to Peru. This hypothesis does not exclude the possibility that Belaúnde was at the same time genuinely afraid of opposition from other Peruvian political leaders. After all, APRA had not inspired much confidence when it had become an ally of General Odría in 1962. From 1952 to 1956, Odría persecuted the Apristas and even tried to do away with Haya de la Torre.

For such domestic and international reasons, the Belaúnde administration decided not to settle the I.P.C. controversy—at least not by the terms which had been worked out during the first half of 1964. The Peruvian government stalled for nearly six months while I.P.C.'s general manager tried to rally support for the agreement from the potential opposition. Ironically, I.P.C. management was as slow to get the Peruvian point of view of La Brea y Pariñas as the Peruvians appeared to be in getting the message behind the American "red tape" delays on aid. By the end of 1964, President Belaúnde presented a "revised" version of the July agreement to the company.

This new proposal of December 30, 1964 substantially changed the July agreement. The principle of exchange of property rights for an operation contract was deleted from the "revised" proposal, and the company got no clear release from claims for back taxes.

More significant perhaps was that the profit ratio was changed to 90-10 percent in favor of the Peruvian government.[48] I.P.C. could have negotiated on the basis of the president's proposal, but instead the company expressed "surprise and consternation,"[49] and rejected it.

In a sense, this rejection sealed I.P.C.'s fate in Peru. Belaúnde received his largest measure of political support in 1964. In January of that year, West Germany's President Lubke visited Lima, and in September, none other than Charles de Gaulle graced Peru with his presence. Belaúnde's ambitious plans for the development of Peru truly captured the imagination of many a foreign leader, as well as of most Peruvians. He had a reservoir of good will which would have made a compromise with I.P.C. politically tolerable.

I.P.C. had more reasons than ever to compromise. The oligarchy deserted the company due to their disenchantment with the Alliance for Progress. American insistence on a more equitable income distribution for the country, and tax and agrarian reforms made it seem as if the United States was sponsoring change at the expense of Peru's traditional establishment. While in the past they looked upon Washington as the protector of property rights, now the United States seemed to support only American-owned property. The oligarchy had successfully avoided a property tax during Peru's republican history. Under the general cover of the Alliance for Progress, Washington pressed for such a tax using the leverage of the International Monetary Fund.[50] As the oligarchy perceived the situation, with allies like the Americans, they needed no enemies. The oligarchy grew at first detached from and eventually antagonistic to the American presence in Peru, and correspondingly, the country's public opinion grew ever more aware of I.P.C. as a source of nationalistic irritation.[51]

Another reason which should have swayed the company towards compromise was the fact that Standard Oil's original investment in Peru had been amortized over the years; a relatively small return should have been acceptable to the company. Yet, the golden opportunity slipped through the fingers of International Petroleum Company and President Belaúnde. Why did both parties to the controversy fail to compromise at a time when it was imperative that they do so to benefit both?

The inability to reach a compromise was due to Peruvian nationalism, and a corporate phenomenon very similar to nationalism—company pride. The essence of Peru's demands on the company was not that more money be given to the state, or that I.P.C. comply with existing general legislation. It was rather that the company be humiliated. Peruvians felt wronged and defrauded by the Laudo of 1922. It was as if with hindsight the country boy suddenly realized that he was cheated by the slick city cousin. Peru's demand for humiliation took the form of a claim for back taxes. While the exact amount varied over

I.P.C. AND BELAÚNDE FACE EACH OTHER 125

the years, the demand that the company pay the alleged taxes remained constant throughout. A payment of the taxes would have been a public acknowledgement that I.P.C. was wrong, and that it owed reparations to Peru. Peruvians also wanted the company to give up its claims over the subsoil of La Brea y Pariñas, and in so doing, again to admit that it was wrong to claim such ownership.

International Petroleum Company consistently refused to acknowledge any debt for back taxes, and furthermore, the company insisted that it would give up its rights over the subsoil of La Brea y Pariñas only in exchange for a contract to operate the fields. If the company successfully exchanged its ownership of the subsoil for a contract from the government of Peru, then the government would implicitly acknowledge the Laudo of 1922 as a legitimate document setting forth I.P.C.'s property rights in Peru. As a matter of principle, every major political group declared the Laudo of 1922 to be anathema to the nation, and Belaúnde was not about to recognize its validity—implicitly or otherwise.

A conversation between the General Manager of I.P.C. and an unidentified Odriista (U.N.O.) senator well illustrated the heart of the problem. After considerable discussion over whether the company owed Peru back taxes, the senator agreed with Espinosa that the company did not. Nevertheless, the senator asked that the company make a settlement of $50 or $60 million and terminate the controversy. To this suggestion, Espinosa replied "but we have proved there is no debt," only to hear the senator in turn declare, "but the matter of the debt is a national psychosis!"[52]

Fernando Espinosa's reasoning for not capitulating to Peruvian demands for debt payment was eminently practical. No private corporation can disburse fifty million dollars as therapy for a national psychosis. The expediency of the senator's suggestion deserved attention, however. The amount of money was not the issue, for if I.P.C. felt that $50 million was too high a price to pay, it might have requested a downward adjustment. Furthermore, since the payments on this debt would have stretched over a period of years, the Peruvian government would have acquired a vested interest in the success of I.P.C.'s operation so that the debt payments could be made. At the end of the payment period, the company could have returned to the fold of Peru's good corporate citizens, having expiated its sins. The company was willing to pay the money, as the frustrated agreements between I.P.C. and the Beltrán Cabinet and the Belaúnde administration proved—these agreements provided for special payments of one sort or another. What the company was unable to do was to acknowledge wrong doing, to humiliate itself.

This is indeed a surprising conclusion given the generally accepted belief that a corporation such as Standard Oil (New Jersey) is interested in profits and nothing else. If the ultimate loyalty of the company is to the dollar sign, how can the company's behavior be explained? I.P.C. risked capital to save face, to preserve its corporate pride. "I.P.C." or "the company" is composed of a group of human beings subject to the full range of emotions—fear, hatred, love, anger, compassion, and pride. They strive to do their job—which might be to protect the profits of the enterprise—but not at the price of their own personal dignity.

While exploring the gamut of options the company had during the Belaúnde administration, research drew this conclusion. John Oldfield, I.P.C.'s top executive officer in Coral Gables, headquarters of Esso Inter-America, acknowledged that International Petroleum Company would not have considered the possibility of relinquishing ownership over the subsoil without an operating contract, and moreover, the company would not have publicly apologized to Peru as a tactical move designed to vent the country's long accumulated hatred for the company.[53] For the group of men who had been responsible for their company's policy during the last thirty years, the men who had made Talara grow from a miserable village into a bustling and prosperous industrial city, it was hard to admit that they had been defrauding the Peruvian nation all along, especially since they certainly bore no more responsibility for the developments than men such as Augusto Leguía or Luis Sanchez Cerro, both Peruvian chiefs of state.

President Belaúnde held Fernando Espinosa in his highest esteem, and the feeling was returned by Espinosa, yet the two men represented incompatible points of view. Compromise was impossible unless either man was willing to alter his viewpoint. Perhaps each man assumed that the other would eventually yield. Unfortunately, they both embarked on a course which only led to the mutual failure of their causes.

NOTES

1. The La Brea y Pariñas Controversy, Vol. I (International Petroleum Company, February, 1969), pp. 7-8.

2. This incident was related by I.P.C.'s former general manager in Peru, Fernando Espinosa, during an interview at his residence in Key Biscayne, Florida, May 28, 1971.

3. Robert Kennedy, brother of the president, is reported to have said: "You Peruvians want to nationalize La Brea y Pariñas. Well, do it. Nothing is going to happen." For Peruvian opinions on the Kennedy administration, see: Augusto Zimmermann Zavala, La Historia Secreta del Petróleo (Lima: Editorial Gráfica Labor, 1968), pp. 153-168.

I.P.C. AND BELAÚNDE FACE EACH OTHER 127

4. Richard N. Goodwin, "Letter from Peru," The New Yorker (May 17, 1969), p. 58.
5. Interview with Fernando Espinosa, Key Biscayne, Florida, May 28, 1971.
6. "Golpe del Año Pasado Retrasó Ayuda de E.U.—Lo Revela Teodoro Moscoso," La Prensa, August 25, 1963, p. 1; "Moscoso Prometi(Más Ayuda al Peru—Hablo 3 horas con Belaúnde," La Prensa, August 27, 1963, p. 1.
7. Banco Central de Reserva del Peru, Plan Nacional de Desarrollo Económico y Social del Peru, 1962-71 (Lima: Banco Central, 1962), p. 87.
8. Enrique Chirinos Soto, "Kennedy y el Hijo Pródigo," La Prensa, November 10, 1963, p. 14.
9. The La Brea y Pariñas Controversy, Vol. I, Exhibit 6.
10. "IPC Dice que Proyecto La Brea Sería 'Confiscación Ecnomica' Dice que nada debe y que nunca se la ha cobrado," La Prensa October 29, 1963, p. 1; "Peru reivindica Brea y Pariñas, El Comercio, October 29, 1963, p. 1.
11. "Gobierno llamó al Gerente IPC y lo Amonesto—Comunicado Oficial," La Prensa, October 29, 1963, p. 1; "El Gobierno amonesta a la IPC por emitir información tendensiosa," El Comercio, October 30, 1963, p. 1.
12. See the advertisement entitled "El Proyecto del Ejecutivo implica Confiscación," La Prensa, October 30, 1963, p. 3.
13. "El Estado absorbería más del 100 por ciento de la Utilidades," La Prensa, October 31, 1963, p. 7; "Dice presidente de International Petroleum Co.—Atternativa del Gbno. a I.P.C. es antieconomica," El Comercio, October 30, 1963, p. 1.
14. "El Proyecto es Confiscatorio Reitera el Gerente de la IPC," La Prensa, October 31, 1963, p. 1.
15. "Gerente de IPC crée Posible se Reinicien Negociaciones," La Prensa, October 31, 1963, p. 4; "Carta Abierta al Señor Presidente de la República," La Prensa, October 31, 1963, p. 10; "Empleados de la IPC apoyan actitud de desacato a Presidente," El Comercio, October 31, 1963, p. 1.
16. "Embajada de E.U. Expresa Desilución con el Caso IPC," La Prensa, October 31, 1963, p. 1.
17. "Repercusion en E.U. e Inglaterra del Proyecto de Brea y Pariñas," La Prensa, October 31, 1963, p. 4.
18. Ibid.
19. See statements by Armando Villanueva in: "En las Cámaras," La Prensa, October 31, 1963, p. 2.
20. The La Brea y Pariñas Controversy, Vol. I, Exhibit 7.
21. Por unanimidad aprobaron las dos Camaras la Derogatoria de ley previa al Laudo," La Prensa, November 6, 1963, p. 4.

22. "Diputados Rechazan Moción Roja contra Embajador de EU e IPC—Senador AP Censura a empleados de esa Empresa," La Prensa, November 5, 1963, p. 1.

23. See the statement by U.N.O. senator Fernando Noriega Calmet in "En las Camaras," La Prensa, October 31, 1963, p. 2.

24. "Los Petroleros Pararán si se Expropia la IPC," La Prensa, November 8, 1963, p. 1.

25. "Senadores Criticaron Duramente la Exposición que Hizo Pestana," La Prensa, November 8, 1963, p. 4.

26. "Belaúnde dice que no Pretende Monopolio Estatal del Petroleo," La Prensa, November 13, 1963, p. 1.

27. Zimmermann, Historia Secreta, p. 180.

28. Ibid.

29. Interview with former president Fernando Belaúnde Terry at his residence in Chevy Chase, Maryland, May 21, 1971.

30. Ibid.

31. Goodwin, "Letter from Peru," p. 60.

32. Ibid.; Interview with Fernando Espinosa, Key Biscayne, Florida, May 28, 1971.

33. Interview with Fernando Belaúnde Terry, Chevy Chase, Maryland, May 21, 1971.

34. Certain minority interests own shares of I.P.C., and some are reportedly British citizens. However, this is a very small portion of I.P.C. stock. Interview with John Oldfield, Coral Gables, Florida, May 25, 1971.

35. The La Brea y Pariñas Controversy, Vol I, Exhibit 8.

36. Ibid., p. 9.

37. Interview with John Oldfield, Coral Gables, Florida, May 23, 1971; Interview with Fernando Espinosa, Key Biscayne, Florida, May 28, 1971.

38. Interview with Fernando Espinosa, Key Biscayne, Florida, May 28, 1971; President Belaúnde also indicated a personal liking for Espinosa in an interview, Chevy Chase, Maryland, May 21, 1971.

39. The La Brea y Pariñas Controversy, Vol. I, pp. 10-11.

40. Interview with Fernando Espinosa, Key Biscayne, Florida, May 28, 1971.

41. Ibid.

42. Zimmermann, Historia Secreta, p. 32.

43. Interview with Fernando Espinosa, Key Biscayne, Florida, May 28, 1971.

44. Ibid.

45. Ibid.

46. Ibid.

47. For figures on Standard Oil of New Jersey's assets, see: Standard Oil Company (New Jersey), 1969 Annual Report (New York: n.p., 1970).

48. The La Brea y Pariñas Controversy, Vol I, pp. 11-13.
49. Ibid.
50. American policy-makers took on the cause of righting Latin American social injustices. For instance, they virtually demanded that industrialists and landowners in Latin America be taxed, a proposition which was particularly difficult to implement in the case of Peru. See the testimony of James Fowler, Acting U.S. Coordinator, Alliance for Progress, Agency for International Development, in: U.S., Congress, House of Representatives Committee on Foreign Affairs, Subcommittee on Inter-American Affairs, New Directions for the 1970's: Toward a Strategy of Inter-American Development, 91st Cong., 1st Sess., 1969, pp. 2-35.
51. In 1962, Peruvian visitors to Talara often asked to be shown the Laudo of 1922 because they had heard so much about it. However, many thought that it was some kind of landmark! Private surveys by I.P.C.'s public relations office showed that 95 percent of the total population was totally ignorant about I.P.C. and La Brea y Pariñas. By 1965, that percentage had dropped to 50 percent—one half of the population was aware of and usually detested the Laudo, a change in public sentiments largely attributable to El Comercio. Confidential interview with I.P.C. executive, Coral Gables, Florida, May 27, 1971.
52. Interview with Fernando Espinosa, Key Biscayne, Florida, May 28, 1971.
53. Interview with John Oldfield, Coral Gables, Florida, May 28, 1971.

CHAPTER

7

THE END OF INTERNATIONAL PETROLEUM COMPANY AND DEMOCRATIC REFORM IN PERU

While the best opportunity to solve the La Brea y Pariñas problem was lost in the 1964-65 period, negotiations continued. Nearly four years of President Belaúnde's term remained, and I.P.C. hoped that political conditions would change sufficiently to make an acceptable settlement more likely. The I.P.C. controversy was a millstone around Belaúnde's political neck throughout the remainder of his term, however, and eventually doomed his efforts to promote development in Peru.

In outline, the Belaúnde administration had several favorite projects. The Peruvian president placed considerable emphasis on agrarian reform, Cooperación Popular, and on various engineering projects, particularly the construction of a highway along the eastern slopes of the Andes—the marginal highway. Since Belaúnde had to contend with an opposition legislature dominated by an APRA-U.N.O. coalition, his programs faced an uphill battle almost from the beginning.

Mindful of the agricultural interests which controlled the large sugar and cotton plantations, the congressional majority chipped away at Belaúnde's agrarian reform until the coastal estates were virtually exempt from its effects. Congress also passed a bill providing for immediate compensation for whatever lands were distributed, thereby placing a very high price tag on the program. The various construction projects which Belaúnde envisioned were, of course, capital intensive projects. Only Cooperación Popular, a self-help program wherein the government provided the organizational and technical expertise, as well as the necessary materials, and the peasants contributed the labor to construct schools, wells, roads, and health facilities, was a relatively inexpensive reform program. The Peruvian congress, however, voted against the necessary funding for this program when it had barely begun.[1]

Since Congress refused to increase taxes adequately to finance the executive's programs, aid from abroad, particularly from the United States, became Belaúnde's only hope for success. His reforms

END OF I.P.C. AND DEMOCRATIC REFORM

were very close to the prescriptions that the Alliance for Progress had issued as a cure-all for Latin American problems. Belaúnde, therefore, expected that the United States would contribute heavily to financing Peru's development through the Alianza. Those expectations were unfulfilled to a large degree because the controversy with I.P.C. remained unresolved throughout most of the 1960s.

As a result of the lack of U.S. aid, and the reluctance of the Peruvian Congress to vote new taxes, Peru began to experience serious inflationary problems in 1965. The rate of inflation increased during 1966 and 1967, forcing a 30 percent devaluation of the sol on September 1, 1967. This devaluation was particularly damaging to President Belaúnde's credibility, for he promised in April of that year that he would uphold the then existing rate of exchange between the sol and the dollar.[2] In spite of this dramatic devaluation, the unofficial rate of exchange continued to drop until by the fall of 1968, the sol had depreciated by about 57 percent in relation to the dollar.[3]

As the Belaúnde administration lost ground, its opposition grew bolder. In mid-June 1965, a guerrilla movement developed in the center of the country, in the La Convención Valley—the area which had witnessed considerable peasant unrest during the early 1960s. The guerrilla movement soon spread to southern Peru as well. Many of the guerrilla leaders were former Apristas who disapproved of Haya de la Torre's moderate position. In Congress, the APRA-U.N.O. coalition passed a law establishing the death penalty for the guerrillas, and voted extraordinary funds for the armed forces to support their effort to wipe out the movement.[4]

The first nine months of 1965 saw little progress in the negotiations between I.P.C. and the Belaúnde administration. Acción Popular and the Christian Democrats reaffirmed their commitment to nationalization of I.P.C. during their respective party meetings in June. In his July 28 annual address to Congress, President Belaúnde made only slight references to La Brea y Pariñas. It was not until September 1965 that the controversy again acquired momentum.

On September 1, 1965, U.S. Under-Secretary of State Jack Hood Vaughn visited President Belaúnde. The Lima press reported that Belaúnde told Vaughn that petroleum was too grave a problem to leave in the hands of the oilmen, and that Peru would take the road to expropriation if no prompt agreement with I.P.C. was possible.[5] Since no progress was made during the month, President Belaúnde made good his threat and sent a "Bill of Expropriation with Bonds" to Congress on September 30. This bill did not mention I.P.C. or La Brea y Pariñas. It merely referred to "expropriations" for purposes of agrarian reform, irrigation projects, enlargement of cities and towns, etc. Among the properties listed for possible long-term expropriation by means of 18- to 22-year bonds there was a category entitled "sources of energy." According to International Petroleum Company, the purpose of the bill was to pressure I.P.C. into reaching a settlement.[6] The United States Embassy in Lima informed the company that it considered the proposed methods of compensation unsatisfactory under the Hickenlooper Amendment to the U.S. Foreign Aid Bill.[7] If the Peruvian government expropriated La Brea y Pariñas and then compensated I.P.C. with long-term local currency bonds, aid to Peru would be discontinued. Since the bulk of American aid was already being withheld, the position of the U.S. Ambassador John Wesley Jones must have been very awkward—he threatened that the United States would officially suspend aid that had already been suspended unofficially.

In December 1965 a new round of negotiations began, and at the end of the month, I.P.C. submitted a draft contract which reflected the areas of agreement up to that point. By January, however, the company encountered what it interpreted as "clear evidence of the President's intention not to press for a solution. . . ."[8] Henceforth, I.P.C. tried to isolate the La Brea y Pariñas ownership dispute from all other related operating problems. The purpose of this new company policy was to press for government permission to proceed with a refinery expansion at Talara, and with a corporate realignment whereby I.P.C. would establish a subsidiary owner of the Talara refinery and the distribution apparatus—Esso Peruana.

In early 1966, a new Assistant Secretary of State for Inter-American Affairs, Lincoln Gordon, assumed office. In an effort to clear up misunderstandings between Washington and Lima, the State Department announced in February for the first time to the Peruvian government that American aid had been suspended pending a solution to the La Brea y Pariñas controversy.[9] In March, U.S. Presidential Assistant Walter Rostow flew to Lima and during conversations with Belaúnde he assured the Peruvian executive that if Peru did not expropriate La Brea y Pariñas, American aid would be resumed promptly. President Belaúnde, in turn, declared that he had never intended to confiscate the company. U.S. aid began to flow into Peru shortly thereafter.[10]

United States aid, however, was destined to another suspension. But this time it had nothing to do with I.P.C. It was the result of a dispute between Washington and Lima over the purchase of jet planes for the Peruvian Air Force. The Peruvian armed forces had proved themselves quite capable in their dealings with the guerrilla movement. In less than a year they had virtually eliminated the guerrilla threat. The military, however had come to look askance upon their role as internal policemen. They envisioned themselves as the defenders of Peru in any potential international conflict. U.S. military aid policy vis-à-vis Peru and other Latin American countries seemed to be one of reinforcing their counterinsurgency roles. The matter came to a head when the Peruvian government attempted to purchase some of Northrop Aviation's F-5 fighters, a relatively inexpensive aircraft with which the Peruvian Air Force planned to replace their aging F-80s. Under U.S. Congressional pressure against aid for military hardware, Washington delayed authorization for the sale, and the Peruvians, in a fit of anger, purchased some very expensive and far more sophisticated French Mirages. In retaliation for the purchase, the U.S. government once more suspended aid to the Belaúnde government.[11] Thus, of his five years in office, President Belaúnde received full U.S. aid for about one year. Between the I.P.C. controversy and the disagreement over the jet fighters, his administration was denied aid for most of its term of office.

On July 28, 1966, President Belaúnde once again addressed the Peruvian Congress, and referred to the La Brea y Pariñas controversy. Belaúnde told the Congress that considerable progress had made in negotiations with the company. He added that in a projected agreement, twenty of twenty-one articles had already been accepted by both sides. Only a single article remained to be ironed out—a task which he expected to complete by early December 1966. President Belaúnde criticized his political opponents, and without directly mentioning APRA, noted that it would not be sensible for those who had been ready to give La Brea y Pariñas away now to demand expropriation.[12]

Andrés Townsend Ezcurra, speaking for the Aprista delegation in Congress, responded by attacking Belaúnde for not pursuing the type of radical solution which his own party, Acción Popular, had advocated while out of office. He pointed out Montesinos's Congressional bill calling for the expropriation of La Brea y Pariñas, and remarked that while APRA backed "progressive nationalization," Belaúnde's Acción Popular engaged in demagoguery, and called for more radical steps. Townsend Ezcurra asked: "What has changed? Has the Company changed? Has the problem changed? Or is it the President of the Republic who has changed?"[13]

The intent of the APRA-U.N.O. coalition was clear—to embarrass President Belaúnde by contrasting the tough position of former prominent Acción Popular members such as Alfonso Montesinos with the current conciliatory politics with which the President hoped to settle the long-standing problem of I.P.C. This intention to embarrass the President became even clearer between August and November 1966, when the Belaúnde Administration agreed to let I.P.C. proceed with an $8 million refinery expansion at Talara, as well as the creation of a wholly-owned subsidiary "Esso Peruana" to act as a holding company for the Talara refinery. The Congressional opposition criticized the Peruvian Executive so severely that approval for the expansion and the creation of a subsidiary was withdrawn.[14]

During November, negotiations proceeded, based on the "Draft of December 1965," and once more, agreement seemed within reach when the President suggested a 60-40 percent profit split with the company's share subject to a 50 percent tax. International Petroleum accepted the president's proposal and returned it to him with minor revisions, without altering the profit split or the tax level. Once again, there was no action, and six months elapsed before negotiations were reinitiated.[15]

By the middle of 1967, the Belaúnde administration faced great economic adversities. Although the President had promised not to devalue the sol, he had no choice but to do so because of Peru's rampant inflation. Against this background of economic unrest, Belaúnde turned to Congress in an effort to raise revenues. However, Haya de la Torre declared his opposition to new taxes in February 1967, and APRA responded to Belaúnde's proposal by unleashing more criticism. On June 20, 1967 the Commission which the Chamber of Deputies had established to deal with the La Brea y Pariñas controversy declared itself in permanent session with the avowed purpose of sifting through all the proposals which had come up over the years, and to make a unanimous recommendation for the best solution.[16] By June 22, the entire Chamber of Deputies was once more debating two bills which would have effectuated expropriation. One was submitted by the Christian Democrats and the other was backed by the APRA-U.N.O. coalition.[17] Because of the pressure, the president's party, Acción Popular, joined in the new wave of pro-expropriation sentiment. On June 23, Acción Popular publicly demanded that the State-owned petroleum enterprise, Empresa Petrolera Fiscal, take over the La Brea y Pariñas fields.[18]

The APRA-U.N.O. majority, however, prevailed with their version of a solution, and by July 8 the bill was approved by the Congress and sent on to the President. Belaúnde signed it into law on July 26, 1967. Law No. 16674 reiterated what a previous law (No. 14696) had already established: the Laudo of 1922 was null and void. But it went on to state that in passing Law No. 14696, Congress intended to transfer ownership of the La Brea y Pariñas oilfields to the state. The new law also instructed the Peruvian executive branch to inscribe the oilfields in the property registries in the name of the state since all other registrations were null and void, and to establish an exploitation plan "most consistent with the national interest." President Belaúnde was also authorized to expropriate equipment, installations, and other assets which either might be needed to operate the fields or to cover the debts owed the Peruvian state by the company. A thirty day period beginning the day the law was enacted was given as the maximum time the president would be allowed to effectuate its provisions.[19]

END OF I.P.C. AND DEMOCRATIC REFORM 135

Once more, Peru was "vindicating" its rights over La Brea y Pariñas. While these rights had been "vindicated" several times over the years, the Peruvian government seemed incapable of seizing the oilfields despite numerous laws and proclamations to that effect. Mirroring past performance, this new offensive merely signaled the beginning of another descent of papers, resolutions, and administrative orders—with little effect on the actual operations of I.P.C.

On July 31, President Belaúnde issued Supreme Decree 61-F, ordering that the oilfields be registered in the name of the State in the Realty Registry in Piura; he also instructed the Energy Bureau of the Ministry of Development to evaluate the worth of the company's investment and to authorize I.P.C. "temporarily" to continue to operate the oilfields.[20] On August 10 the Petroleum Bureau issued Directional Resolution No. 76. I.P.C. was to continue operating La Brea y Pariñas.[21] For its part, the company began to flood all available legal and administrative channels with appeals which argued that Law No. 16674 was unconstitutional because it deprived the company of its property without due process. I.P.C. also argued that the 1922 Laudo had merely settled the question of taxation and that the property rights of the company had nothing to do with the Laudo. Hence, the invalidation of the Laudo had no bearing on its property rights.[22]

There was an electoral campaign under way in the background of this new paper war. An Acción Popular deputy from Lima died, and a special election was scheduled for November 12 to fill his seat. The by-election developed into a key test of Belaúnde's political strength. Running against the Belaúndista candidate was APRA's Enrique Chirinos Soto, the man who had articulated so well Peruvian upper-class frustrations with the Alliance for Progress. Like another prominent leftist, Eudocio Ravines, Chirinos Soto had been co-opted into the fold of La Prensa by Pedro Beltrán. However, unlike Ravines, who had broken completely with his former allies, the Communists, Chirinos Soto could maintain both his upper-class connections and his APRA membership, for APRA had become closely identified with the upper-class.

On election eve, the Peruvian government published what I.P.C. termed "measures of great demagogic appeal" in the Official Gazette. The Tax Court ruled that I.P.C. would have to pay the Peruvian government its profits for the last fifteen years. President Belaúnde issued Supreme Resolution 1609-H ordering the attorney-general to institute a suit against the company for "unjust enrichment."[23] November 12 brought ominous news to President Belaúnde. Aprista Enrique Chirinos Soto won the election, thus confirming what had been suspected for some time—Belaúnde's popular appeal had declined considerably and his personal endorsement could no longer carry an election. Furthermore, since the Aprista candidate ran on a platform openly hostile to the president's policies, the election was a test which did not go unnoticed.

President Belaúnde, who has always held I.P.C. largely responsible for his political misfortunes, shifted from a policy of negotiation to one of open confrontation.[24] The company was still in the process of preparing one of its appeals against the pre-election decrees when on November 17 Belaúnde issued an official communique declaring that the National Superintendency of Taxation had calculated the amount owed by I.P.C. to the government as U.S. $144,015,582.22. The figure was the government's calculation of I.P.C.'s profits during the last fifteen years. Eight days later, a new Supreme Resolution (No. 1770-H) ordered the company to pay "complementary taxes" of 26 million soles within three days "under warning of attachment."[25] On November 24, 1967 International Petroleum filed an appeal against the government's last collection order. This appeal was first rejected and then accepted by the Peruvian government, but on November 29, I.P.C. learned through the news media that the company's assets had been frozen.[26] I.P.C. immediately paid the tax bill to free its bank accounts. This was the first time that the company was directly affected by the Peruvian government's drive to "vindicate" the La Brea y Pariñas oilfields!

A long string of government decrees rejecting the company's appeals came in December 1967 and January 1968. On December 19 the attorney general was authorized to bring about full "restitution" and to sue I.P.C. for "unjust enrichment." On January 27, the Empresa Petrolera Fiscal (E.P.F.) was designated as the representative of the Peruvian government in all dealings with I.P.C. Negotiations between the managements of I.P.C. and E.P.F. began, and even though the Peruvian government had already expropriated the oilfields I.P.C. still negotiated on the position that it would cede Peru its rights and title to La Brea y Pariñas only in consideration of a cancellation of all debt claims and for an operating contract whereby the company could continue to work the fields. The Belaúnde government was willing to drop the debt claims in exchange for La Brea y Pariñas, but it would not give I.P.C. an operating contract. By mid-February negotiations between I.P.C. and E.P.F. broke down. Neither side was willing to yield on the question of the operating contract.[27]

With his political footing badly shaken, President Belaúnde faced unsurmountable odds. On the one hand, the opposition-controlled Congress had decreed the expropriation—it was his responsibility to carry it out. How could Belaúnde undertake such a battle with the American giant and its allies at a time when he was so lacking in political support? At the same time, the company showed an unyielding face to the Peruvian president, making what amounted to a demand

END OF I.P.C. AND DEMOCRATIC REFORM 137

for Belaúnde's political head. There was little question that the president could not have risked in 1968 what he did not want to risk in 1964 when he had far greater political strength.

During the last round of negotiations in January and February 1968, President Belaúnde appealed to the company to yield—to give up its rights to the oilfields and to the surface installations. According to I.P.C., Belaúnde assured the company that by yielding La Brea y Pariñas without an operating contract, it would gain a new "certificate of legitimacy."[28] Belaúnde's anxiety perhaps stemmed from the early 1968 rumor that General Doig, then Peru's Military Chief of Staff, was preparing a coup d'etat.[29] But I.P.C.'s General Manager Fernando Espinosa felt less urgency. He had held personal meetings with Generals Julio Doig Sanchez and Francisco Morales Bermudez, and found them well-disposed toward the company.[30] General Doig's coup never materialized, and mandatory retirement soon removed him from the political scene. His replacement was General Juan Velasco Alvarado—a man reportedly antagonistic to I.P.C. for political and personal reasons.[31]

On March 28, 1968 El Comercio carried a story declaring that the Empresa Petrolera Fiscal recommended to President Belaúnde that it be allowed to take over the La Brea y Pariñas oilfields. The article stated that the recommendation was unanimously approved by the E.P.F. Board of Directors, on which General Jorge Maldonado represented the armed forces. The article also revealed that prior to the final vote on the recommendation, General Maldonado asked for a twenty-four hour delay so that he could consult with the armed forces command, and that the command was in favor of the recommendation.[32] While the contents of the E.P.F.—Armed Forces recommendation was never made public, the Miró Quesadas must have interpreted the document as being quite radical, for on the following day, El Comercio editorially applauded the document of which it had very limited knowledge.[33]

While many of the actual details of these developments were obscure, there was evidence to the effect that these events in late March were very significant. According to President Belaúnde, he requested the E.P.F. Board of Directors and its President, Carlos Loret de Mola, to draw up a recommendation for a final solution to the La Brea y Pariñas problem. On March 21, Loret de Mola forwarded a proposed decree to President Belaúnde. The proposal was remarkably mild. It ordered E.P.F. to take over the nonproducing areas of La Brea y Pariñas and develop them, while I.P.C. would continue to operate the existing facilities. The proposed resolution provided that all proceeds from the operation be banked. I.P.C. would be compensated for operating costs, but the profits would remain in the bank pending a later agreement with company. Included with the proposed resolution, was a covering letter from E.P.F. Director Carlos Loret de Mola in which he assured Belaúnde that General Maldonado supported the resolution and that both E.P.F. and the armed forces were behind it.34

It is possible that Empresa Petrolera Fiscal took this position because Carlos Loret de Mola actually doubted the ability of the state enterprise to run the complex operation at La Brea y Pariñas. It is also possible that the armed forces acquiesced to Loret de Mola in a effort to trap President Belaúnde. Since a coup had been in the works for some time, the military might have wanted to encourage Belaúnde to reach a compromise, and then use the compromise itself as an excuse to take the reins. Someone leaked information to El Comercio to the effect that E.P.F. and the armed forces wanted to take over La Brea y Pariñas immediately. The details, however, were withheld. If Belaúnde had interpreted the position of the armed forces on the I.P.C. problem as rather lax or even favorable to the company, he might have been tempted to yield to I.P.C.'s demands for an operating contract. Once the agreement had been arrived at, the armed forces could have overthrown Belaúnde and denied ever agreeing to such a concession, and the story in El Comercio on March 28 would have corroborated their denial. General Juan Velasco Alvarado was, in his capacity as army chief, involved with the proposed resolution. Perhaps the "banana peel" which President Belaúnde feared from Haya de la Torre in 1964 had actually been dropped in his path by the armed forces command in 1968.

President Belaúnde decided to ignore the solution proposed by E.P.F. and the armed forces. He kept it confidential, perhaps hoping that the version of the story carried by El Comercio would provide additional pressure on I.P.C. Fernando Espinosa indeed took note of the El Comercio article, and on April 1 the company filed a report with the Minister of Development giving its own version of the negotiations with E.P.F. up to that point. According to this statement, Loret de Mola remained adamant on the question of an operating contract. He had, however,

> ...tried to persuade I.P.C. to assign in a definitive manner all its producing assets located on La Brea y Pariñas to the State, declaring that the company would continue in point of fact to operate the oil field until there might be formalized the above-mentioned operating contract with I.P.C., which could be finalized within a year or a year and a half.35

In other words, Loret de Mola wanted I.P.C. to yield its claims on the promise that an operating contract could be secured in the future. The company refused.

April, May, and June went by without further meaningful action on the petroleum front. The Peruvian government was preoccupied with the economic and political problems of the day. On June 1, Acción Popular selected Edgardo Seoane as its presidential nominee for the 1969 elections. On July 7, Haya de la Torre announced his own candidacy. Fernando Belaúnde, constitutionally barred from running, became a "lame duck" executive. But as the candidates lined up on crucial issues, the question arose as to whether President Belaúnde's government would endure until the end of its constitutional term.

Realizing the vulnerability of constitutional order in Peru, I.P.C. decided at last to yield to the President's demands.[36] On July 25, three days before Belaúnde was to present his annual address to Congress, an I.P.C. executive walked into the office of Belaúnde's Minister of Development and announced that the company was now ready to transfer La Brea y Pariñas and the installations thereon to the Peruvian State. The company also agreed to renounce its claims over the subsoil, and would abandon its insistence on an operating contract as a condition of the agreement. In exchange for its concessions, I.P.C. expected the government to drop all debt claims against the company, and to agree to have E.P.F. sell I.P.C. the petroleum from La Brea y Pariñas so that the company could continue its refining and marketing operations in Peru. The government reacted "first with incredulity, and subsequently with unsurpassed delight."[37]

In his July 28 address to Congress, President Belaúnde dedicated considerable time to the announcement of the settlement. Only the details of the transfer, as well as subsequent arrangements for supplying the I.P.C. refinery at Talara, remained to be worked out. The chief difficulty would be the price at which E.P.F. would sell I.P.C. the petroleum it extracted from the nationalized La Brea y Pariñas. Belaúnde also announced to Congress that he would travel to Talara to sign the final agreement with the company as soon as the remaining details had been worked out.

Arriving at an agreement on the selling price proved more difficult than anticipated. By Monday, August 5, no agreement had been reached, but Belaúnde, anxious to bring the deal about, declared to the press that he would travel to Talara during that week. Saturday still brought no agreement, and the President summoned the negotiators to the Executive Palace in an effort to pressure them into agreement. Joining I.P.C.'s Lima management was the President of I.P.C., James Dean; joining E.P.F.'s management were several Cabinet members as well as the President. Belaúnde reportedly told the negotiators that he wanted to keep his promise to go to Talara. No progress was made during the long day of negotiation. I.P.C.

wanted E.P.F. to supply it with at least 80 percent of the oil produced at La Brea y Pariñas—at the price of $1.80 per barrel. The company also wanted the State enterprise to retain more La Brea y Pariñas workers than E.P.F. was willing to accept. Finally, speaking for I.P.C., James Dean insisted that Peru should give the company a concession to exploit certain tracts in the Selva region. This demand was later dropped.[38]

Saturday's negotiations broke down late that night when Belaúnde announced that he was being forced to take stern measures. There was no movement on Sunday, Belaunde's self-imposed deadline for his trip to Talara with the agreement. On Monday morning, El Comercio came out with a prominently displayed front page headline announcing an "impasse" in the negotiations, and also stating that I.P.C. demanded a concession in the Selva region of Eastern Peru as well as a contract to purchase E.P.F. petroleum for $1.80 per barrel.[39]

On Monday, August 12, International Petroleum again attempted to resume negotiations. The government's position was now that since the company's demands had been made public knowledge through an unidentified leak to El Comercio, the government could no longer accept these terms.[40] I.P.C. dropped its demands for a concession in the Selva region but came to no agreement on the price it would pay for E.P.F. petroleum. By mid-night, the negotiations broke down again. President Belaúnde then ordered that a decree of expropriation be drawn up, and at three o'clock in the morning of August 13, 1968, the Cabinet approved the expropriation. In a final effort to reach an agreement, Belaúnde's Prime Minister, Osvaldo Hercelles, telephoned the U.S. Ambassador, John Wesley Jones, to inform him of the step the Peruvian government was about to take. The ambassador asked for a three- or four-hour delay, and within that time he persuaded I.P.C.'s general manager, Fernando Espinosa, to return to the Presidential Palace and accept the government's terms. E.P.F. would take only 167 I.P.C. workers and the rest would remain with the American company. I.P.C. would pay $1.97 per barrel for E.P.F. petroleum, and the state enterprise would determine how much petroleum it would sell I.P.C. The company would supply E.P.F. with water, and maintenance services from its utility plants in Talara at a price to be determined later. The final agreement was signed at 5:30 A.M. on August 13, 1968.[41] Later the same day, the President and several members of his Cabinet, the Presidents of both chambers of Congress (both Apristas) and I.P.C. management flew to Talara and in a brief ceremony signed the Acta de Talara—the official document by which the Peruvian state acquired the La Brea y Pariñas oilfields.[42]

The Act of Talara was indeed an historic document, but one which outlined only formally the details of the agreement. The actual terms were delineated in the contract signed earlier that morning at the Presidential Palace. Unfortunately, E.P.F.'s Loret de Mola and I.P.C.'s Fernando Espinosa signed different contracts. Since I.P.C. was to supply La Brea y Pariñas with certain services, and the price of these services was not immediately determined, Loret de Mola insisted that I.P.C. could not make deductions for those services so as to bring the price of crude oil below a certain minimum level— $1.0835. Espinosa refused to bind the company to provide the services on such terms.

Each subscriber to the contract maintained that the document he signed reflected his position on the minimum price question. The typed contract contained no provision for a minimum price. While it had eleven pages the text ended at the bottom of the tenth page. The E.P.F. Director later claimed that he wrote: "In any event, the price for crude oil shall be no less than $1.0835," and then signed his name near the top of page eleven. Richard Goodwin, who investigated the matter in great detail and interviewed both Espinosa and Loret de Mola, speculated that while the document was in transit from one room to the other page eleven was removed. Espinosa then signed at the bottom of page ten. The lawyers who handled the contract asked Loret de Mola to sign each page on the margin, so that Espinosa assumed that his E.P.F. counterpart merely signed the document in that manner. The end result was a ten page contract signed at the margin of every page by Loret de Mola and at the bottom of page ten by Fernando Espinosa, with no provision for a minimum price.[43]

On September 6 Carlos Loret de Mola and three other members of the Board of Directors of Empresa Petroleo Fiscal resigned. In their letter of resignation they alleged a lack of cooperation from Minister of Development, Pablo Carriquiry. More specifically, Loret de Mola and his supporters argued that when they tried to assume the administrative duties over the oilfields I.P.C. turned them away saying that the agreement reached in August called for the company to operate the fields until the end of 1968. Furthermore, the former E.P.F. Director objected to the Peruvian government's permission for I.P.C. to expand its Talara refinery.[44] <u>El Comercio</u>, which had been itching to attack Belaúnde openly, seized on the resignation of Loret de Mola and other Board members to initiate a campaign against the Act of Talara. Through its front page headlines and its editorials, Don Luis Miró-Quesada once more dug into one of his favorite topics, the I.P.C. controversy.

On the evening of September 10, almost a month after the actual signing of the contract between I.P.C. and E.P.F., Carlos Loret de Mola appeared on television to publically denounce the disappearance of page eleven—that page of the contract on which he claimed to have set a minimum price of $1.0835 for the crude oil

I.P.C. would purchase from E.P.F. The following morning both major Lima newspapers, which were by then quite antagonistic to Belaúnde, carried large headlines suggesting foul play.[45]

On September 6, the day Loret de Mola resigned from E.P.F., a group of political leaders gathered in a ceremony to mark the publication of Augusto Zimmermann's book, <u>Historia Secreta del Petróleo</u>, a frankly anti-I.P.C. work by the protege of Don Luis Miró Quesada, to whom the book is dedicated. The book, which at the time covered the controversy through the Act of Talara, was critical of President Belaúnde for not giving credit to the Miró Quesadas and the other anti-I.P.C. leaders during his Talara speech. Present at the meeting were some of the campaigners of the early 1960s, such as Alberto Ruíz Eldredge and Alfonso Benavides Correa. More importantly, two major political leaders were also present: Hector Cornejo Chavez, the leader of the Christian Democrats, and Edgardo Seoane, Acción Popular's Presidential nominee.[46] The meeting which introduced a book openly hostile to President Belaúnde was in itself a sign of the government's troubles. The Christian Democrats ended their coalition with Acción Popular just prior to the November 1967 by-election, and Acción Popular itself had veered left in support of its more radical leader, Edgardo Seoane.

With the administration almost bereft of political support, one of Belaúnde's top advisors, Manuel Ulloa, apparently attempted to forge an alliance of loyal Belaundistas and Haya de la Torre's Apristas. While there was no absolute proof of this alliance, the evidence indicated its existence. For instance, in June 1968, the APRA majority passed Law No. 17044 giving the President extensive powers for a period of sixty days "to solve the structural unbalanced conditions of public finances, to strengthen the international balance of payments of the country and to promote the complete development of our economy."[47] The law allowed Belaúnde to take extraordinary measures by decree to deal with the deteriorating economic conditions of the country. It was this law which allowed Belaúnde to negotiate the Act of Talara without Congressional approval. In fact, part of the urgency to conclude the agreement with I.P.C. was that the sixty day period giving the President extraordinary powers had nearly expired in early August. Not only did APRA give Belaúnde carte blanche to deal with Peru's problems, but it defended his use of the extraordinary powers. In a television interview, the Aprista President of the Chamber of Deputies praised the government for acting sensibly during the sixty days.[48] While Belaúnde's former allies, the Christian Democrats villified his emergency measures, APRA defended them.[49] On September 1, an Aprista Deputy who accused the government of dishonesty was suspended. While Belaúnde's own party opposed the suspension, APRA pressed for it.[50] A Peruvian magazine, <u>Oiga</u>,

END OF I.P.C. AND DEMOCRATIC REFORM 143

had denounced the covert Belaúnde-APRA alliance for some time, and by the middle of 1968 La Prensa joined in these denunciations, thus prompting APRA's Secretary Armando Villanueva to go on television to deny the existence of an understanding between his party and President Belaúnde.[51]

El Comercio remained strangely silent through most of this period. Given the strong antagonism the Miró Quesadas harbored for APRA, El Comercio's boss could not have failed to notice the apparent warming relations between Belaúnde and APRA. When the Aprista President of the Chamber of Deputies, Armando Villanueva, visited Rome in August, Carlos Miró Quesada, Belaúnde's Ambassador to Italy, refused to receive him. The Peruvian Congress demanded an apology, and when the Ambassador refused, the Belaúnde government apologized on his behalf. Carlos Miró-Quesada immediately resigned,[52] and the fate of Belaúnde in the pages of El Comercio was sealed. On August 15, that newspaper carried both a rather hostile statement by the former Ambassador, and an editorial in which El Comercio suspended judgment on the Act of Talara pending a clarification of the conditions of the contract.[53]

When Carlos Loret de Mola resigned and then denounced the alteration of the contract, El Comercio, La Prensa, the Christian Democrats, and even the Odriistas (U.N.O.), who had earlier broken their coalition with APRA, joined their voices to attack Belaúnde. The Act of Talara and the "missing page" became their battle cry as they rushed to destroy what had the potential of being a formidable political alliance between Peru's two most appealing political leaders, Fernando Belaúnde Terry and Víctor Raúl Haya de la Torre.

The day after Loret de Mola made his "page eleven" denunciation on television, a group of thirty-six Army generals met to study the developments surrounding the Acta de Talara. They were led by Juan Velasco Alvarado. The Peruvian Navy and Air Force were reported to be studying the matter separately. Only the Army generals reached a conclusion. They disapproved of the measures taken by the Peruvian government after the Act of Talara and sent a communication to Belaúnde via the Minister of War, with a request that it be passed on the Chamber of Deputies.[54] By September 15, neither the Navy nor the Air Force had joined the Army in disapproving of Belaúnde's petroleum policies, but General Velasco Alvarado publically affirmed that the Joint Command (Army, Navy and Air Force chiefs) would issue a communique on the I.P.C. controversy.[55]

With the armed forces on a collision course with the Belaúnde administration, the political parties hurried to realign their positions. In an effort to pacify the Army, APRA demanded that I.P.C. pay for the privilege of exploiting La Brea y Pariñas until the end of the year. Aprista Congressional leaders also joined in the criticism of

Cabinet members most closely identified with the Act of Talara. The Christian Democrats intensified their attacks on the Act, and even the Catholic Church, in an obvious effort not to be left out of what promised to be the political cause of the century, demanded through Cardinal Juan Landazuri that the contract be clarified.[56]

To complicate the president's already desperate situation, Acción Popular's presidential candidate Edgardo Seoane made a stinging attack on the Cabinet and demanded that the agreement on La Brea y Pariñas be annulled.[57] The following day, September 21, Belaúnde ousted Seoane from the party and ordered a "reorganization" of Acción Popular. This action split the party into two groups —one siding with Seoane and the other Belaúnde respectively.[58] At one point, Seoanistas and Belaúndistas battled for the Acción Popular headquarters, with the latter gaining control of the offices with support from the police.[59] Through this interparty fighting, APRA's leadership remained loyal to Belaúnde, and attacked the Seoanistas as people "acting without moral courage."[60]

With every major political group except APRA attacking the Act of Talara, and even the Cardinal of Lima demanding an explanation, President Belaúnde's Minister of War General Jose Gagliardi moved to cool the rampant rumors of a coup. On September 20, General Gagliardi declared that the armed forces would not assume "an attitude of force, outside the Constitution," and neither would they take a position on the controversy. The following day, however, General Velasco declared: "The announcement by Minister Gagliardi has no validity. Neither the Armed Forces nor the Joint Command depends on one Minister."[61] The writing was on the wall—the military was ready to seize the opportunity to take over the Peruvian government.

In a token effort to prevent the inevitable coup, APRA's Secretary General Armando Villanueva declared that Apristas would not tolerate such an act. He warned the military to pay no heed to the extremists of right or left who promoted a coup, and he encouraged the Apristas to take arms against any such attempt.[62] Despite Deputy Villanueva's statements, the end of the Belaúnde administration was just a matter of time.

On October 2, Belaúnde appointed a new Cabinet in the hope of stemming the coup, but in the early hours of the following day, the old routine around the Presidential Palace was staged once more. President Belaúnde was rudely awakened by the Peruvian Rangers. The morning issue of La Prensa carried a front page picture of a lieutenant and a captain pushing President Belaúnde out of the Palace.

On October 4, the junta guided by General Juan Velasco Alvarado issued a decree declaring the I.P.C.-E.P.F. contract and the Act of Talara null and void. On October 9, another decree expropriated the

Talara refinery as well as La Brea y Pariñas. This action was justified by the new government as an effort to collect the "debt" which I.P.C. owed the Peruvian nation. Unlike previous government decrees on the problem, this one was backed by action. Forty officers and a thousand troops moved in to take the oil fields, and a Rear Admiral of the Peruvian Navy was assigned to take Talara.[63]

After the seizure, I.P.C. was left with its 50 percent ownership of the Lima Concessions (jointly owned with Compañía Petrolera Lobitos) as well as its network of gas stations, storage facilities, and offices. But on January 28, 1969 everything—including the company's Lima offices—was expropriated. The Peruvian government took the position that I.P.C. would be compensated for the expropriated property as soon as the company paid the alleged debt of U.S. $690,524,283. This sum represented the government's calculation of the value of all products extracted from La Brea y Pariñas from March 1, 1924 to October 9, 1968.[64]

After fifty years of involvement in Peru, Standard Oil (New Jersey), one of the world's largest corporations with enormous annual profits and assets, was humiliated by the Peruvian government, as it had once humiliated Peru by threatening to shut off its fuel supplies. Troops took over I.P.C. property and eventually the government issued warrants for the arrest of its management personnel. It took Peru half a century to grow from a primitive society which could easily be manipulated by foreigners with superior technology and power, into a self-assertive nation ready not only to correct the injustices, but to administer what it considered just retribution to the foreign company which overstayed its welcome by several decades.

NOTES

    1. Selden Rodman, "Peruvian Politics Stalls Belaúnde's Reforms," The Reporter, Vol. 35, No. 1 (July 14, 1966), pp. 37-40.
    2. Sir Robert Marett, Peru (New York: Praeger, 1969), p. 192.
    3. Ibid.
    5. "Dijo Belaúnde al Sub-Secretario de Estado de E. U.," El Comercio, September 2, 1965, p. 1.
    6. The La Brea y Pariñas Controversy, Vol. I (February, 1969), p. 13. The entire text of the bill appears as Exhibit 11 in the same volume.
    7. Ibid., pp. 13-14.
    8. Ibid., p.14.
    9. La Decada del 60-Del Colonialismo Liberal a la Revolucion," Oiga (January, 1970) p. 47: Richard Goodwin, "Letter from Peru," The New Yorker (May 17, 1969), p. 60.

10. Goodwin, ibid.
11. Luigi Einaudi, Peruvian Military Relations with the United States, (Santa Monica, Calif.: The Rand Corporation, 1970), pp. 33-36.
12. For the text of President Belaúnde's remarks on the subject see: Augusto Zimmermann Zavala, La Historia Secreta del Petróleo (Lima: Editorial Gráfica Labor, 1968), pp. 183-184.
13. Andrés Townsend Ezcurra, Respuesta a un Discurso Presidencial (Lima: Ediciones Pueblo, 1966), p. 8.
14. The La Brea y Pariñas Controversy, p. 16; U.S., Department of State, Annual Petroleum Report—1966—Peru, U.S. Department of State Document No. A-639 (Washington: U.S. Government Printing Office, 1966), p. 6.
15. The La Brea y Pariñas Controversy, Vol. I., p. 17.
16. "En sesion permanente se declaró Comisión de la Brea de la Cámara Baja," El Comercio, June 21, 1967, p. 1.
17. "Expropiar Brea y Pariñas se discute en diputados—Hay dos proyectos en Mesa: de la Coalición y de la D.C.," El Comercio, June 24, 1967, p. 1.
18. "AP pide que la EPF explote La Brea y Pariñas," El Comercio, June 24, 1967, p. 1.
19. The entire text of Law No. 16674 appears in The La Brea y Pariñas Controversy, Vol. I, Exhibit 13.
20. Ibid., Exhibit 16.
21. Ibid., Exhibit 17.
22. For example, see "Administrative Appeal filed against Law 16674 with Ministry of Development and Public Works, August 1, 1967," Ibid, Exhibit 15.
23. Ibid., pp. 27-28; Exhibits 25 and 26.
24. Interview with Former President Fernando Belaúnde Terry, Chevy Chase, Maryland, May 21, 1971.
25. The La Brea y Pariñas Controversy, Vol. I., Exhibit 30.
26. Ibid., pp. 29-30.
27. Ibid., pp. 32-33.
28. The La Brea y Pariñas Controversy, Vol. II (February 1969, International Petroleum Company), p. 1.
29. Goodwin, "Letter from Peru," p. 72.
30. Interview with Fernando Espinosa, Key Biscayne, Florida, May 28, 1971.
31. In 1941, Peru was at the brink of war with Ecuador. There were rumors that the Ecuadorian Air Force was about to bomb Peru. I.P.C.'s personnel knew better, for in their capacity as gasoline suppliers to the Ecuadorian air bases, they had noted that Ecuador's planes were grounded because of poor maintenance. At the height of this crisis, a Peruvian army captain arrived at Talara, endeavoring to commandeer motor vehicles to take his troops to the front. The

END OF I.P.C. AND DEMOCRATIC REFORM 147

I.P.C. manager in Talara refused to cooperate with the captain until he had had a chance to consult the authorities in Lima. Communications being what they were then, it took some 24 hours to secure an answer from the capital. After what must have seemed an interminable wait, the furious captain received the equipment he needed and proceeded to the front 24 hours behind schedule. The captain became a General— Juan Velasco Alvarado. Confidential source.

    32. "Reversión al Estado de los yacimientos de Brea y Pariñas pide E.P.F.," El Comercio, March 28, 1968, p. 1.

    33. "El Directorio de E.P.F. ha cumplido con su deber," El Comercio, March 28, 1968, p. 2.

    34. Photostatic copies of both the proposed resolution and the letter were shown to this researcher by Former President Belaúnde, who stated that he had never before released this information. Interview with Fernando Belaúnde Terry, Chevy Chase, Maryland, May 21, 1971.

    35. The La Brea y Pariñas Controversy, Vol. II, Exhibit 47.

    36. The La Brea y Pariñas Controversy, Vol. II, pp. 1-2.

    37. Ibid., p. 2.

    38. For almost an hour by hour account of the few days preceding the agreement of August 13 see: Zimmermann, Historia Secreta, pp. 11-19.

    39. "Impasse sobre La Brea y Pariñas—La IPC estariá pidiendo una concesion en la Selva. . ." El Comercio, August 12, 1968, p. 1.

    40. Ibid.; Goodwin, "Letters from Peru," pp. 80-82.

    41. Zimmermann, pp. 11-19; Richard Goodwin, pp. 80-82.

    42. For the text of the Act of Talara, see The La Brea y Pariñas Controversy, Vol. II, Exhibit 48.

    43. For a more detailed analysis of this contract mystery, see: Goodwin, "Letters from Peru," pp. 82-86.

    44. For the complete text of the letter, see: "'Por Falta de Coordinación' Renuncio Directorio de EPF," La Prensa, September 8, 1968, p. 8.

    45. "Grave denuncia de Loret de Mola—Contrato firmado el 13 de Agosto fue alterado y le falta und pagina," El Comercio, September 11, 1968, p. 1; "Loret de Mola Denunció quo no Aparece una Pagina del Contrato con la IPC," La Prensa, September 11, 1968, p. 1.

    46. "'Historia Secreta del Petróleo" reunión ayer a Seoane y Cornejo," El Comercio, September 7, 1968, p. 3.

    47. The La Brea y Pariñas Controversy, Vol. II, Exhibit 50.

    48. "Townsend Dice Actual Gabinete Actua con Acierto y Mesura," La Prensa, August 4, 1968, p. 2.

    49. "PDC Critica los Impuestos; El Apra Defiende al Ejecutivo," La Prensa, August 30, 1968, p. 1.

50. "Suspended 2 Dias a Diputado Villaran Por Decir 'Deshonesto' al Gobierno," La Prensa, September 1, 1968, p. 1.

51. "Alianza con A.P. o el P.S.D. Negó Villanueva por T.V.," La Prensa, September 2, 1968, p. 2.

52. "Miró Luesada Cesó en Cargo," La Prensa, September 1, 1968, p. 2.

53. "Exposición del Embajador del Peru en Italia," El Comercio, August 15, 1968, p. 1; "La Recuperación de La Brea y Pariñas," El Comercio, August 15, 1968, p. 2.

54. "El Ejército emite opinión sobre La Brea y Pariñas," El Comercio, September 13, 1968, p, 1.

55. "Solo el Ejército ha opinado hasta ahora sobre La Brea," La Prensa, September 16, 1968, p. 1.

56. See El Comercio and La Prensa, September 17-19, 1968; The La Brea y Pariñas Controversy, Vol. II, pp. 13-16.

57. "Dura crítica de Seoane a Ministros Populistas," La Prensa, September 21, 1968, p. 1.

58. "Belaúnde destituyó a Seoane," La Prensa, September 21, 1968, p. 1.

59. "Seoanistas Sitiaron Local AP; Policía Golpeó a Diputado." La Prensa, September 25, 1968, p. 1.

60. "No Votarán Moción de Censura; Incidente Frustró la Sesión," La Prensa, September 27, 1968, p. 1.

61. "La FA no Tomará actitud de Fuerza declaró ayer el Ministro Gagliardi," La Prensa, September 21, 1968, p. 1; "General Velasco dijo que la FA ne depende de un Ministro, Desautorizo a Gagliardi," La Prensa, September 22, 1968, p. 1.

62. "Villanueva autorizó Ayer a los Apristas a combatir si hay un Golpe de Estado," La Prensa, September 22, 1968, p. 1.

63. The La Brea y Pariñas Controversy, Vol. II, pp. 17-18.

64. Ibid., p. 30.

CHAPTER

8

CONCLUSIONS

In taking over the assets of International Petroleum Company in Peru the military junta headed by General Juan Velasco Alvarado argued that I.P.C.'s was a "unique" case—the company existed under historical circumstances unlike those facing any other company in Peru.[1] This argument did not originate with the junta, however. It was part of El Comercio's policy for years to report favorably on the activities of other U.S. companies, including oil companies, while attacking I.P.C. This vehement anti-I.P.C. policy was echoed in official circles and eventually suceeded in isolating I.P.C. from other American enterprises in Peru, who came to view the company as a potential spoiler of their good standing in the host country.[2]

But the anti-I.P.C. argument had more than tactical value as a means of dividing potential opponents. It had logical validity. Asked why he disliked I.P.C., an unidentified Peruvian general with the present government responded: "They bribed ministers, corrupted governments, and promoted revolutions."[3] Evidence pointed to the truth of this charge, at least during the period covered in the available Department of State diplomatic correspondence between the U.S. Government and the American Embassy in Lima up to 1939. As Richard Goodwin stated, however, "it takes two to make a bribe, and you cannot corrupt the incorruptible."[4] Nevertheless, the generals who carried out the coup and subsequent seizure of La Brea y Pariñas in 1968 were aware of I.P.C.'s historic role in Peruvian politics—as the rescuer of doomed incompetent Cabinet officials, as the underwriter of any government which promised no interference with the company, and as the promoter of international intrigues designed to bend the will of Peru's public officials. Luigi Einaudi suggested that during the 1960s Peruvian military intelligence began electronic surveillance of I.P.C.'s telephone communications, and they disliked their discovery of the company's financial largesse towards nearly every major political party.[5] I.P.C. was well aware that their telephones were being bugged, but they denied making contributions to Peruvian political parties during the 1960s.

Simple nationalistic pride, wounded by an awareness of the historic political role of I.P.C., did not entirely explain the decision by the military to expropriate I.P.C.'s assets. For years Peru's military trained itself through the Center for Higher Military Studies (CAEM) to formulate and carry out developmental plans for Peru. In 1962, they made a brief attempt at social planning but then decided to give civilian leadership a final chance. When President Belaúnde's program did not progress as quickly as they had envisioned, the generals once more became restless to carry out reforms. Many developments in 1968 prompted the military to take over the government. The "page eleven" scandal weakened the already feeble Belaúnde government. The possibility of a Civilista-type coalition including APRA and the Belaúndistas would have provided a formidable counterbalance to the military's influence in Peruvian political life, a state of affairs not seen since the 19th century. The possibility of such a bloc, or "frente único" as La Prensa called it, had to be aborted at the earliest possible moment if the CAEM plans were ever to become operable.

Whatever the motive for the coup itself, the reason for the seizure was clearly one of immediate political expediency. For years the Peruvian leftists such as the Social Progressists and the members of the Front for the Defense of Petroleum, and some conservatives, notably the Miró Quesada family and some Odriistas, had sold the Peruvian people on the importance of nationalizing I.P.C.'s La Brea y Pariñas. For almost ten years the Peruvian radical left and El Comercio built up a political savings account payable only to the person, group, or political party which nationalized La Brea y Pariñas. That gigantic pay check of national political goodwill awaited the "vindicator" of the property. Naturally, I.P.C.'s staunch enemies hoped to be a party to that final payment. But International Petroleum Company, knowing that someone would benefit tremendously by the nationalization of La Brea y Pariñas, decided that so long as the benefit would be at the company's expense, I.P.C. should have the power to determine the beneficiary. That was why I.P.C. yielded to Belaúnde on July 25, 1968, for the company knew that by then the question was not whether the property would be nationalized, but rather, by whom. In an effort to save what was in fact its least antagonistic political opponents, I.P.C. attempted to make President Belaúnde and APRA the political beneficiaries of the long awaited "vindication."

CONCLUSIONS 151

It was precisely because I.P.C. jumped the gun on its would-be executors that El Comercio and the radical left reacted with anger and frustration when the achievement of their goal was finally announced by President Belaúnde on July 28, 1968. Had they not been clamoring for the "vindication" of La Brea y Pariñas? The answer of course was yes, but by then, Fernando Belaúnde and the APRA leadership in Congress that gave him the authority to reach the agreement, would have become the recipients of a huge payoff of political goodwill. It was after all Fernando Belaúnde and the Aprista leaders of the Senate and the Chamber of Deputies who travelled to Talara to officiate in the actual ceremony of "vindication." How could the arch enemies of APRA sit by and see that party share in the glory of the Acta de Talara at the expense of the radical anti-I.P.C. leaders who had fought the company for a seemingly interminable ten years?

What a relief to the radical left and to El Comercio when the scandal over "page eleven" developed! Assuming that the page did exist and that Carlos Loret de Mola did write in a minimum price for the oil I.P.C. would purchase from E.P.F., the provision was relatively insignificant compared to the magnitude of the agreement reached. In fact, the minimum-price provision might have been irrelevant, since I.P.C.'s utility service charges might not have reduced its oil payments below that minimum price. In any case, there was a clause in the contract whereby Empresa Petrolera Fiscal could stop sales in two years if the price was not agreeable. Furthermore, the price of I.P.C.'s services to E.P.F. had to be negotiated in the future, and I.P.C. certainly would not have been free to manipulate the price of petroleum in such a way as to cause E.P.F. to lose money in La Brea y Pariñas. But these considerations were ignored. To Peruvians, what mattered was that I.P.C. allegedly conspired to defraud their country, an accusation which found a sympathetic hearing from people long conditioned to viewing I.P.C. in the worst possible light. During the month of September, the campaign of innuendos tagged responsibility for the scandal on the Cabinet. Although President Belaúnde tried to rid himself of the suspected Cabinet, his own political head came rolling down.

International Petroleum's last gamble, foiled by the military coup, would have been a masterful move had it taken place before— even as late as 1967, but preferably in 1964-65. The company could have given President Belaúnde a substantial boost that in turn might have generated American aid funds and success in many of his programs. But I.P.C. did not, perhaps could not, bring itself to yield earlier than July 1968. By that time, it was already too late; not even the devolution of La Brea y Pariñas could stop the impending coup. In fact, the company's acquiescence precipitated the coup by providing a "now or never" situation which the generals could not overlook. They had to sieze power before Belaúnde rallied political support for the agreement.

In spite of the fact that President Belaúnde reaped the consequences of the forceful overthrow of the Peruvian government, and to this day appears to be the only significant Peruvian political figure living in exile by order of the junta, the military coup had a greater effect on APRA than on the Belaúndistas. For instance, the junta has given top priority to the agrarian reform program for the large sugar plantations of Trujillo and Chiclayo, traditional strongholds of Aprista unionism. Its purpose is said to be "that of weakening the agricultural union of the northern seaboard. . . ."[6]

Since a coup designed to keep APRA out of power could hardly be justified, the seizure of I.P.C.'s La Brea y Pariñas, the Talara complex, and later on the company's remaining assets, became the legitimizing element. The junta was forced to go beyond a mere seizure of La Brea y Pariñas because, after all, Belaúnde had already arranged for its transfer to the state. Assisted by the same radicals who had led the anti-I.P.C. campaign in the early 1960s, the military junta charged the company with a tax claim so large (over $690 million) that I.P.C.'s assets in Peru could never match the alleged debt. By sparing most other American investments, and compensating the few that were also nationalized, such as International Telephone and Telegraph, the junta insured the further isolation of I.P.C. from the native Peruvian and American business communities.

By following a limited confiscation, the junta managed to reap bountiful support from the left, while maintaining the neutrality of and even securing support from the right. Alberto Ruíz Eldredge, one of the radical champions in the anti-I.P.C. offensive and leader of the Social Progressists, actively participated in the shaping of the junta's postcoup petroleum policy. He later wrote a pamphlet lavishing praise on General Velasco Alvarado and designated October 9 as "The Day of National Dignity."[7] The Soviet weekly <u>New Times</u> began to carry highly favorable articles written by Peruvians—hailing the new Peruvian anti-imperialist policy.[8] Evidence of the junta's support from the right of the Peruvian political spectrum was more difficult to find, but according to Richard Goodwin:

> Velasco has found support among the conservative banking and commercial families, who see his accession as a way to increase their wealth and have encouraged him to place new restrictions on their foreign banking competitors.[9]

Support from traditional conservatives in Peru is difficult to gauge, since the newspapers that in the past articulated these interests,

CONCLUSIONS

particularly La Prensa, have operated under less than complete freedom since the coup.

Perhaps the most frustrated of all Peruvian groups involved in the I.P.C. controversy was the Miró Quesada family. The junta forced El Comercio to accept and deal with a union, that has the statuatory right to space in the editorial page of the paper to answer or refute editorials with which it disagrees. The proud Don Luis Miró Quesada has been forced to print material which is uncomplimentary to his own family. The threat of union-sponsored editorials and the possibility of a government shut-down of El Comercio and all other newspapers has deprived the Miró Quesadas of their power to make and unmake Peruvian governments.

Clearly, Don Luis Miró Quesada did not foresee that his anti-I.P.C. campaign would have the effects it had. He hoped that with the creation of a powerful state petroleum monopoly the power of the government would increase, and since El Comercio's power is but a function of its ability to influence, veto, or promote government policy, he believed that his paper's power would grow accordingly. Peruvian chief of state Juan Velasco Alvarado appears to be unwilling to allow the Miró Quesadas or Pedro Beltrán to hold the enormous power they held during the Prado and Belaúnde administrations.

Not satisfied with being the managers who act out the directives of a board composed of prominent Peruvians issuing their memoranda in the form of editorials and paid announcements in the Lima dailies, the generals have become the actual policy-makers of Peru. Unlike the junta of 1962-63, which set out to repress Communists because La Prensa said the country was in danger from them, the 1968 junta has repressed the news media. It is the generals who define Peru's enemies.

International Petroleum Company's former general manager Fernando Espinosa suggested that the La Brea y Pariñas controversy was encouraged by and kept alive with the blessings of the Peruvian oligarchy—a group which calculated that as long as a highly visible foreign company could be made the object of popular hatred, Peru's pressing socioeconomic problems would remain out of the political vortex.[10] If his assessment is correct, that strategy indeed did work for some time. The I.P.C. controversy, however, eventually developed into a catalyst for reform. Having billed themselves as radical reformers on the I.P.C. issue, the generals had to keep up the momentum by enacting programs which are dramatically eroding the oligarchy's power.

Beyond the immediate causes and effects of the 1968 coup and seizure of I.P.C.'s property lies the far more important lesson of that company's impact on Peru during its half century tenure. It was easy for Peruvians to become enraged over the foreign exploitation of their oilfields; as of 1966 it was estimated that the country's known petroleum reserves would last only fourteen more years.[11] To them, Standard Oil (New Jersey) and its subsidiary International Petroleum Company were nothing more than the thieves of their natural resources.

While a great deal of petroleum extracted from La Brea y Pariñas was exported, even larger amounts were used for domestic consumption at the lowest prices in the world. I.P.C. provided Peru with an efficient and virtually selfcontained petroleum industry which encompassed every phase of the business, from extraction of the crude oil to the final sale at the gas station pump. In 1968, Peru was able to seize the entire industry, knowing that it would not have to depend on a refinery or an oilfield located outside the country.

I.P.C. provided training and technical education for the thousands of Peruvians who worked in the various phases of their company's operation. When the government expropriated I.P.C., it also took over its Peruvian work force, an asset of greater value than the wells, tubes, and buildings that would have been useless without it. I.P.C. probably gave more technical and managerial training to Peruvians than the Peace Corps could ever hope to give. By raising the living standards of its work force in Talara, the company showed both the Peruvian elite and the Peruvian working-class that poor housing, inadequate health services, and lack of educational opportunities were not necessary conditions of a worker's lot. How great an impact this example had on the expectation level of Peruvian workers has not been measured, but given the enormous amount of publicity which I.P.C. handed out about its work force, chances are that the impact was very significant.

International Petroleum Company's influence was not limited to employers and employees. It extended into nearly every intellectual endeavor of the Peruvian nation. In its quest for legitimization, I.P.C. supported and encouraged nationalistic art and literature. The company provided a vehicle, <u>FANAL</u>, for Peruvians' best literary efforts. Through open essay competitions, I.P.C. encouraged an interest in Peruvian history and national heroes. Yet, not even these contributions to Peruvian arts and letters could undo the accumulated hatred and suspicion with which two generations of Peruvians had come to view I.P.C.

If anything, the company's efforts as a benefactor of Peruvian intellectual and cultural pursuits reinforced the conviction among Peru's leaders that I.P.C. had something to hide, some burden of guilt which drove it to give part of its ill-acquired profits to the victim of its "fradulent" dealings. While most of Peru's leaders were not well informed of the facts of I.P.C.'s history in Peru, they automatically chose to believe the worst. Ironically, most of the actual rumors circulated among Peruvians concerning I.P.C. were not factual. For example, the company was charged with using double-bottomed ships to carry twice as much oil as it declared, with "inventing" the Laudo of 1922 and the Swiss judge who presided over its formulation. In all such cases, the charges against I.P.C. were false. The company's actual machinations in Peru went unnoticed by its detractors. During the last days of José Pardo's Civilista government, I.P.C. withdrew ships to force the Peruvian Congress to yield to the company demands; yet, Peruvians remain unaware of this interference. The fact that the company helped finance the administration of Luis Sanchez Cerro during the early 1930s was also ignored. Ironically, I.P.C. has been convicted in the minds of most Peruvians of crimes the company never committed, while its actual transgressions remain unpublicized.

Small countries such as Peru have great difficulty trusting a multinational corporation dedicated to its own enrichment. Even when International Petroleum Company was willing to negotiate factually with the government, the Peruvian officials distrusted I.P.C.'s management on every point. The dispute over the 1968 contract and the Act of Talara was a result of the fact that the president of Empresa Petrolera Fiscal, Carlos Loret de Mola, wanted to cover every possible contingency. He assumed that I.P.C. would maneuver with whatever loopholes existed to deprive E.P.F. of its just share of the proceeds from the nationalized La Brea y Pariñas. In a sense, what E.P.F. management feared was the superior expertise of I.P.C.'s personnel—a fear not reduced by the knowledge that E.P.F. had the whole weight of the Peruvian government behind it in the negotiations.

Fernando Espinosa, I.P.C.'s General Manager during the 1960s, recalled that whenever he attempted to have Peruvian political leaders examine contract proposals or any other documents connected with the controversy, they declined such an examination and requested an oral explanation, since the details would be far too bothersome.[12] The fact was that the Peruvian government did not have the expertise necessary to deal with an organization as sophisticated as I.P.C. Whatever Peruvian talent existed was probably under hire to I.P.C. and other foreign companies. Deprived of expert advice, the government was unable to gauge accurately the reasonableness of I.P.C.'s or even its own proposals. When agreement seemed near in 1964, President Belaúnde backed away because he sincerely believed that he would be granting too much to the company. In his view, I.P.C. was attempting to operate under a promotional petroleum law—one highly favorable to oil companies which were initiating their business operations.[13] However, Belaúnde determined his action on the basis of a "gut feeling" that the deal was too favorable to the company. He did not really know and could not know if such was really the case because his only source of information was I.P.C., an obviously interested party. His uninformed advisors lacked the technical knowledge to determine with accuracy how much the Peruvian government was yielding. In the end, the very fact that the company favored the agreement seemed to suggest that there was something rotten lurking in the intricate fine print of the incomprehensible proposal. This is not to say that the Peruvian political leadership was incompetent. On the contrary, Peru had many highly educated and intelligent leaders, with Fernando Belaúnde Terry in the forefront. Peru also had an abundance of legal scholars. What Peru lacked was technical expertise of the business and industrial variety, the kind of knowledge necessary to determine whether or not, for instance, the price of a barrel of oil was fair—taking into consideration the costs of production, transportation, storage, processing, etc.

Peruvians knew that the large multinational oil concerns set up machinery to fix prices in the international market, and that the big oil corporations got together in 1928 and signed the Ashnacarry Convention by which they all agreed to set a world price of oil based on the Texas Gulf Coast rate. But Ashnacarry and oil's "seven sisters" were well out of Peru's jurisdiction. The effects of such complex agreements on the daily life of a small country like Peru remained an enigma to its leaders.[14]

The U.S. Government has the power and resources necessary to expose the full consequences of whatever the "seven sisters" agree to. While consumer advocates have argued that the U.S. Government does not exercise this power enough, one has only to look through Congressional records to find that under subpoena, the American oil companies have been forced to reveal some of their secrets. But the government of Peru has no such powers. In the last analysis, Peru seized I.P.C. records in the Lima offices, but the company records in Coral Gables and elsewhere would never fall into the hands of a Peruvian official.

The ability to operate across international borders and outside the complete jurisdiction of any one government except the "home" country allows the multinational corporation to function as a state within other states. Governments are supposed to command the supreme allegiance of their citizens, yet Peru's largest taxpayer, International Petroleum Company, owed its allegiance to a foreign corporation. General Marco Fernandez Baca, current chief of E.P.F., grasped this problem when he declared:

> No people can live in dignity and with respect for its sovereignty . . . when it tolerates the insolent arrogance of another state within its own frontiers.[15]

One need not accept the value judgment contained in the statement to see that I.P.C. was indeed responsible not to Peru, but to its parent company and to its stockholders.

Because the operation of I.P.C. was primarily the extraction and export of oil, during its early years the company was safe in the assurance that without its ships and its marketing facilities throughout the world, Peru could not export its oil. As the company became primarily a supplier of domestic needs, however, its strategic position weakened. Peru ceased to be a net exporter and became a net importer of oil in 1962. From that point on, I.P.C.'s position was extremely precarious. It was to the credit of its very capable management that the company survived as long as it did.

International Petroleum Company contributed to the development and national consciousness of Peru. It provided a common enemy against which Peruvians who might otherwise have had nothing in common united to fight on behalf of their nation. Unwittingly, I.P.C. bestowed on Peru a modern petroleum industry, a competent work force, and a national unity that has brought together the most unlikely alliance of intellectuals, technicians, soldiers, and middle-class elements ever to grace that country.

NOTES

1. Peru, Petróleos del Peru, Departamento de Relaciones Públicas, El Petróleo en el Peru: Historia de un Caso Singular para que el Mundo lo Juzgue. (Lima: Petróleos del Peru, 1969).

2. Both President Belaúnde and General Manager Fernando Espinosa agreed on this assessment. Interview with Fernando Belaúnde Terry, Chevy Chase, Maryland, May 21, 1971; Interview with Fernando Espinosa, Key Biscayne, Florida, May 28, 1971.

3. Richard Goodwin, "Letter from Peru," The New Yorker (May 17, 1969), p. 54.

4. Ibid.

5. Conversation with Luigi Einaudi at the 67th Annual Meeting of the American Political Science Association, Chicago, Illinois, September 7, 1971.

6. Marcel Niedergang, "Revolutionary Nationalism in Peru," Foreign Affairs, 49, No. 3 (April, 1971), pp. 459-460.

7. Alberto Ruíz Eldredge, El Diá de la Dignidad Nacional (Lima: Ministerio de Transportes y Comunicaciones, 1971).

8. Gustavo Valcarcel, "Peruvian Paradoxes," New Times (Moscow), No. 2 (January 13, 1969), pp. 20-22.

9. Goodwin, "Letters from Peru," p. 100.

10. Interview with Fernando Espinosa, Key Biscayne, Florida May 28, 1971.

11. U.S., Department of Commerce, Bureau of International Commerce, Overseas Business Reports: Basic Data on the Economy of Peru, prepared by Bruce B. Sever (Washington: U.S. Government Printing Office, 1969).

12. Interview with Fernando Espinosa, Key Biscayne, Florida, May 28, 1971.

13. Interview with Fernando Belaúnde Terry, Chevy Chase, Maryland, May 21, 1971.

14. For a Peruvian view of the "seven sisters" and their agreement see Cesar Levano, "Por la nacionalización del Petróleo," Tareas del Pensamiento Peruano, I, No. 3 (May-June, 1960), pp. 55-83.

15. General Marco Fernandez Baca, as quoted by Goodwin, "Letters from Peru," p. 48.

BIBLIOGRAPHY

BASIC SOURCES—PUBLIC DOCUMENTS

Government of Peru. La Cuestión "Brea y Pariñas," Discursos Parlimentarios. Lima: Imprenta del Estado, 1917.

Peru, Cámara de Diputados. Diario de los Debates, Tomo I, Legislatura Ordinaria de 1960. Lima: Publicación Oficial, 1960.

Peru, Dirección General de Información del Peru. Petróleo. Lima: n.p., 1965.

Peru, Dirección de Petróleos. Estado del Padrón General de Petróleo.

Peru, Ministerio de Fomento y Obras Publicas Dirección de Petróleo. Boletín del Registro de las Concesiones Petroleras, Número 1, Leyes 11780 y 12376. Lima: Imprenta Torres Aquirre S.A., 1956.

Peru, Petróleos del Peru, Departmento de Relaciones Públicas. El Petróleo en el Peru: Historia de un Caso Singular para que el Mundo lo Juzgue. Lima: Petroleos del Peru, 1969.

Peru, Petróleos del Peru, Department of Public Relations. Petroleum in Peru: History of a Unique Case for the World to Judge (Lima: Petróleos del Peru, 1967).

U.S. Department of Commerce, Bureau of Foreign and Domestic Commerce. Peru—A Commercial and Industrial Handbook. Trade Promotion Series No. 25 (Washington: U.S. Government Printing Office, 1925).

U.S. Department of Commerce, Bureau of International Commerce. Foreign Economic Trends, Peru. Document No. ET-71-030. March, 1971.

U.S. Department of Commerce, Bureau of International Commerce. Overseas Business Reports: Basic Data on the Economy of Peru, prepared by Bruce B. Sever. Washington: U.S. Government Printing Office, 1969.

U.S. Department of State. <u>Annual Petroleum Report—1961—Peru</u>.
U.S. Department of State Document No. 551.

U.S. Department of State. <u>Annual Petroleum Report—1962—Peru</u>.
U.S. Department of State Document No. A-718.

U.S. Department of State. <u>Annual Petroleum Report—1963—Peru</u>.
U.S. Department of State Document No. A-784.

U.S. Department of State. <u>Annual Petroleum Report—1964—Peru</u>.
U.S. Department of State Document No. A-664.

U.S. Department of State. <u>Annual Petroleum Report—1966—Peru</u>.
U.S. Department of State Document No. A-639.

U.S. Department of State. <u>Annual Petroleum Report—1967—Peru</u>.
U.S. Department of State Document No. A-592.

U.S. Department of State. <u>Annual Petroleum Report—1968—Peru</u>.
U.S. Department of State Document No. 249.

U.S. Department of State. <u>Supplement to Annual Petroleum Report—1962—Peru</u>. U.S. Department of State Document No. A-717.

U.S. House of Representatives, Committee on Foreign Affairs, Subcommittee on Inter-American Affairs. <u>New Directions for the 1970's: Toward a Strategy of Inter-American Development</u>. 91st Cong., 1st Sess., 1969.

U.S. House of Representatives, Committee on Foreign Affairs, Subcommittee of National Security Policy and Scientific Developments. <u>Reports of the Special Study Mission to Latin America on Military Assistance Training and Developmental Television</u>. 91st Cong., 2nd Sess., 1970.

U.S. Senate, Committee of the Judiciary and Committee on Insular Affairs. <u>Emergency Oil Lift Program and Related Oil Problems</u>. 85th Cong., 1st Sess., 1957.

U.S. Senate, Committee on Foreign Relations, Subcommittee on Western Hemisphere Affairs. <u>United States Military Policies and Programs in Latin America</u>. 91st Cong., 1st Sess., 1969.

U.S. Senate, Committee on Foreign Relations, Subcommittee on Western Hemisphere Affairs. <u>United States Relations with Peru</u>. 91st Cong., 1st Sess., 1969.

SELECTED BIBLIOGRAPHY   161

U.S. Senate, Special Committee Investigating Petroleum Resources. American Petroleum Interests in Foreign Countries. 79th Cong., 1st Sess., 1945.

U.S. Senate, Committee on Foreign Relations, Subcommittee on Western Hemisphere Affairs. Hearings with Under Secretary of State for Western Hemisphere Affairs. 91st Cong., 2nd Sess., 1970.

U.S. Federal Trade Commission. The International Petroleum Cartel. Washington: U.S. Government Printing Office, 1952.

BASIC SOURCES—
PUBLISHED BOOKS, PAMPHLETS, AND REPORTS

Banco Central de Reserva del Peru. Plan Nacional de Desarrollo Ecónomico y Social del Peru, 1962-1971. Lima: Banco Central, 1961.

Banco Central de Reserva del Peru. Cuentas Nacionales del Peru, 1950-1965. Lima: Banco Central, 1966.

Barros, Oscar C. Discursos Parlamentarios: Asunto Brea y Pariñas. 2nd Ed. Lima: Imprenta Minerva, 1960.

Belaúnde Terry, Fernando. Peru's Own Conquest. Lima: American Studies Press, S.A., 1965.

Benavides Correa, Alfonso. Oro Negro del Peru—La Brea y Pariñas: Problema para la I.P.C. y Solución para el Peru. Lima: El Escritorio, S.A., 1963.

_____. El Petróleo Peruano . . . ó "La Autopsia de un Clan. Lima: Papel Gráfica Editora, 1961.

El Caso de la I.P.C.: Historia de una Incomprensión. Lima: International Petroleum Company, Ltd., 1969.

Deustua, Ricardo A. El Petróleo en el Peru. Lima: Imprenta Americana, 1921.

Elejalde Vargas, Eduardo, et. al. La Brea y Pariñas—Examen Jurídico de los Proyectos de Ley Presentados en el Parlamento.

Lima: International Petroleum Company, "Noticias de Petróleo," 1963.

Frente Nacional de Defensa del Petróleo. Declaración de Principios y Exposición de Motivos. Lima: Technograf, S.A., 1960.

Heysen, Luis E. El ABC de la Peruanización. Lima: Editorial APRA, 1931.

Historia de la Standard Oil Company (N.J.). Lima: International Petroleum Company, 1949.

Historia de La Brea y Pariñas: Artículos y Documentos Publicados en 1916 por la London & Pacific Petroleum Company, Ltd. Lima: International Petroleum Company, 1960.

Historical Resumé of "La Brea y Pariñas." International Petroleum Company, August, 1967.

The La Brea y Pariñas Controversy, 3 Vols. International Petroleum Company, February, 1969.

Lauri Solis, Luis. La Diplomacia del Petróleo y el Caso de "La Brea y Pariñas." Lima: Universidad Nacional de Ingeniería, Departmento de Publicaciones, 1967.

Macedo Mendoza, José. ¡Nacionalicemos el Petróleo! Lima: Ediciones Hora del Hombre, 1960.

Osores, Arturo, el al. La Brea y Pariñas: Discursos ante el Senado, (Legislatura Extraordinaria de 1917) y Dictámenes Jurídicos. Lima: International Petroleum Company, "Noticias de Petróleo," 1963.

Petróleo: Aspectos de su Industrialización en el Peru y en el Mundo. Lima: International Petroleum Company, 1954.

Ramirez Novoa, Ezequiel. Recuperación de la Brea y Pariñas: Soberanía Nacional y Desarrollo Economico. Lima: Ediciones "28 de Julio." 1964.

Ruíz Eldredge, Alberto. El Día de la Dignidad Nacional. Lima: Ministerio de Transportes y Comunicaciones, 1971.

Seoane, Manuel Alejandro. Crédito Externo y Justicia Social-Un Discurso Polémico. Lima: Editorial Atahualpa, 1946.

_____. La Revolución que el Peru Necesita. Arequipa, Peru: Gráfico J. Quiroz, S.A., 1965.

Sociedad Nacional de Minería y Petróleo. Boletín. Lima: n.p., 1955.

Standard Oil Company (New Jersey). 1969 Annual Report. New York: n.p., 1970.

Townsend Ezcurra, Andrés. Pan y Libertad; Ensayos y Discursos Entorno al APRA. Lima: Ediciones Pueblo, 1968.

_____. Respuesta a un Discurso Presidencial (Pronunciado por Fernando Belaúnde Terry). Lima: Ediciones Pueblo, 1966.

Ugarte Elespuru, Juan Manuel. Lima y lo Limeño. Lima: Editorial Universitaria, 1966.

Zimmermann Zavala, Augusto. La Historia Secreta del Petróleo. Lima: Editorial Gráfica Labor, 1968.

BASIC SOURCES—ARTICLES AND PERIODICALS

El Comercio (Lima). 1946-1948; 1955-1969.

FANAL (International Petroleum Company, Lima), 1953-1969.

La Prensa (Lima). 1957-1969.

Noticias de Petróleo (International Petroleum Company, Lima). 1958-1963.

BASIC SOURCES—PERSONAL INTERVIEWS

Confidential Interviews with an International Petroleum Company Executive. May 23-28, 1971, Coral Gables, Florida.

Interview with Fernando Belaúnde Terry, President of Peru 1963-1968. May 21, 1971. Chevy Chase, Maryland.

Interview with Fernando Belaúnde Terry. January 27, 1972, Cincinnati, Ohio.

Interview with Fernando Espinosa, General Manager of International Petroleum Company in Peru, 1963-1969. May 28, 1971. Key Biscayne, Florida.

Interviews with John Oldfield, Director, Esso Inter-America, Inc. May 23-28, 1971. Coral Gables, Florida.

Interview with Philip Gillette, May 18, 1971. Washington, D.C.

BASIC SOURCES—ARCHIVES

Decimal Files, United States Department of State, Washington, D.C.

SECONDARY SOURCES—

PUBLISHED BOOKS, PAMPHLETS AND REPORTS

Astiz, Carlos A. *Pressure Groups and Power Elites in Peruvian Politics.* Ithaca: Cornell University Press, 1969.

Bellani Nezeri, Rodolfo. *Faustino G. Piaggio, Creador de la Industria Petrolera Peruana.* Lima: La Inmediata, 1949.

Bourricaud, François. *Power and Society in Contemporary Peru.* Translated by Paul Stevenson. New York: Praeger, 1970.

Carey, James C. *Peru and the United States, 1900-1962.* Notre Dame, Ind.: University of Notre Dame Press, 1964.

Ceresole, Norberto. *Peru: Una Revolución Nacionalista.* Buenos Aires: Ediciones Sudestada, 1969.

Delgado, Luis Humberto. *Drama del Peru.* Lima: Ariel, 1963.

_____. *Historia de Antonio Miró Quesada 1875-1935*, 3 Vols. Lima; American Express, Ltd., 1938.

Einaudi, Luigi R. *Peruvian Military Relations with the United States.* Santa Monica, Calif.: Rand Corporation, 1970.

_____. *Revolution from Within? Military Rule in Peru since 1968.* Santa Monica, Calif.: Rand Corporation, 1971.

SELECTED BIBLIOGRAPHY 165

Fanning, Leonard M. Foreign Oil and the Free World. New York: McGraw Hill, 1954.

Fuentes Alvarez, Enrique. La Realidad Política del Pueblo Peruano; Neonacionalismo de los Pueblos Oprimidos. Lima: Talleres Gráficos de Linotipo "Los Rotarios," 1968.

Gerassi, John. The Great Fear in Latin America. London: Collier MacMillan, Ltd., 1965.

Hannifin, Reick B. Expropriation by Peru of the International Petroleum Company: A Background Study of the Legal Issues, Political Considerations, and Possible Consequences of the Controversy. Legislative Reference Service, Library of Congress, No. F-360. April 15, 1969 (Addenda, March 26, 1969).

Horowitz, Irving Louis (ed.). Masses in Latin America. New York: Oxford University Press, 1970.

Kantor, Harry. The Ideology and Program of the Peruvian Aprista Movement. New York: Octagon Books, 1966.

_____, ed. Patterns of Politics and Political Systems in Latin America. Chicago: Rand McNally, 1969.

Kilty, Daniel R. Planning for Development in Peru. (Praeger Special Studies in International Economics and Development). New York: Praeger, 1967.

Larson, Magali Sarfatti and Arlene Eisen Bergman. Social Stratification in Peru. Berkeley, Calif.: Institute of International Studies, University of California Press, 1969.

Manual del Elector. Lima: J. Mejía Baca, 1962.

Marett, Sir Robert. Peru. New York: Praeger, 1969.

Mariategui, José Carlos. Obras Completas de José Mariategui. Lima: Empresa Editora Amauta, 1967.

Martin Saunders, Cesar. Dichos y Hechos de la Política Peruana: Una Descripcion Auténtica, Sobria y Condensada de los Procesos Electorales y las dos Juntas Militares. Lima: Tipografía Santa Rosa, 1963.

Martinez, S. Ideario y Plan de Gobierno de los Partidos Políticos. Lima: n.p., 1962.

Martinez de la Torre, Ricardo. Apuntes para una Interpretación Marxista de Historia Social del Peru. 2nd. ed. Lima: Empresa Editora Peruana, 1947.

Miró Quesada de la Guerra, Luis. Albores de la Reforma Social en el Peru. Lima: Talleres Gráficos P. L. Villaneuva, 1965.

Miró Quesada Cantuarias, Francisco. Las Estructuras Sociales. Lima: Tipografía Santa Rosa, 1961.

──────. La Otra Mitad del Mundo, 2 vols. Lima: Tipografía Santa Rosa, 1959.

Miró Quesada Laos, Carlos. Intorno Agli Scritti e Discorsi di Mussolini. Milano: Fratelli Treves Editori, 1937.

──────. Lo que he Visto en Europa. Lima: Imprenta Torres Aguirre, 1940.

──────. Radiografía de la Politica Peruana. 2nd. ed. Lima: Ediciones "Paginas Peruanas," 1959.

North, Liisa. Civil-Military Relations in Argentina, Chile, and Peru. Berkeley, Calif.: Institute of International Studies, University of California Press, 1966.

O'Connor, Harvey. World Crisis in Oil. New York: Monthly Review Press, 1962.

Partido Comunista Peruano, Congreso Nacional. Resoluciones del Partido Comunista del Peru. Lima: n. p., 1964.

Payne, Arnold. The Peruvian Coup D'Etat of 1962: The Overthrow of Manuel Prado. Washington: Institute for the Comparative Study of Political Systems, 1968.

Payne, James L. Labor and Politics in Peru. New Haven: Yale University Press, 1965.

Penrose, Edith T. The Large International Firm in Developing Countries: The International Petroleum Industry. Cambridge, Mass.: Massachusetts Institute of Technology Press, 1968.

SELECTED BIBLIOGRAPHY

Peterson, Harries Clichy and Tomas Unger. Petróleo: Hora Cero. Lima: n.p., 1964.

Petras, James. Political and Social Structure in Latin America. New York: Monthly Review Press, 1970.

Pike, Fredrick B. The Modern History of Peru. New York: Praeger, 1967.

Ramirez Gaston, José M. Medio Siglo de la Política, Economica y Financiera del Peru, 1915-1964. Lima: La Confianza, 1964.

Ramirez y Berrios, M. Guillermo. Examen Expectral de las Elecciones del 9 de Junio de 1963. Lima: n.p., 1963.

Rippy, James Fred. British Investments in Latin America, 1822-1949: A Case Study in the Operations of Private Enterprise in Retarded Regions, 2nd. ed. Hamden, Conn.: Archon Books, 1966.

Roca Sanchez, Pedro Erasmo. El Nacionalismo Económico y la Justicia Social. Lima: Universidad Mayor de San Marcos, Facultad de Ciencias Económicas y Comerciales, 1961.

Salazar Larrain, Arturo. Las Estructuras Sociales de Francisco Miró Quesada: Gato por Liebre. Concepto Cientifico o Bandera Política? Lima: Empresa Gráfica T. Scheuch, S.A., 1961.

Stocking, George and Myron W. Watkins. Monopoly and Free Enterprise. New York: Greenwood Press, 1968.

Tungendhat, Christopher. Oil—The Biggest Business. London: Eyre and Spottiswoode, 1968.

Ugolotti Dansay, Humberto. Las Elecciones de 1963 y la Elección del 62. Lima: N.P., 1963.

Valencia Cardenas, José. El Problema del Petróleo en el Peru. Lima: Congreso Económico Nacional, 1946.

Vernon, Raymond. How Latin America Views the United States Investor. New York: 1960.

_____. Sovereignty at Bay. The Multinational Spread of U.S. Enterprises (New York: Basic Books, 1971).

Villanueva, Victor. El Militarismo en el Peru. Lima: Empresa Gráfica T. Scheuch, S.A., 1962.

Volski, Victor. America Latina: Petróleo e Independencia Buenos Aires: Cartago, 1966.

SECONDARY SOURCES—ARTICLES AND PERIODICALS

Bravo Bresani, Jorge. "Mito y Realidad de la Oligarquía Peruana," Revista de Sociología, III (1966), 43-71.

Bunker, Rod. "Linkages and the Foreign Policy of Peru, 1958-1966," Western Political Quarterly, XX (June, 1969), 280-297.

Chandler, Geoffrey. "Myth and Oil Power: International Groups and National Sovereignty," International Affairs, XLVI, No. 4 (October, 1970), 710-718.

Chaplin, David. "Peru's Postponed Revolution," World Politics, XX, No. 3 (April, 1968), 393-420.

Clear, Val. "Report from Lima," Fortune, LXXIX, No. 3 (March, 1969), 55-58.

Cobo, Juan. "The Peruvian Phenomenon," New Times (Moscow), No. 11 (March 17, 1970), 21-24.

Cotler, Julio. "Internal Domination and Social Change in Peru," Irving Louis Horowitz, ed. Masses in Latin America. New York: Oxford University Press, 1970. 407-444.

"La Década del 60—Del Colonialismo Liberal a la Revolución," Oiga (January, 1970), 20-23, 46-50.

DiTella, Torcuato S., "Populism and Reform in Latin America," Claudio Veliz, ed. Obstacles to Change in Latin America. New York: Oxford University Press, 1965.

Engelhof, Joseph. "Big Business in Future Seen for Multinational Firms," Chicago Tribune, August 2, 1971.

――――――. "Profit Necessary in Social Activity Too: Rockefeller," Chicago Tribune, October 4, 1971.

SELECTED BIBLIOGRAPHY

Espejo, Julio Augusto. "1968: Modernización o Revolución?" Oiga (April, 1971), 20-23, 50.

Furtado, Celso, "La Concentración del poder económico en Los EEUU, y sus proyecciones en América Latina," Estudios Internacionales, I, No. 3-4 (1968).

"Generals Pull Two Surprises," Economist, 229, No. 6529 (October 12, 1968), 22, 25.

Glade, William P. and John G. Udell. "Marketing Concept and Economic Development: Peru," Journal of Inter-American Studies, X, No. 4 (October, 1968), 533-546.

Gomez, Rosendo A. "Peru: The Politics of Military Guardianship," Martin Needler, ed. Political Systems of Latin America. 2nd. ed. New York: Van Nostrand Reinhold, 1970. 325-354.

Goodwin, Richard N. "Letter from Peru," The New Yorker (May 17, 1969), 41-109.

Grayson, George W., Jr. "Peru's Military Government," Current History, LVIII, No. 342 (February, 1970), 65-72, 114-115.

"In a Hickenlooper of a Hole," Economist, 230, No. 6550 (March 8, 1969), 31.

Levano, Cesar. "Por la Nacionalizacion del Petróleo," Tareas del Pensamiento Peruano, I (May-June, 1960), 50-83.

The New York Times. 1968-1969.

Niedergang, Marcel. "Revolutionary Nationalism in Peru" Foreign Affairs, XLIX, No. 3 (April, 1971), 454-463.

Payne, James L. "Peru: The Politics of Structured Violence," Robert D. Tomasek, ed. Latin American Politics. Garden City, N.J.: Anchor Books, 1970.

Peruvian Times. 1957-1968.

Rodman, Selden. "Evolution of the Political Role of the Peruvian Military," Journal of Inter-American Studies, XII, No. 4 (October, 1970), 539-564.

_____. "Peruvian Politics Stalls Belaúnde's Reforms" The Reporter, XXXV, No. 1 (July 14, 1966), 37-40.

Seers, Dudley. "Big Companies and Small Countries," Kyklos, XVI, No. 4 (1963), 601-615.

Sigmund, Paul. "Nationalism and Nationalization (Bolivia, Chile, Peru, Zambia)," New Leader, 52 (October 27, 1969), 9-12.

Smith, Goeffrey. "As They See It, Expropriation: Why They Do It?" Forbes, CVIII, No. 1 (July 15, 1971).

"Soldier in a Hurry," Economist, 235, No. 6615 (June, 1970), 28.

"Special Report on Peru," Latin American Report, VII, No. 5 (May, 1969), 1-3.

Sunkel, Osvaldo. "Big Business and 'Dependencia,' A Latin American View," Foreign Affairs, L, No. 3 (April, 1972).

"Those without Beards," Economist, 234, No. 6600 (February 21, 1970), 41-42.

Valcarcel, Gustavo. "Peruvian Paradoxes," New Times (Moscow), No. 2 (January 13, 1969), 20-22.

SECONDARY SOURCES—UNPUBLISHED PAPERS

Astiz, Carlos A. "The Peruvian Armed Forces as a Political Elite: Can They Develop a New Developmental Model?" Paper delivered at the 1969 Round Table of the International Political Science Association, Rio de Janeiro, Brazil, October 27-31, 1969.

Cotler, Julio. "El Populismo Militar como Modelo de Desarrollo Nacional: El Caso Peruano," Paper delivered at the 1969 Round Table of the International Political Science Association, Rio de Janeiro, Brazil, October 27-31, 1969.

Galloway, Jonathan F. "Multinational Enterprises as Worldwide Interest Groups," Paper delivered to the 66th Annual Convention, American Political Science Association, Los Angeles, California, September 8-12, 1970.

Schiller, Herbert I. "The Multinational Corporation as International Communicator," Paper delivered at the 66th Annual Convention,

American Political Science Association, Los Angeles, California, September 8-12, 1970.

SECONDARY SOURCES—ORAL PRESENTATION

Einaudi, Luigi. Oral Presentation at the 67th Annual Convention, American Political Science Association, Chicago, Illinois, September 7, 1971. (Panel: Comparative Military Regimes in Developing Societies).

ABOUT THE AUTHOR

ADALBERTO JOSÉ PINELO is Assistant Professor of Political Science at Northern Kentucky State College. Prior to his appointment there in 1972, he taught part time at Northeastern Illinois State College and Kendall College (1970 - 1971). While a graduate student at the University of Massachusetts, Mr. Pinelo held both teaching and research assistantships (1966 - 1970). He received his B.A. from Lake Forest College in 1966, his M.A. from the University of Massachusetts in 1968, and his Ph.D. from the University of Massachusetts in 1972.

Mr. Pinelo is a member of Pi Sigma Alpha, Phi Kappa Phi, the American Political Science Association, and the Latin American Studies Association. He is a native of Cuba, came to the United States in 1961, and recently became an American citizen.